Performing Artists

Performing Artists

Volume 2 ★ G–M

Molly Severson

*An imprint of Gale Research Inc.,
an International Thomson Publishing Company*

I(T)P

NEW YORK • LONDON • BONN • BOSTON • DETROIT • MADRID
MELBOURNE • MEXICO CITY • PARIS • SINGAPORE • TOKYO
TORONTO • WASHINGTON • ALBANY NY • BELMONT CA • CINCINNATI OH

Performing Artists: From Alvin Ailey to Julia Roberts

Molly Severson, *Editor*

Staff

Carol DeKane Nagel, *U·X·L Developmental Editor*
Thomas L. Romig, *U·X·L Publisher*

Mary Kelley, *Production Associate*
Evi Seoud, *Assistant Production Manager*
Mary Beth Trimper, *Production Director*

Cynthia Baldwin, *Art Director*

H. Diane Cooper, *Permissions Associate (Pictures)*
Margaret A. Chamberlain, *Permissions Supervisor (Pictures)*

Marty Somberg/Somberg Design, Ann Arbor, MI *Cover Design*
The Graphix Group, Fenton, MI *Typesetting*

∞™ This book is printed on acid-free paper that meets the minimum requirements of American National Standard for Information Sciences—Permanence Paper for Printed Library Materials, ANSI Z39.48-1984.

ISBN 0-8103-9868-0 (Set)
ISBN 0-8103-9869-9 (Volume 1)
ISBN 0-8103-9870-2 (Volume 2)
ISBN 0-8103-9871-0 (Volume 3)

Printed in the United States of America

I(T)P™ U·X·L is an imprint of Gale Research Inc.,
an International Thomson Publishing Company.
ITP logo is a trademark under license.

Contents

Volume 3: N-Z

Performing Artists by Field of Endeavor

Comedy:

Dance:

Film and Television:

Music:

Reader's Guide

Performing Artists: From Alvin Ailey to Julia Roberts features biographies of 120 popular singers, actors, dancers, comedians, musicians, and television personalities who have made an impact on the performing arts. Selected and written especially with students in mind, the entries focus on the early lives and motivations of the performers as well as highlights (and lowlights) of their careers.

Arranged alphabetically over three volumes, the biographies open with the birth dates and places of the individuals and, where necessary, with death dates and places. Each entry features a portrait of the biographee, a three- to nine-page essay on the performer's life and career, and a list of sources for further reading. Additionally, sidebars containing interesting details about the performers are sprinkled throughout the text, as are 25 movie stills and other action shots. A cumulative index providing easy access to the people and works mentioned in *Performing Artists* concludes each volume.

Comments and Suggestions

We welcome your comments on this work as well as your suggestions for individuals to be featured in future editions of *Performing Artists: From Alvin Ailey to Julia Roberts*. Please write: Editor, *Performing Artists,* U·X·L, 835 Penobscot Bldg., Detroit, Michigan 48226-4094; call toll-free: 1-800-877-4253; or fax 1-313-961-6348.

Andy García

Born April 12, 1956
Bejucal, Cuba

ACTOR

From a young age, Andy García had hopes of growing up to be a professional basketball player. When he was a senior in high school, however, he was benched for weeks because he contracted mononucleosis. While he was recovering from the long-term illness, he began to think about acting as a career. Although he had performed in several school plays, he had never considered it as a profession. Once he made up his mind to pursue it, though, he never looked back. "From then on," he related to Jennet Conant in *Redbook*, "acting was a hunger in the pit of my stomach, and if I didn't cater to it, it got worse."

"There's nothing that I cherish more than my culture and what I am. But to call me the great Hispanic actor is ridiculous; it's racism. They don't call Dustin Hoffman the great Jewish-American actor."

Andrés Arturo García Menendez was born in 1956 in Bejucal, Cuba, the youngest of three children. His mother, Amelie, taught English while his father, Rene García Nuñez, was a prominent lawyer. His family enjoyed a comfortable life in the small town outside of the capital city of Havana until the Cuban Revolution broke out in the late 1950s. Rebels led by Fidel Castro and Ernest "Ché" Guevara sought to overthrow the brutal Cuban dictator Fulgencio Batista. After the rebels were victorious and Castro came to power in December 1959, all private property was seized by the new government. Having lost all they had, the García family fled to Miami.

García remembers his early years in Florida as difficult ones. He was only five when he came to America and could speak no English. His parents took what work they could, and began to rebuild life for the family. Even the children helped out. On his way home from school, the young García picked up pop cans for change. When he grew older, he helped at night by sweeping out the hosiery factory where his father worked.

Sports give way to acting

Because he initially had trouble speaking English and was short for his age, García was in a fight almost every day in grade school. By the time he reached high school, however, his greatly improved English and his athletic abilities had won him many friends. Then came the illness that changed his life. For García, the switch from sports to acting was not that dramatic. "Acting is very much like a game of basketball," he explained to Stephanie Mansfield in *Gentlemen's Quarterly*. "There's a moment-to-moment, spontaneous thing about it. You don't know what's going to happen."

García enrolled in Florida International University and majored in theater. After he left college without graduating, he found that Florida offered little acting work, so he moved to Los Angeles in 1978. While looking for acting parts, he worked at odd jobs like loading trucks and waiting on tables. When he could, García did improvisational comedy at clubs around Los Angeles. His first television role, a small part as a gang member, was on the premiere episode of *Hill Street Blues* in 1981.

García found roles in motion pictures much harder to come by. Although he had small parts in a few movies in the early 1980s, he was denied many more parts because of his ethnic background. As he told Mansfield, "I was rejected. And in the rudest of ways.... All the racist kinds of things." His first big film role finally came in 1985, when he played an Hispanic detective in *The Mean Season*.

Commands attention with breakthrough role

The following year García landed the part of a charming but brutal drug dealer in *8 Million Ways to Die*. His excellent portrayal captured the attention of film critics and the director Brian De Palma, who wanted García to play the villain in his next movie, *The Untouchables*. Fearing he would always be typecast as an Hispanic bad guy, García convinced De Palma to let him play a good-guy FBI agent instead. His performance in the 1987 film won him international acclaim.

Subsequent parts in *Black Rain* (with Michael Douglas) and *Internal Affairs* (with Richard Gere) also cast García in law enforcement roles, but he proved he was capable of acting out a range of intense emotions. Critics noticed and commented on his presence in even small supporting roles. They praised him for portraying a wide variety of cops—good, bad, sensitive, quiet, or friendly.

García achieved star status in 1990 with his appearance as the illegitimate nephew of Don Corleone in *The Godfather Part III*. He received an Academy Award nomination for his role. He quickly went on to star in other major films, including *Hero, Jennifer Eight,* and *When a Man Loves a Woman.* None of these roles had García playing a cop or an Hispanic, roles he quickly tired of. "There's nothing that I cherish more than my culture and what I am," García told Charla Krupp of *Glamour.* "But to call me the great Hispanic actor is ridiculous; it's racism. They don't call Dustin Hoffman the great Jewish-American actor."

In 1993 García moved behind the camera to direct a Spanish-language documentary film about Cuban musician Israel "Cachao" Lopez. In the future, he hopes to do a film about Cuba entitled *The Lost City.* Based on a work by Cuban novelist Guillermo Cabrera Infante, it will tell the story of a young man forced to leave Cuba at the time of the revolution.

Family comes first

García is married to Marivi (short for Maria Victoria), another Cuban exile whom he met while in college. They have three daughters, and García insists their lives are very normal despite his stardom and wealth. To be near his family, he and his wife purchased a home in Key Biscayne, Florida, in 1991.

Part of the reason García moved back to Florida is that he believes it is important for his children to grow up in an environment that stresses their Cuban identity. He still considers himself a political exile of Cuba. "I had a great childhood in Miami Beach, but ultimately it's like having a stepmother," he explained to Conant. "If you are ripped from the womb of your real mother at the age of five, you can love your stepmother, but your mother is missing. You can't touch her, only love her from afar."

Sources

Gentlemen's Quarterly, December 1990.

Glamour, January 1991.

Hispanic, January/February 1994.

Redbook, January 1993.

Time, May 16, 1994.

Judy Garland

Born June 20, 1922, Grand Rapids, Minnesota
Died June 22, 1969, London, England

"The history of my life is in my songs."

ACTRESS, SINGER, AND DANCER

To most Americans Judy Garland will always be Dorothy, the little girl who traveled over the rainbow in the musical classic *The Wizard of Oz*. She was the original triple threat—her voice was spectacular, she danced with the best in the business, and she demonstrated a remarkable sensitivity in her acting. Yet, despite her wonderful gifts, Garland's life was rife with suffering. Under the advisement of powerful studio executives, Garland began taking diet pills, sleeping pills, and sedatives. She became addicted to the drugs, as well as to alcohol, and her dependence hounded her throughout her life until it finally killed her, leaving legions of fans and the movie and music industries to mourn.

Born Frances Gumm

Garland was born Frances Gumm in Grand Rapids, Minnesota, in 1922. Her parents, Frank Avent and Ethel Marian Gumm, were vaudeville performers. (Vaudeville was a type of entertainment, popular in the early twentieth century, that combined music, comedy sketches, and dance.) There is a story that at the age of 30 months, Frances was placed onstage to sing "Jingle Bells" for a Christmas program. Apparently, she was so entranced by the applause that her parents had to drag her off the stage. By the time she was three years old she had joined the family act and they had headed out to Los Angeles, California. When Garland's father became ill, the three daughters toured as a singing trio. They were billed as the "Three Garlands," and it was at this point that Frances changed her name to Judy Garland.

Although the "Three Garlands" were a popular act, it was really Judy's ability to infuse her songs with emotion and style that won over the audiences. Soon her sisters' singing was confined to the background, as Judy herself became the main attraction. By 1935 Judy's sisters had married and her father had died. After touring for a short while as a solo act, she was signed to a seven-year contract with the MGM studio. She first won recognition in the 1938 movie *Broadway Melody,* when she serenaded a picture of the actor Clark Gable. The following year she played the role of Dorothy in *The Wizard of Oz,* which was based on the Frank Baum children's book of the same name. She enchanted millions as the little girl from Kansas who travels to a strange and magical land, "over the rainbow," only to discover that "there's no place like home." Her rendition of the song "Over the Rainbow" soon became her trademark and the film her legacy.

Garland graduated from juvenile to adult roles in 1942, when she played opposite Gene Kelly in the movie musical *Me and My Gal.* Critics and fans alike were impressed by her transition, and she went on to make a series of moneymaking films for MGM throughout the 1940s. Among the most successful were *Meet Me in St. Louis* (1944), *The Harvey Girls* (1946), and *Easter Parade* (1948). The musical comedy *Meet Me in St. Louis* was set in St. Louis in 1904, and has often been mentioned as providing Garland with her favorite role. In *The Harvey Girls,* a story about Fred Harvey's chain of restaurants located along the Santa Fe railroad, Garland sang the show-stopping number "The Atchison, Topeka and the Santa Fe." And in *Easter Parade,* Garland was paired with the famous dancer Fred Astaire, and she gave what many consider her finest performance of the 1940s.

Begins taking prescription medicine

Despite her professional success, Garland battled severe feelings of loneliness and depression. She often felt as if her worth were tied only to her ability to make money—first for her ambitious mother, then for MGM.

Her stress led to insomnia, beginning when she was only 17. The insomnia was heightened by the diet pills the studio prescribed for her to slim down her natural plumpness. Because she couldn't sleep, she was prescribed sleeping pills, and when the mixture of these two prescriptions caused her to be anxious, she was prescribed yet another set of pills. Her feelings of isolation, combined with the excessive medication, eventually led to a series of mental breakdowns throughout the 1940s. She was prematurely released from her contract with MGM in 1950.

Garland also had two failed marriages during the 1940s. In 1941, when she was only 19, Garland married the music composer David Rose. The marriage ended in 1943, when the 32-year-old Rose asked for a divorce because he felt Garland was too immature. The divorce magnified Garland's negative self-image and led to her first nervous breakdown. In 1945 Garland married the motion picture director Vincent Minnelli, and in 1946 their daughter Liza was born. Their marriage had problems from the beginning, and the two were divorced in 1951.

With no film contract in hand, Garland returned to the stage in April 1951. She had put together a program of songs from her movies, and the highlight of the show was her signature song, "Over the Rainbow." Audiences were overwhelming in their support, and Garland played to sold-out houses in London and New York. Many found her to be an even better performer onstage than she had been in the movies and her renewed popularity led to a five-year contract with RCA Victor Records.

Makes comeback

The early 1950s, then, were a time of renewed hope for Garland. She became engaged to Sidney Luft, a former test pilot, in July 1951 and the two were married in 1952. They had a daughter, Lorna, born in 1952, and a son, Joseph, born in 1955. Her early years with Luft were happy and she quit taking many of the medications that had been prescribed by the studio's doctors. In 1953 she made a triumphant return to the screen in the film *A Star Is Born*. Considered by many to be her finest performance, *A Star Is Born* allowed Garland the chance to demonstrate the full range of her talents.

As discussed in David Shipman's *Judy Garland: The Secret Life of an American Legend*, many critics drew parallels between Garland's own life and that of the actress she portrayed. "There are things in this story that

Garland with Jack Haley, Ray Bolger, and Bert Lahr in *The Wizard of Oz*, 1939.

must have touched her deeply," wrote Campbell Dixon in the *Daily Telegraph*. "The little girl who wandered singing through the wonderland of Oz has known more setbacks than most, and this gives her performance an emotional depth rare in this kind of picture. *A Star is Born* is a glorious comeback, a triumph of skill and sincerity where a glossier performer might have failed." Most critics were overwhelmed by the depth of Garland's acting ability. Dilys Powell of the *Sunday Times* commented: "Pathos she has always had; but today the pathos has deepened, and her acting has a nervous tension which, when I saw the film, held the audience silent and tear-stained." Virginia Graham, of the *Spectator*, was also overcome: "[Garland] has lost a little in looks but gained enormously in talent. Warm, sensitive, touching she always was, but now her pathos has a poignancy and her singing a passion." Garland was nominated for an Academy Award for her performance, and many thought she was cheated when she lost to Grace Kelly for her role in *The Country Girl*.

Throughout most of the 1950s, Garland was able to keep her use of prescription drugs under control. She narrowed her use of drugs to sedatives and sleeping pills, which she felt she needed to keep her from suffering any more breakdowns. In 1959 she almost died from a rare form of hepatitis, which her doctors thought was linked to a build-up of drugs in her system. When she was released from the hospital she made an effort to quit using drugs altogether. Despite predictions that her illness would leave her a semi-invalid, unable to return to work, Garland returned to the stage in 1960. In 1961 she won the "Performer of the Year" Award given by *Show Business Magazine*. She also acted in the dramatic films *A Child Is Waiting* and *Judgment at Nuremberg*, receiving an Academy Award nomination for her work in the latter.

In 1963 Garland had difficulties in her marriage and separated from her husband, just as she was beginning a television series of 26 shows. Before the shooting began for the series, Garland had been assured that her hours would be limited so that she might spend time with her children. When the show unexpectedly began changing producers and cast members, Garland was required to spend far more time on the set than she had ever imagined. As a consequence, her husband sued for custody of the children on the grounds that she was rarely at home. When his suit turned into a sensational and public court case, Garland was devastated and turned to pills for escape. In addition to her usual sleeping pills and sedatives, Garland was prescribed the drug Ritalin so that she would have the energy to continue working. When her work on the series ended, she was in a terrible state of emotional and physical health.

Dies in London

In 1964, while attempting a concert tour in Australia, Garland came down with pneumonia and pleurisy and almost died. She was in a coma for 14 hours, and in order to save her, doctors performed a tracheotomy. Because of the surgical incision in her trachea, Garland's voice began to suffer and her ability to earn money was impaired significantly. The last five years of her life were burdened by failing health and few financial resources. After her divorce from Sid Luft, she was briefly married for six months to Mark Herron in 1965. In 1969 she married the manager of a New York discotheque, Mickey Deans. Only three months after they married, Garland was found dead in the bathroom of their rented London house. An autopsy revealed the equivalent of six sleeping pills in her system, which when combined with her generally weakened state, was sufficient to cause her death.

Her body was flown back to New York for her funeral, which over 20,000 people attended. The entertainer Bing Crosby is quoted in *Judy*

Garland: The Secret Life of an American Legend as giving her the following tribute: "The most talented woman I ever knew was Judy Garland. She was a great, great comedienne and she could do more things than any girl I knew. Act, sing, dance, make you laugh. She was everything. I had a great affection for her. Such a tragedy. Too much work, too much pressure, the wrong kind of people as husbands." Crosby also added: "There wasn't a thing that gal couldn't do—except look after herself."

Sources

Edwards, Ann, *Judy Garland: A Biography*, New York, 1975.

Shipman, David, *Judy Garland: The Secret Life of an American Legend*, New York, 1993.

Smith, Lorna, *My Life Over the Rainbow*, New York, 1987.

Danny Glover

Born in 1948
Georgia

ACTOR

"I was in the right place in the right time. I was coming along at a time when the roads were available.... It's a very simple correlation."

In an industry that offers limited screen opportunities for blacks, Danny Glover managed to be one of the busiest actors at work in the 1980s and into the 1990s. He began on the stage in the late 1970s and within ten years had made a successful transition to the screen, starring in some of the biggest films of the 1980s, including *Places in the Heart, Witness, The Color Purple, Lethal Weapon,* and *Lethal Weapon 2.* His stage career had also been quite successful and was highlighted by his acclaimed role in the 1982 award-winning Broadway play *"Master Harold" ... and the Boys;* throughout, Glover has made frequent appearances on television. The talented actor has displayed great versatility in the roles he has tackled and is regularly noted for his empathetic treatment of the characters he has portrayed, which have ranged from the hard–hearted farmer Mose of *Places in the Heart* to the villainous and abusive husband Mister in *The Color Purple.*

Born in rural Georgia and raised in California, Glover had early ambitions to become an economist, but was exposed to acting while a politically active student at San Francisco State University in the late 1960s. "My [acting] interest began simultaneously with my political involvement," Glover explained to Aldore Collier in *Ebony*. "My acting is also an extension of my involvement in community politics, working with groups like the African Liberation Support Committee, tutorial programs.... All of these things, at some point drew me into acting." While in college he obtained roles in several plays by Amiri Baraka, who had traveled to San Francisco to stage new theater productions as part of the Black Arts movement. "I did activist roles in many of the plays," Glover told Collier. "I felt I was making a statement in the plays."

In addition to his stage experience Glover studied acting formally while in college, yet did not pursue it as a career until years later. After graduation he continued his political activism by working within city government and was employed for five years as an evaluator of community programs for the mayor's office in San Francisco. He continued to dabble in local theater, however, and even eventually decided that his calling was to be an actor, not a bureaucrat. Glover studied at the American Conservatory of Theater and the Black Box Theater Company, moonlighted as a taxi driver, and quickly amassed a great amount of stage experience. He appeared in South African antiapartheid playwright Athol Fugard's *The Island* and *Sizwe Bansi Is Dead* at the Eureka Theater in San Francisco and the Los Angeles Actors Theater, and later was seen at New York City's Roundabout Theater in Fugard's *The Blood Knot*. He also performed in Sam Shepard's *Suicide in B Flat* at the Magic Theater in San Francisco and played Shakespeare's Macbeth at the Los Angeles Actors Theater.

In 1982 Glover received recognition for his performance in Fugard's three-person *"Master Harold" ... and the Boys,* which premiered at the Yale Repertory Theatre in New Haven, Connecticut, and eventually moved to Broadway. Glover's performance as Willie, a good-hearted waiter whose white friend turns on him and a fellow black waiter in a vicious barrage spurred by self-hatred, won him a Theatre World Award as one of the most promising new talents of 1992. *"Master Harold"* was heralded by the *New York Times*'s Frank Rich as one of the best and most well-written plays of recent times, which, he speculated, "may even outlast the society that spawned it—the racially divided South Africa of apartheid." Rich noted that "as the easygoing Willie, Mr. Glover is a paragon of sweet kindliness—until events leave him whipped and sobbing in a chair, his low moans serving as forlorn counterpoint to the play's main confrontation."

Places in the Heart *earned film respect*

Glover's performance in *"Master Harold"* was seen by film director Robert Benton, who cast Glover in the role of Mose in his 1984 film, *Places in the Heart.* Although the role originally called for an older man, Benton was so impressed with Glover's reading for the part that he had the script rewritten. Glover portrays a hobo-farmer who helps to save the farm of a white southern widow played by Sally Field; for character reference Glover drew upon the many years of his youth spent on his grandparents' farm in Georgia. He told Lisa Belkin in the *New York Times* that in playing Mose he continually looked to the image of his 90-year-old grandfather "picking cotton and trusting in God." Glover was more profoundly influenced, however, by the tragedy of his mother's death in an automobile accident days before he went to work on the film. "She was with me in so many ways," he told Charlene Krista in *Films In Review,* especially in the film's poignant farewell scene. "I mean, she was there when I gave the handkerchief to Sally.... I think as actors, we probably would have found ways to get what we wanted, but what happened with my mother gave us the thrust. At a time I was mourning, it gave me strength."

Places in The Heart was nominated for a best-picture Oscar, as was the next film Glover appeared in, *Witness* (1985), a romance-thriller set amid the Amish communities of Pennsylvania. *Witness* provided Glover the opportunity to create a completely different type of character—a dapper ex-police officer turned murderer. Also in 1985 Glover appeared in Lawrence Kasdan's acclaimed western, *Silverado,* playing the role of Malachi, a cowboy hero. Glover told Belkin that feedback from the role, especially from children, reinforced for him the importance of his image as a black screen actor. "I've run into black kids who flash their two fingers at me like guns and who say, 'This ought to do' or 'I don't want to kill you and you don't want to be dead,'" he remarked, citing two of his lines from the film. "They're watching me. That's a responsibility."

The Color Purple *stirred controversy*

The following year Glover appeared in *The Color Purple,* which provided one of his most complex roles and certainly his most controversial. In the Steven Spielberg-directed film based on Alice Walker's Pulitzer Prize-winning novel, Glover plays Mister, a southern widower who marries a young woman, Celie. Not only does he cruelly separate Celie from her beloved sister, but he intercepts and hides her sister's letters over a number of years. Mister is an abusive husband who exploits Celie ruthlessly, openly carrying on a love affair with a sultry blues singer named Shug.

The Color Purple was protested by the NAACP, which felt the film type-cast black characters in stereotypical roles—in particular, Glover's Mister, which allegedly projected a negative image of black men as violent and insensitive. Glover, who'd been criticized by some friends and relatives in the South, held, however, that the character accurately depicted life in the early 1900s. "I hear the criticism," he told Belkin, "... [and] prefer to remember the reaction of older black women who say, 'That's the way it was.'" Glover nonetheless understood the disapproval and explained his character in a broader context. "Mister was an adequate representation of one particular story," he told *People*. "He's a product of his past and his present and I think we showed that he has some capabilities for changing." Glover's empathy with the reprehensible Mister translated onto the screen in a manner that was noted by many critics. Donald Bogle in *Blacks in American Films and Television* wrote that Glover "gave a tightly drawn, highly charged performance of a man who's both brute and simp," while Janet Maslin of the *New York Times* said that Glover "somehow makes a very sympathetic villain."

In 1987 Glover teamed up with screen idol Mel Gibson for the biggest movie hit of the year, the comic action film *Lethal Weapon*. In it Glover portrays Roger Murtaugh, a homicide detective and dedicated family man, whose partner is a reckless—to the point of suicidal—officer named Martin Riggs (Gibson). Glover's stable character serves as a successful counterpoint to Gibson's crazed persona; their rapport made the movie a blockbuster at both the box office and with critics. Roger Ebert in *Roger Ebert's Movie Home Companion 1988 Edition* claimed that although Glover had important film roles in the past, his performance in *Lethal Weapon* "makes him a star. His job is to supply the movie's center of gravity, while all the nuts and weirdos and victims whirl around him." Two years later Glover and Gibson teamed up again for the equally successful *Lethal Weapon 2*, and in 1993 the duo made *Lethal Weapon 3*. Paul Baumann, in a review of *Lethal Weapon 2* in *Commonweal*, noted the film "is well written and competently acted.... It's blood drenched fluff, but there is real chemistry between these two accomplished actors."

Glover's performance in the little-noticed 1990 Charles Burnett film *To Sleep with Anger* has been judged by some critics to be among his best. Glover plays a superstitious and manipulative man named Harry from the Deep South who pays a visit to old friends who have had a family and settled in Los Angeles. Slowly but surely, Harry works to stir up simmering disputes within the family, which eventually come to a head. David Ansen wrote in *Newsweek* that "Glover, in what may be the best role of his film career, makes [Harry] an unforgettable trickster, both frightening and a little pathetic." Terrence Rafferty in the *New Yorker* noted that Glover turns in "an elegantly suggestive performance." In 1992 Glover played a tow truck driver in Lawrence Kasdan's *Grand Canyon*—a film that explores the problems of modern life. Glover's next role was that of a homeless man in *The Saint of Fort Washington.*

Sense of responsibility as black role model

Throughout the diverse roles of his career Glover has been aware of his responsibility as a role model for blacks. Echoing the political activism of his earlier days, Glover was quoted as saying in *Jet:* "I've always felt my experience as an artist is inseparable from what happens with the overall body of Black people.... My sitting here now is the result of people, Black people and people of good conscience in particular, fighting a struggle in the real world, changing the real attitudes and the real social situation." This awareness results in a special discretion regarding the roles he plays. "I have to be careful about the parts I take," he told Belkin. "Given how this industry has dealt with people like me, the parts I take have to be political choices."

As busy as Glover is with work, he still manages to devote his time and energy to helping others. He works for the Coors Foundation for Family Literacy. He is also cochair of the Fund for Democratic Elections in South Africa. In early 1994 he toured U.S. colleges with African National Congress official Jeff Radebe to raise money toward fostering South African elections. Glover still lives in his hometown of San Francisco in a house in the Haight-Ashbury district that he purchased years ago. He commented to Ebert in an interview: "I remember, when I was driving a cab and acting at night, I was in seventh heaven. I'm no happier today than I was in those days when I was living in a house in San Francisco and fixing it up, and I got a paycheck and spent it on sheet rock and worked with a guy putting it into the house, and went out and acted, and I was getting paid for it. How could I be happier than that?"

Sources

Bogle, Donald, *Blacks in American Films and Television: An Illustrated Encyclopedia,* Simon & Schuster, 1988.

Commonweal, October 6, 1989.

Ebert, Roger, *Roger Ebert's Movie Home Companion 1988 Edition,* Andrews, McMeel & Parker, 1987.

Ebony, March 1986.

Films In Review, April 1985.

Gentleman's Quarterly, July 1989.

Jet, March 17, 1986; April 6, 1987; October 31, 1988; September 18, 1989; March 5, 1990; November 15, 1993; February 21, 1994.

Maclean's, November 19, 1990.

Newsweek, October 22, 1990.

New Yorker, November 5, 1990.

New York Times, May 5, 1982; May 6, 1982; May 16, 1982; December 18, 1985; January 26, 1986.

People, March 10, 1986; February 10, 1992.

People Weekly Magazine Guide to Movies on Video, edited by Ralph Novak and Peter Travers, Macmillan, 1987.

Premiere, February 1992.

Whoopi Goldberg

Born in 1955
New York, New York

"What I am is a humanist before anything—before I'm a Jew, before I'm black, before I'm a woman. And my beliefs are for the human race—they don't exclude anyone."

COMEDIAN, ACTRESS, AND SOCIAL ACTIVIST

A comedian and actress, Whoopi Goldberg is one of the most bankable, talented, and unique stars in Hollywood. Throughout her acting career, she has not forgotten the lessons she learned in her difficult early life. There is, in a sense, no division between Whoopi Goldberg the actress and Whoopi Goldberg the person, as Paul Chutkow pointed out in *Vogue:* "She seems much the same way she has often appeared on-screen: fresh, direct, exuberant, no cant, no can't." Goldberg's modesty and determination affect her best characterizations—they are direct and empathetic. She is committed to her art. "Simply, I love the idea of working," she admitted to Aldore Collier in *Jet.* "You hone your craft that way." And she is committed to helping change harmful social conditions affecting the unfortunate, and to which she was once subjected.

Born Caryn E. Johnson in New York City in 1955, Goldberg wanted to be a performer from the very beginning. "My first coherent thought was probably, I want to be an actor," she recount-ed to Chutkow. "I believe that. That's just what I was born to do." She was acting in children's plays with the Hudson Guild Theater at the age of eight and throughout the rest of her childhood immersed herself in movies, sometimes watching up to three or four in a single day. "I liked the idea that you could pretend to be somebody else and nobody would cart you off to the hospital," Goldberg explained to *Cosmopolitan*'s Stephen Farber.

During the early 1970s Goldberg went by the name "Whoopi Cushion," sometimes using the French pronunciation "Kushon." After her mother pointed out how ridiculous the name sounded, Goldberg finally adopted a name from her family's history.

But by the time she reached high school, Goldberg had lost her desire and vision. It was the 1960s, and she was hooked on drugs. "I took drugs because they were available to everyone in those times," she told Farber. "As everyone evolved into LSD, so did I. It was the time of Woodstock, of be-ins and love-ins." Goldberg dropped out of high school and became lost in this culture, delving further into the world of drugs and ending up a junkie. Finally she sought help, cleaned herself up, and, in the process, married her drug counselor. A year later, Goldberg gave birth to her daughter, Alexandrea. Less than a year afterward, she was divorced. She was not yet 20 years old. In 1974 Goldberg headed west to San Diego, California, pursuing her childhood dream of acting. She performed in plays with the San Diego Repertory Theater and tried improvisational comedy with a company called Spontaneous Combustion. To care for her daughter, Goldberg had to work as a bank teller, a bricklayer, and a mortuary cosmetologist. She was also, for a few years, on welfare.

Developed insightful comic routine

In a significant step, Goldberg moved north to Berkeley, California, in the late 1970s and joined the Blake Street Hawkeyes Theater, a comedic troupe. With this group, Goldberg was able to realize her powerful acting and comedic abilities, developing a repertoire of 17 distinct characters in a one-woman show that she labeled *The Spook Show.* She performed the show on the West Coast, then toured the country and Europe in the early 1980s before landing in New York City.

Among her sketches were four characters: Fontaine, a profanity-spewing drug dealer with a Ph.D. in literature who travels to Europe looking for hashish, only to weep openly when he comes across the secret hiding place of Anne Frank, the young diarist who eventually died in a Nazi concentration camp; a shallow 13-year-old surfing "valley girl" who is left barren after a self-inflicted abortion with a coat hanger; a severely handicapped young woman who tells her prospective suitor, who wants to go dancing, "This is not a disco body"; and a nine-year-old black girl who bathes in bleach and covers her head with a white skirt, wistfully hoping to become white with long blonde hair so she can appear on *The Love Boat.*

Although Brendan Gill of the *New Yorker* decided Goldberg's sketches were "diffuse and overlong and continuously at the mercy of her gaining a laugh at any cost," the majority of critical and popular reaction was positive. Cathleen McGuigan, writing in *Newsweek,* believed that Goldberg's "ability to completely disappear into a role, rather than superficially impersonate comic types, allows her to take some surprising risks." And Enid Nemy, in a review of Goldberg's show for the *New York Times,* found the performer's abilities extended beyond mere comic entertainment and that her creations—seemlessly woven with social commentary—"walk a finely balanced line between satire and pathos, standup comedy and serious acting." These realistic and far-ranging performances also caught the attention of famed film director Mike Nichols. After seeing Goldberg's premiere performance in New York, Nicholas offered to produce her show on Broadway in September 1984.

Film debut earned critical praise

Another Hollywood figure impressed by Goldberg's sensitive performances was director Steven Spielberg, who at the time was casting for the film production of author Alice Walker's *The Color Purple.* Spielberg offered Goldberg the lead role of Celie—her first film appearance. Goldberg told Audrey Edwards of *Essence* how badly she wanted to be a part, any part, of the film: "I told [Alice Walker] that whenever there was an audition I'd come. I'd eat the dirt. I'd play the dirt, I'd be the dirt, because the part is perfect."

"As Celie, the abused child, battered bride, and wounded woman liberated by Shug's kiss and the recognition of sisterhood's power, Whoopi Goldberg is for the most part lovable and believable," Andrew Kopkind wrote in a review of the movie for the *Nation.* "She mugs a bit, pouts and postures too long in some scenes, and seems to disappear in others, but her great moments are exciting to behold." *Newsweek'*s David Ansen concurred in assessing Goldberg's film debut: "This is powerhouse acting, all the more so because the rage and the exhilaration are held in reserve." For this performance, Goldberg received a Golden Globe Award and an Academy Award nomination.

Increased exposure allowed greater social activism

Despite the lukewarm reception to *The Color Purple* as a whole, Goldberg's fortunes rose. In addition to her awards for her film portrayal, she won a Grammy Award in 1985 for her comedy album *Whoopi Goldberg* and received an Emmy nomination the following year for her guest appearance on the television show *Moonlighting*. The increased exposure, recognition, and acceptance allowed Goldberg to pursue social activities focusing on issues that affected her when she required public assistance and that she has tried to call attention to since her early stand–up routines.

Beginning in 1986, Goldberg hosted, along with Billy Crystal and Robin Williams, the annual Comic Relief benefit that raises money for the homeless through the Health Care for the Homeless project. "People would like the United States to be what we're told it can be, without realizing that the price has gone up—the price, you know, of human dignity," she explained to Steve Erickson in *Rolling Stone*. "Homelessness in America is just disgusting. It's just disgusting that we could have this big, beautiful country and have families living in dumpsters. It makes no sense." Her protests are not limited to this one social imbalance; Goldberg also campaigns on behalf of environmental causes, the nation's hungry, AIDS and drug abuse awareness, and women's right to reproductive freedom. She has been recognized with several humanitarian awards for her efforts.

Increased exposure, though, did not translate into increased success for Goldberg, as she went on to star in a succession of critically assailed movies: *Jumpin' Jack Flash, Burglar, Fatal Beauty, The Telephone, Clara's Heart,* and *Homer and Eddie*. It seemed that as soon as she had risen, she had fallen. "On the strength of her past work as a stand-up comic, Goldberg deserves better," Lawrence O'Toole wrote in a review of *Burglar* for *Maclean's*. "If she keeps making thumb-twiddling movies like this one, she is unlikely to get it."

Goldberg was frustrated by gossip and rumors that Hollywood was ready to write her off. "In less than five years she went from Hollywood's golden girl to a rumored lesbian/Uncle Tom with a bad attitude and a career on the skids," Laura B. Randolph reported in *Ebony*. "In Hollywood, that combination is almost always terminal, and insiders whispered that she should pack it in and be happy to do guest spots on the Hollywood Squares."

Still, Goldberg remained steady. "I've just stopped listening to them," she explained to Chutkow. "I've taken crazy movies that appeal to me. I don't care what other people think about it. If it was pretty decent when I did it, I did my job." The thread that connects her box-office disappointments seems to be her strong performance marred by poor direction or a poor final script. The *New York Times*'s Janet Maslin, reviewing *Fatal Beauty*, wrote what could be taken as an overall assessment of Goldberg's failed showings: "It isn't Miss Goldberg's fault, because Miss Goldberg is funny when she's given half a chance."

Ghost *revived career*

Her chance came with the 1990 film *Ghost*. "Thank God Whoopi finally has a part that lets her strut her best stuff," Ansen proclaimed. Although some critics didn't fully embrace the film—the *New Yorker*'s Terrance Rafferty called it a "twentysomething hybrid of *It's a Wonderful Life* and some of the gooier, more solemn episodes of 'The Twilight Zone'"—most critical and popular response was overwhelmingly positive, especially to Goldberg's portrayal of the flamboyant yet heroic psychic Oda Mae. It was a part for which she lobbied studio executives for more than six months, and her persistence paid off. Considered a sleeper when it was released, *Ghost* was the highest-grossing movie of 1990. And Goldberg won an Oscar as best supporting actress for her performance, becoming only the second black female in the history of the Academy Awards to win such an honor. (The first was Hattie McDaniel, who won for *Gone with the Wind* in 1939.)

To demonstrate her acting range, Goldberg immediately followed her comedic role in *Ghost* with a dramatic role in *The Long Walk Home*. The film is about the bus boycott in Montgomery, Alabama, in 1955—a pivotal event in the American civil rights movement. Goldberg portrays Odessa Cotter, a housekeeper who, because of the boycott, is forced to walk almost ten miles to work, regardless of blistering or bleeding feet. Throughout, the character maintains her composure and integrity. Chutkow quoted Richard Pearce, the director of the film, on Goldberg's successful characterization: "What her portrayal of Odessa revealed about Whoopi was a complex inner life and intelligence. Her mouth is her usual weapon of choice—to disarm her of that easy weapon meant that she had to rely on other things. It's a real actress who can bring off a performance like that. And she did."

Goldberg's success in television has been somewhat more limited. Beginning with the 1988-89 season, she earned praise for appearing on an irregular basis as a crew member on the successful series *Star Trek: The Next Generation*. But her 1990 stint in the series *Bagdad Cafe* was short-lived, as was her talk show, which ran only for the 1992-93 season.

The year 1992 brought a series of successes to Goldberg. She began the year portraying a homicide detective in director Robert Altman's highly anticipated and subsequently acclaimed Hollywood satire *The Player*. In mid-year Goldberg donned a nun's habit as a Reno lounge singer seeking refuge from the mob in a convent in the escapist comedy *Sister Act*. One of the biggest box-office draws of the summer of 1992, the film, according to *Detroit Free Press* film critic Judy Gerstel, worked "as summer whimsy mainly because of Goldberg's usual witty, lusty screen presence." Goldberg won a Golden Globe Award for best actress for this film. And in the fall she turned again to a dramatic role, starring in *Sarafina: The Movie;* a film adaptation of the musical about black South African teenagers and their struggle against apartheid, *Sarafina* was shot entirely on location in Soweto, South Africa.

Goldberg also kept up a full and successful schedule in 1993. She began the year by being named Harvard's "Woman of the Year" and by winning a People's Choice Award as favorite comedy film actress. She then costarred with Ted Danson in the comedy *Made in America,* and the two became romantically linked. Their relationship drew significant media attention when Danson performed in blackface at a Friar's Club roast for Goldberg. Some felt his act was vulgar and racist, but Goldberg defended it as being in the tradition of a roast. Despite this controversy, the year continued well for Goldberg. She revealed that she was paid $8 million for appearing in *Sister Act 2*—making her, at that time, the highestpaid actress in the movie industry. In early 1994 Goldberg was given the job of hosting the Academy Awards. She was both the first African American and the first woman to host this prestigious event. In August of that year *Corinna, Corinna,* a romantic comedy-drama set in the 1950s in which Goldberg plays opposite Ray Liotta, was released. And in October Goldberg wed union organizer Lyle Trachtenberg.

Goldberg's constant quest for a range of roles which led Maslin to label her "one of the great unclassifiable beings on the current movie scene," is not the mark of a Hollywood prima donna but of an actor committed to her craft. "None of my films cure cancer," Goldberg explained to Chutkow. "But they have allowed me to not just play one kind of person, which is important to me. Nobody knows how long this stuff is gonna last, and you want to have it and enjoy as much of it and be as diverse as you can."

Sources

Christian Science Monitor, March 27, 1986.

Cosmopolitan, December 1988; March 1991; April 1992.

Detroit Free Press, May 29, 1992.

Ebony, March 1991.

Essence, March 1985.

Harper's, January 1987.

Interview, June 1992.

Jet, April 24, 1989; August 13, 1990; April 22, 1991; January 13, 1992; June 1, 1992; January 18, 1993; February 1, 1993; February 22, 1993; March 8, 1993; June 14, 1993; June 21, 1993; October 25, 1993.

Ladies' Home Journal, June 1993.

Maclean's, April 6, 1987.

Nation, February 1, 1986; December 10, 1990.

New Republic, January 27, 1986.

New Statesman, August 23, 1991.

Newsweek, March 5, 1984; December 30, 1985; October 20, 1986; July 16, 1990.

New York, December 12, 1988; April 2, 1990.

New Yorker, November 5, 1984; December 30, 1985; July 30, 1990.

New York Times, October 21, 1984; October 30, 1987; February 14, 1988; February 9, 1990.

Parade, November 1, 1992.

People, October 17, 1988; April 2, 1990.

Rolling Stone, May 8, 1986; August 9, 1990.

Time, December 17, 1990; June 1, 1992.

USA Weekend, August 5-7, 1994.

Vogue, January 1991.

Amy Grant

Born in 1961
Augusta, Georgia

SINGER AND SONGWRITER

A my Grant is one of the first Christian singers to attract the attention of mainstream pop music fans. After gaining prominence in the early 1980s for her gospel songs, Grant released *Unguarded* in 1985, an album which propelled her into the realm of pop stardom. Grant and her back-up band have appeared in concert throughout the United States, garnering a steady following. Her award-winning albums have sold in the millions and spawned hit singles and videos. Grant has appeared often on talk shows and has been featured on a televised Christmas special.

"[Love] (and not just love for Jesus) has value. If we could get over that hump in our songwriting we could still communicate with Christ."

The youngest of four daughters of a prominent radiologist, Grant was born in Augusta, Georgia, and raised in Nashville, where she and her family attended the local Church of Christ. She did not become particularly interested in music until her teenage years. One summer, away at camp, she was mesmerized by a fellow camper who played John Denver songs on the guitar. She cut her nails and convinced the friend to give her lessons. She never had a formal

Grant Recalls Her First Big Break

"I made the tape for my parents. And without my knowing it, someone called Word Records took the tape, and Word Records said, hey, this is contemporary Christian music. I didn't know what I was doing was contemporary Christian music. Then they called me and said, "We want you to do an album.' And I thought it was a practical joke. We never thought it would go anywhere. We were probably five or six albums into it when I realized, hey, you know, I'd kind of like to do this as my life."

music teacher. While attending Harpeth Hall, an exclusive girl's prep school, Grant worked part-time at a recording studio, demagnetizing tapes and doing janitorial chores. She used the facilities at hand to make a tape for her parents of her own songs, which she accompanied on guitar. Unknown to Grant, someone at the Texas-based Word Records heard the tape, and she was later approached about recording an album.

Established a musical following

Released in 1976 on Word Records' Myrrh label, Grant's self-named debut album became an immediate best-seller in the field of Christian music. During the following years, the teenage singer tried to balance a recording career with her education. After graduating from Harpeth Hall, she attended Furman University in South Carolina before transferring to Vanderbilt University, where she majored in English. She dropped out during her senior year, however, to concentrate on her career and to marry Gary Chapman. She met Chapman at an industry gathering in 1979 after hearing a cassette tape of his song "Father's Eyes," which she later recorded. Today Chapman plays rhythm guitar in her ten-piece touring band.

At this stage in her budding career, Grant performed solo in churches to her own guitar accompaniment. Two of her albums comprised of concert performances became best-sellers in their field. She recalled how she felt leaving that context in an interview with the *Gavin Report:* "The only time I felt myself changing was when I got my first band, then I quit playing churches. But it wasn't a moral decision. It's just that churches are built for a man to stand on a pulpit and to speak and be heard. You get eight people up there with amplifiers and everything else and it doesn't sound good. So we made a decision based on a musical problem and some people say, 'Oh, no!' And that's when it can appear that you're trying to be a maverick." Grant's managers (including Harrell, her brother-in-law) began suggesting that interested churches sponsor the band in a civic hall or at colleges. "It was helpful for all of us to meet on neutral territory," Grant asserted in the *Gavin Report* interview.

Chartered new territory

While at Vanderbilt University in 1983, Grant recorded *Age to Age,* the first of her albums to see sales figures rise dramatically. In 1985 Word Records signed a distribution deal with A&M Records to launch various gospel artists. Grant was one of them. With its synthesized sound and upbeat songs expressing subtle Christian lyrics, her album *Unguarded* received much airplay and sold more than a million copies. When the single "Find a Way" hit the pop charts, and a duet with Peter Cetera (of the band Chicago), "The Next Time I Fall," topped *Billboard*'s pop chart in 1987, Grant garnered criticism from some Christians who thought that in her quest for success, she had lost sight of her spiritual roots. Grant countered by suggesting that her songs need not mention Jesus by name in order to portray the message of love that he taught. Critics generally maintain that in concert, Grant aims to entertain her audience; she does not overtly attempt to convert listeners to Christianity.

At the end of the tour to promote *Unguarded,* Grant and her entourage needed a rest. Following a three-year recording hiatus, she released the 1988 album *Lead Me On,* which represents an even further departure from Grant's previous efforts. Unlike the upbeat synthesized sound of *Unguarded, Lead Me On* primarily uses acoustic instrumentation, and the songs revolve around somber themes. The album reflects many of Grant's concerns during her absence from the concert stage: accusations that she had sold out her faith, the trauma of a miscarriage, a difficult period in her marriage that was overcome through counseling, and the birth of her son, Matthew. Because none of its songs lent themselves readily to radio airplay, the album was largely ignored by radio stations. Nonetheless, Grant's following remained loyal.

Topped the pop charts

Grant made a distinct attempt to find a place in the pop market with her 1991 release *Heart in Motion,* which contains songs that contemplate the earthly side of human love. "I did that for a few different reasons," she told Chris Willman of the *Los Angeles Times.* "I have invested so much of my time and creative energy [in] writing contemporary Christian songs, and I was really wanting to try something new." To answer her critics in the Christian community she added, "It had nothing to do with a loss of faith or change of lifestyle.... I think that Christians, no matter where they are, should be the same person whether they're singing Gospel music or writing and performing a pop album.... We just ought to get out there and live life and be true to what we believe, and for those of us that write, just let what we do reflect that."

Fans had a chance to see Grant's efforts portrayed on the small screen as well. When her video "Baby, Baby" aired on MTV, it caused considerable controversy and sparked both positive and negative criticism. While the song was inspired by Millie, the singer's daughter, in the video Grant is seen singing romantically to a handsome actor—not her husband, with whom Grant has often performed in concert. In spite of the uproar surrounding the release, *Heart in Motion* brought Grant several 1992 Grammy nominations and a legion of new listeners.

In 1994 Grant continued to expand her audience, releasing *House of Love*, which rose to Number 13 on the *Billboard* 200 pop album chart. The record also scaled the Top Contemporary Christian chart, indicating that Grant's core-fans were still behind her.

Sources

Atlanta Journal, March 1, 1986; November 25, 1988.

Christian Herald, September/October 1991.

Focus on the Family Parental Guidance, June 1991.

Gavin Report, June 7, 1985.

Indianapolis Star, October 22, 1988.

Los Angeles Herald Examiner, May 2, 1986.

Los Angeles Times, April 16, 1991.

Nashville Banner, July 28, 1989.

News and Observer (Raleigh, NC), March 16, 1986.

New York Daily News, October 7, 1984.

New York Tribune, July 25, 1989.

People, July 15, 1991.

Plain Dealer (Cleveland), August 9, 1985.

Providence Journal, October 5, 1984.

St. Paul Pioneer Press-Dispatch, October 27, 1988.

Saturday Evening Post, November/December 1991.

Tennessean (Nashville), August 3, 1985; December 14, 1986; October 15, 1988.

Today's Christian Woman, May/June 1991.

Tulsa World, March 16, 1986.

Washington Post, November 2, 1982; December 11, 1983, June 9, 1985.

Cary Grant

Born January 18, 1904, Bristol, England
Died November 29, 1986, Davenport, Iowa

ACTOR

One of the most charming, elegant, and likeable of Hollywood leading men, Cary Grant created a light, comic style that many have tried to imitate but none can surpass. In 72 films made over four decades, Grant served as both a romantic ideal for women and a dashing role model for men.

Grant was born Archibald Alexander Leach on January 18, 1904, in Bristol, England. His parents were poor, and they quarreled often as they struggled to raise their children. Grant's father pressed trousers in a factory, and when war broke out between Italy and Turkey in 1911 and England increased its production of armaments (though they weren't involved directly in the war), he temporarily moved to another town to make uniforms at higher pay.

"I think that being relaxed at all times, and I mean relaxed, not collapsed, can add to the happiness and duration of one's life and looks. And relaxed people are fun to be around."

With his father gone and an increase in the family's income, Grant and his mother enjoyed their time together. After six months, however, his father lost his job and returned to Bristol. Family life was again tense. Grant's father came home from work late, if at all, and spent his time avoiding confrontations with his wife. Although it was unknown to Grant at the time, his father had fallen in love with another woman.

Through all this, Grant found escape in the newly emerging "picture palaces." There he would lose himself in the exciting adventures of movie heroes and heroines and laugh at the comic antics of silent-screen stars.

Mother sent to mental institution

At the age of ten, Grant received news that would forever change his life and influence his future relationships with women. Arriving home from school one day, Grant was told his mother had left for a seaside resort. In reality, she had been locked away in a nearby mental institution where she remained for 20 years. Grant was an adult before he learned of his mother's true whereabouts. Until then she was a topic never discussed, and Grant was left to wonder why she had abandoned him. "There was a void in my life," Grant reflected on this time, "a sadness of spirit that affected each daily activity with which I occupied myself in order to overcome it."

In later years, Grant surmised that his mother had had a nervous breakdown, having never recovered from his elder brother's death. Aged only two months, this child died as a result of convulsions brought on by gangrene. Others have speculated, however, that Grant's father locked her away because at that time divorce was costly and socially unacceptable, and he wanted to provide a home for his pregnant mistress.

In 1915 Grant won a scholarship to Fairfield Academy. There he received good grades with the exception of those in Latin and mathematics, which he disliked. He also received a reputation for playing jokes and getting in trouble. During the summer of 1916 Grant volunteered to use his Boy Scout training to help with the war effort. World War I was well under way and England needed the help of all volunteers. Grant became a messenger and errand boy at the military docks of Southampton. Here, Grant was filled with wanderlust as he watched the ships depart for new and exciting destinations. At summer's end, Grant roamed the Bristol waterfront and fantasized about a life far away.

Decides to become an actor

It was at the Hippodrome, Bristol's premier vaudeville theater, that Grant realized just how he would escape his working-class environment and have some adventures. After being allowed backstage during a Saturday matinee, Grant decided to become an actor. "I suddenly found my inarticulate self in a land of smiling, jostling people wearing all sorts of costumes and doing all sorts of clever things," Grant remembered. "And that's when I knew! What other life could there be but that of an actor? They happily traveled and toured. They were classless, cheerful and carefree. They gaily laughed, lived and loved."

In 1919 Grant ran away from home and joined the Bob Pender Troupe of comedians and acrobats. He was soon forced to return home when they discovered that he had lied about his age and about having his father's permission to work. At 13, Grant was a year too young to obtain a work permit and work legally. Undeterred, Grant waited until he turned 14 and then tried to get expelled from school so that his father might let him rejoin the group. Grant's plan worked.

Grant learned comedy, gymnastics, and pantomime from Pender's group. His later skill at physical comedy and timing owed much to this very early training. Grant traveled with the troupe throughout Europe and in July 1920 arrived in New York to tour the United States. When the rest of the troupe returned to England, Grant decided to stay and seek success in America. He worked as a barker on Coney Island, a stilt walker at Steeplechase Park, and in vaudeville as a straight man (the "unfunny" half of a comedy duo). He also won roles in light musicals and in plays. In 1932 Grant took the advice of actress Fay Wray and went to Hollywood to find work. After a screen test, Paramount offered Grant a contract but insisted he change his name from Archie Leach. So the more glamorous Cary Grant was chosen—and a great film career begun.

Even in his earliest film roles, Grant demonstrates the elegant sophistication that is the very opposite of his working-class background. His credentials as a traditional leading man were established with his appearances opposite Marlene Dietrich in *Blond Venus* and Mae West in *She Done Him Wrong* and *I'm No Angel*. The full range of Grant's talent was used most successfully with the directors George Cukor, Howard Hawks, and Leo McCarey.

The perfect format for displaying Grant's verbal and physical agility was in the screwball comedies of the 1930s. These films are marked by their fast pace, unconventional characters, and absurd situations. Grant's romantic sparring with Irene Dunn in McCarey's *The Awful Truth,* Rosalind Russell in Hawks's *His Girl Friday,* and Katharine Hepburn in Cukor's *Holiday* and Hawks's *Bringing Up Baby* displayed Grant's deft comic touch. His role as the daredevil flyer in *Only Angels Have Wings* and his Oscar-nominated performances in *Penny Serenade* and *None But the*

Lonely Heart show that Grant was a capable dramatic actor as well, but it was in sophisticated comedy that his real strength lay. Throughout his career, Grant continued to successfully play the charming leading man, even as late as 1964, with the film *Charade*.

Works with Hitchcock

Although Grant's comedies represent the majority of his best-remembered roles, his work with the director Alfred Hitchcock in several classic films offers a departure from his usual image. Hitchcock deliberately played against Grant's familiar persona by introducing psychological twists that are in startling contrast to the actor's smooth surface elegance. *To Catch a Thief* is probably the Hitchcock film in which Grant plays a character closest to his trademark style—that of a glamorous and well-known jewel thief. In *Suspicion* Grant plays a seemingly loving husband who may or may not be trying to kill his wife. While Grant's wise-cracking character in *North by Northwest* has a surface charm, the audience gradually discovers that underneath lies a man with a basically selfish nature whose only lasting relationship is his amusing but obsessive bond with his mother.

It is in *Notorious*, however, that Hitchcock fully uses the conflict between Grant's image and his character's personality. As Devlin, an emotionally repressed American agent, he sends the woman he has unwillingly come to love into the arms of a Nazi collaborator. Devlin's struggle against his attraction to this woman nearly causes her death when he blindly ignores signs that she might be in danger. The bizarre love triangle in this film hinges on the woman's attraction to Grant despite his unfeeling behavior, and his performance is both fascinating and disturbing.

Although Grant achieved tremendous success as an actor, his personal life had some disappointments. His first four marriages ended in divorce and Grant speculated that this poor record was tied to the disappearance of his mother. "I was making the mistake of thinking that each of my wives was my mother, that there would never be a replacement after she left," he said. "I had even found myself being attracted to people who looked like my mother—she had olive skin for instance. Of course, at the same time I was getting a person with her emotional makeup, too, and I didn't need that." In 1981 Grant married Barbara Harris. This marriage was reported to be happy, and with her he was said to find contentment. Harris was at his side when he died of a massive stroke in 1986.

Until his retirement from the screen in 1966, Grant continued to play romantic leads while other actors of his generation often found themselves cast in supporting roles and character parts. Today Grant's name remains a symbol of the stylish sophistication that was his trademark, and repeated viewings of his films reveal an actor whose ability to delight an audience is timeless.

Sources

Interview, January 1987.

Newsweek, December 8, 1986.

New York Times, July 3, 1977; December 1, 1986.

People, December 15, 1986.

Time, December 15, 1986.

Graham Greene

Born c. 1953
Six Nations reserve, Ontario, Canada

"Graham has a chameleon-like ability to change himself into any character he chooses. And he's a master clown."
—Tomson Highway

ACTOR

Graham Greene first won widespread recognition in the highly acclaimed role of Kicking Bird in the 1990 film *Dances with Wolves.* Critics praised his performance, and he became the first North American Indian to receive an Academy Award nomination since the Canadian Chief Dan George was nominated for the 1970 film *Little Big Man.* Since then Greene has continued to work in a variety of film and television roles, most notably as the wise medicine man on the popular CBS series *Northern Exposure.*

Grew up on a reservation

Greene was born the second of six children, to John and Lillian Greene. Although he was raised on the Six Nations reserve, his family did not teach him any Native American tribal customs or language. Green's early days were spent happily running through the woods and playing in the creeks. Never a fan of schoolwork, Greene dropped out of school at the age of 16 and went to Rochester, New York, to look for work. He found a job in a carpet warehouse, but began to drift from town to town, first studying welding in Toronto, then working in Hamilton at a railway car factory. He became interested in music, working first as a sound man and then running a recording studio.

The direction of his life changed in 1974, when a friend asked him to participate in a workshop run by the Ne'er-Do-Well Thespians company in Toronto, Ontario. Greene was bitten by the acting bug. Greene described for *Maclean's* magazine his appreciation for acting: "You dress up in funny clothes, stand around in bright lights and tell lies. You don't have to carry nothing. Someone sweeps up after you. No whining musicians to deal with—I can be a whiny actor. I thought that was fabulous."

In 1982 Greene appeared in the award-winning play *Jessica*, which explored Native American assimilation into mainstream culture. Work in two films followed. In the 1984 movie *Running Brave*, Greene played the friend of the native track star Billy Mills. And in 1984 he was an extra in the box-office disaster *Revolution*, which centered on the American Revolutionary War.

Father dies

Greene took a break from acting after his father's death in 1984. He was very close to his father and his loss drove him to what he now calls his "period of fast cars and guns." He went into the wilds of Canada to try and live off the land by hunting. Eventually he gave up the guns and the countryside and returned to the city. He began serious work with Toronto's inventive theater company Theatre Passe Muraille. His time there provided a serious training ground for his subsequent acting. Clarke Rogers, former artistic director of Theatre Passe Muraille, told *Maclean's*: "[Greene's] success is not some kind of accident. He has worked very hard with some of the best original playwrights in the country."

When his acting work didn't provide enough money to pay the bills, Greene turned to welding sets and working behind the lights. For a while he and his actor friend Michael Copeman resorted to selling hand-painted T-shirts on the streets of Toronto. Greene told *Maclean's*, "Whenever we sold a T-shirt, we'd go to the hot-dog stand. It was literally hand-to-mouth."

Cast in Dances with Wolves

Greene's luck began to turn in 1989. He won a role in the play *Dry Lips*

Greene as Kicking Bird in *Dances with Wolves*, 1990.

Oughta Move to Kapuskasing, which premiered at Passe Muraille. His role was that of a toothless, beer-swilling Indian buffoon. Soon after, Greene was cast in the role of the Sioux medicine man Kicking Bird in Kevin Costner's *Dances with Wolves.* Surprisingly, Costner originally turned down

Greene for the part, saying he looked too "white." After the casting director combined Greene's picture with a sketch of Kicking Bird's costume, Costner reconsidered and gave Greene the role.

In addition to acting, Greene has also worked as a carpenter, landscape gardener, bartender, roadie, high-steelworker, and welder.

Dances with Wolves tells the story of an Army officer (Costner) who befriends the Sioux people—and is ultimately adopted by them. The film, which won seven Academy awards, was praised for its historical accuracy and its affectionate treatment of the Sioux. Kicking Bird's part was central to the film, and many critics singled out Greene's performance. According to Brian Johnson of *Maclean's,* "Much of the movie's magic rests on Greene's performance, captured in rapturous close-ups."

While shooting the film, Greene and Hilary Blackmore, a stage manager from Toronto, exchanged rings in the hills of South Dakota. They were legally married when they returned to Toronto. While Greene had not been married before, he does have a daughter with the Toronto actress Carole Lazare.

Since *Dances with Wolves,* Greene has been involved in a number of projects. He played a kidnapper in the 1991 Canadian movie *Clearcut.* He has also done some work for television. He played a Navajo lawyer in an episode of the television series *L.A. Law,* and he appeared in *Cooperstown* in January 1993. He has a recurring role on the offbeat *Northern Exposure,* playing a shaman who understands some medical mysteries more clearly than the show's Columbia University-trained doctor. Not one to get carried away with the success of his career, Greene told *Maclean's,* "It's only a job. If I want to, I can go back to welding."

Sources

Entertainment Weekly, January 22, 1993.

Maclean's, March 25, 1991.

Variety, January 25, 1993.

Jasmine Guy

Born c. 1964
Boston, Massachusetts

"I've worked hard and, having achieved a little, I find it hard not to want to work harder to achieve even more."

ACTRESS, DANCER, AND SINGER

Jasmine Guy made a name for herself playing snobby Whitley Gilbert on the highly rated television show "A Different World." The part made Guy a star, but it demonstrates only a small facet of her talent—she can dance, sing, and pull off a tense dramatic role with equal finesse. As Whitley, Guy fairly seethed with prissiness and propriety. As a would-be pop singer, however, the former Alvin Ailey dancer radiates excitement and moves flawlessly from jazz to hip-hop to the R&B-tinged "New Jack Swing." The actress told *Essence* magazine that her success has not come on easy terms. "I've been so driven that whole chunks of my life are blurs," she said. "I'm trying to live in the present, trying to enjoy reaping the benefits of eight years of perseverance."

The gifts of beauty and talent were not enough to assure Guy a happy childhood. She was born in Boston but raised in Atlanta. Her father, a minister and college professor, is black. Her mother, a high school English teacher, is white. Guy told *People* that she was often the target of criticism from darker-skinned classmates in the Atlanta public schools. "I remember getting into several fights in grade school because black kids would think I thought I was pretty because I had light skin and long hair," she recalled. "They said I always tried to talk properly. But I wasn't trying to seem better, I just wanted to be me."

Even now Guy often finds herself addressing the issue of her skin color. "I'm tired of hearing about the plight of the mulatto," she told *Essence.* "It's old news. Sure, it's caused me pain. Just the other day, a dark-skinned friend was saying how she'd always envied me. Well, I told her I'd always been envious of the shade of her skin. It's important that chocolate women of the world know they're beautiful." She added: "I spent years worrying about these things, crying in my diary. But I finally stopped myself, stopped finding fault with my big eyes or my blemishes. Like so many other people, I had to fight feeling ugly."

Guy helped bolster her self-image by singing in her father's church choir and by performing in stage musicals. "I always sang in church," she told *Jet* magazine. "I was the loud alto in the back." Her talents landed her a spot at Atlanta's prestigious Northside High School of the Arts, where she studied dance, drama, and voice. "I was Anita in *West Side Story* when I was 13 and that really opened my eyes to what was out there and what I was capable of doing," she said.

Guy's parents were rather dismayed when she won the opportunity to study dance with the Alvin Ailey company in New York City. At the tender age of 17, Guy left Atlanta to make her own way in the world on $75 a week. She performed with Ailey's second and third companies and auditioned frequently for Broadway and Off-Broadway dancing roles. "New York was a rude awakening," she told *Essence.* "It was lonely and scary, but I just couldn't afford those big city fears.... I was pursuing my dream of becoming a dancer. So I put my paranoia in my pocket, fought the smelly ol' subway and just kept training."

Frustrated with her poverty wage and with the fact that she was refused black roles because she was too light-skinned, Guy went to Los Angeles to work as a dancer on the television show *Fame.* That too proved disappointing. "They treated us like scenery," she said of *Fame's* producers, "and I knew in my heart I could do better. Besides, I missed the discipline of dance training. So I quit. I tucked my tail between my legs and returned to Ailey. I went from making $750 a week to making $75." Eventually Guy landed small parts in musicals and variety shows such as *The Wiz, Bubbling Brown Sugar,* and *Leader of the Pack.* Her touring schedule took her all over Europe and the United States, sometimes leaving her near exhaustion.

Struggled to obtain significant film roles

Guy's first movie role was in Spike Lee's 1988 film *School Daze,* about life in an all-black college. Ironically, Guy was cast as a light-skinned black woman who is shunned by her dark-skinned classmates. "The role was difficult for me because it brought back ugly memories," she told *People.* "Again I had to face the reality of how the world sometimes views people only on outward appearances. I don't like being prejudged." Painful as the role was for her, Guy drew notice for her portrayal of a "Wannabee," a vain, spoiled beauty queen.

Even after the film was released, Guy still had trouble getting cast in any sort of substantial role. "When you're light skinned you get it coming and going," she said. "How black do I have to be to play a black woman?" She read for a part on a new television comedy, *A Different World,* and was turned down. Discouraged, she took a position in a 1960s-style review in Paris for six months. "That nearly did me in," she further revealed to *Essence.* "I was so burned out I couldn't stop crying." To her surprise, she was called back to the set of *A Different World,* this time to read for a new character. "When I got to California to read for the show the second time, there was a roomful of people, including the head of the network," she remembered. "I swallowed hard, gave it all I had, and 15 minutes later was told to start working."

Gained popularity on the small screen

The role Guy won was that of Whitley Gilbert, a prim and spoiled southern belle at Hillman College, a fictitious all-black school. *A Different World* originally starred Lisa Bonet and was a spin-off of *The Cosby Show* based on Bonet's character, Denise Huxtable. Bonet left the show in the second season, and Guy slowly emerged as the series' principal female character. *A Different World* never garnered good reviews from the critics, but by virtue of its placement behind the popular *Cosby Show,* it enjoyed high ratings almost from the time it first aired. In 1993 the series ended after a successful six-year run.

Guy admitted that she fought hard to flesh out the role of Whitley. She told *Essence:* "At first I worried that all she had were drop-dead lines—funny lines, for sure, but I knew there was more to her than humor.

Gradually the writers have let her develop. And I've been able to give her more colors; I've tried to shade her personality. I worried whether black women would accept or despise her, and I've been gratified to learn that sisters seem to like her. Maybe that's because she's so funny, or maybe it's because her preoccupation with femininity is universal. Deep down, Whitley's not a bad person—she's egotistical, but good-hearted."

Comic roles can be very confining, especially extreme ones like Whitley Gilbert. Fans expect Jasmine Guy to have a strong southern accent, and they expect her to be a terrible singer, because Whitley is. At every opportunity Guy counters her Whitley image by appearing in projects that accent another side of her nature. In 1989 she took a movie role in the Eddie Murphy vehicle *Harlem Nights* that allowed her to play a sultry Creole conniver named Dominique Lanue, and in 1991 she played a housewife-turned-detective in a chilling television movie, *A Killer Among Us.* Guy told *Glamour* that her dramatic roles leave her far more vulnerable. "Whitley is definitely not me, so I've always felt removed from any criticism or compliments," she said.

Showcased broad range of talent with debut recording

In 1991 Guy released her debut album, *Jasmine Guy,* on the Warner Bros. label. Intended for the pop market, the work blends jazz and hip-hop styles in danceable, upbeat numbers. The first single, "Try Me," did well in heavy rotation on MTV, where Guy's dance training helped her turn in an electrifying music video. A *Jet* reviewer noted that Guy's album, above all, "has proven she's not the pretentious, pampered princess she portrays but a serious, steadfast singer on the rise." Guy has also continued her work on television. In 1992 she appeared in *Stompin' at the Savoy.* Set in 1939, the movie examines the lives of four poor, black single women who live together as roommates and whose only fun is jitterbugging at the famous Savoy Ballroom. Guy also worked on the television movie *Queenie,* which aired in 1993.

Commenting on the young performer's versatility, Betsy Bums theorized in *Mademoiselle:* "Whether [Jasmine Guy] is a singer, dancer or actress is becoming more and more unclear. What is clear is that with all these talents lies the promise of many more projects." Guy is very likely to forge a path for herself that will lead to top-level stardom—she has the proven qualities of determination, discipline, and talent. The actress told *Essence:* "I want to do something commercial, but something of indisputable quality.... I'm fanatical about high standards in every aspect of my work."

Sources

Ebony, June 1988.

Essence, August 1988.

Glamour, February 1991

Jet, December 17, 1990; May 10, 1993.

Mademoiselle, December 1989.

New York, February 15, 1993.

People, November 9, 1987; April 13, 1992.

Arsenio Hall

Born February 12, 1955
Cleveland, Ohio

"I'm not going after Johnny [Carson]'s crowd. I'm going after Johnny's crowd's kids."

ACTOR AND FORMER TALK
SHOW HOST

After five successful years with his late-night talk show, *The Arsenio Hall Show*, Arsenio Hall closed up shop in 1994. He took the world by storm when he entered the late-night arena in 1988. His show was markedly different from other talk shows at that time. In an effort to be less formal, he abandoned the desk and couch that graced the other shows, and instead he and his guests sat on comfortable chairs. His audience was young and hip and he was a master at bringing up their energy by shouting whoops and yelps and through barking-dog imitations—all mainstays of Hall's late-night format. His manner was casual and he became known for asking his guests easy questions, thereby giving them a virtual soapbox from which to pitch their latest projects.

That Hall had a late-night talk show is no surprise; he prepared for it ever since the Cleveland native was a child growing up in a strict Baptist household. His father, Fred Hall, pastor of Cleveland's Elizabeth Baptist Church, was 20 years older than Arsenio's mother. And their house was often a hotbed of disagreement. Fred Hall listened to gospel radio; his wife liked Top 40. He wanted his son to become a preacher; the boy wanted to be an entertainer. "It wasn't unusual for me to see my dad go for a gun during the arguments," Hall told *Time* magazine. "It wasn't just screaming—much deeper and more traumatic. I developed a rash and started sleepwalking. They'd find me in the garage in the morning, sleeping in the car." Hall's mother and father divorced when he was six years old (Fred Hall died in 1979), and Arsenio went to live with his grandmother.

Always hoped to be a talk show host

A lonely only child, Hall spent much of his time in front of the television. But while other kids watched cartoons and other children's shows, Hall was fixated on talk show hosts Dinah Shore, Merv Griffin, and Johnny Carson. After being put to bed, Hall would sneak back out to the living room and watch Carson's *Tonight Show,* whose host Hall, as quoted in the *New York Times Magazine,* still unabashedly refers to as "the architect for a lot of my dreams." As a 12-year-old, Hall arranged chairs in his house to make a makeshift *Tonight Show* set and pretended to be Johnny. This was also about the time he took music lessons, studied puppetry, and learned a few magic tricks so that he could work parties, bar mitzvahs, and weddings as Arsenio the Magician. Soon Hall began appearing on local television programs and he knew entertainment was the field he would devote himself to. "One day the high school basketball coach asked me to try out for the team," Hall told the *New York Times Magazine.* "I said, 'No.' I know what I want to do, and I'm not wasting my time. I'm not going to be here after school for basketball practice when I should be at home working on my magic tricks so I can become an entertainer."

Although Hall was a good student, school was merely a training ground for his routine. He graduated, stayed away from the wrong crowd and avoided drugs. But he liked to cut up. "Everyone else had nine brothers and sisters," he told the *New York Times Magazine.* "School was my only audience. Teachers used to say, "Arsenio comes to school and he fights to make the class laugh." But people didn't realize, I am here to work this room. I'm here to perform."

After he graduated, Hall enrolled at Ohio University in Athens, then transferred to Kent State University, from which he graduated with a degree in speech. "At Kent," Hall told the *New York Times Magazine,* "I stood up in front of a speech class and said, 'I plan on making a living with my oratory skills, and I'd like to be a talk-show host.' There was a pause, then the most incredible laughter you've ever heard in your life. I guess they thought I was crazy. No one stands up in a speech class at Kent State and says he wants to be the next Johnny Carson." But his first job gave no indication that he would reach his goal. He went to work for Noxell, makers of Noxzema skin cream. Then one night, while watching *The Tonight Show,* Hall decided to quit and pursue his dream. He left his job the next day, moved to Chicago, and started working comedy clubs for $10 a night. He began to build a name for himself, and was soon getting bookings to warm up for touring rock bands. Then, in 1979, singer Nancy Wilson hired Hall to host her stage show in Chicago. She arrived late, and Hall had to improvise for 20 minutes. It went so well that Wilson hired him as her regular warm-up act.

Moves to LA

In the early 1980s Hall moved to Los Angeles and continued his climb to fame. He became a familiar face on ABC's *Half Hour Comedy Hour* and in 1983 appeared as Alan Thicke's sidekick in the ill-fated *Thicke of the Night* late-night talk show. "I think I recognized that if anyone was going to be the Jackie Robinson of late night, it was Arsenio," Thicke told *Time.* Later, Hall became host of Paramount's syndicated rock and roll television show *Solid Gold* and continued to open for touring headliners. In 1986, when Patti Davis (President Ronald Reagan's daughter) canceled her interview on Joan Rivers's *The Late Show,* Rivers asked the Carson staff specifically to "get Arsenio," according to the *Los Angeles Times Magazine.* Then, in 1987, he got an eleventh-hour call from the Fox network. Musician Frank Zappa had backed out at the last minute as a fill-in host for Joan Rivers. Hall agreed to appear and did well enough to be called back twice the following week, and was given a 13-week contract. But the show was already scheduled to be canceled. In a way, that show's fate liberated Hall. "My thing was get attention," he told the *New York Times Magazine.* "I took chances. I played with the band, took cameras on the street, did improv, sang, wrote sketches, asked provocative questions, so that when it was over maybe somebody would give me a job. Sure enough, one night two execs from Paramount came to my dressing room and said, 'We'd like to talk to you about a movie deal.' I was ready."

After *The Late Show* came *The Wilton North Report,* another short-lived effort. When that failed, Paramount wanted Hall to try his own show, but the comedian was already committed to other projects. He had just finished *Coming to America,* the first of a three-picture contract with Paramount, in which he costarred with Eddie Murphy. The studio asked him again about trying his own talk show, and again he turned it down. Then, during a guest appearance on *The Tonight Show* to promote *Coming to America*, Hall changed his mind. "It was really kind of eerie, something I had wanted all my life," he told the *New York Times Magazine*. "During a commercial, Johnny showed me a coin trick and I said, 'I got one for you.' We kinda exchanged moves. It was that night [July 21, 1988] I decided to take the offer from Paramount to do the new talk show."

Produces and hosts his own show

Hall didn't just host *The Arsenio Hall Show;* he was also executive producer. He approved the guests, hired the staff, and even wrote the theme music. He would arrive at Studio 29 around 11 a.m., review the mail, look at the newspapers, and begin getting ready for the show. By 5 p.m. he was ready to take the stage. Afterwards, he would review the program with his staff and later take a videotape of the show home to study before finally dozing off at around 2 a.m.

Hall entered a crowded field that was littered with former talk show hosts who had tried to unseat Johnny Carson. But Hall had a few things going for him that the others did not. He was the first successful black late-night talk show host. And his show was considered fresher, *hipper,* than the rest. He did away with the desk and couch—which he found set the host apart from the guests—in exchange for some plush chairs like those you might find in someone's living room. Indeed, he tried to lend his program a party atmosphere, in which he might sing along with the band or run up into the audience. Guests knew they wouldn't get a grilling on *The Arsenio Hall Show,* but instead would have an easy time plugging their latest work. And while the level of conversation on the program was criticized for being light, boring, and non-controversial, Hall maintained that he was an entertainer, not a journalist; that his role was to entertain and not pressure people to discuss topics they probably would rather not. Nevertheless, Hall did see a New York media consultant to hone his interviewing skills.

His guest mix was eclectic. Actor George Hamilton could find himself sharing the gabfest with pro athlete Bo Jackson or the Reverend Jesse Jackson; wrestler Captain Lou Albano and basketball great Kareem Abdul-Jabbar might find themselves sitting next to cultural phenomena like Yahoo Serious or Weird Al Yankovic; Jason, from the *Friday the 13th* series of movies, might be listening to singers and rap groups, including De La Soul, 10,000 Maniacs, or Kool Moe Dee. "There used to be a feeling that late at night people wanted to be put to sleep by a talk show," Hall's producer, Marla Kell Brown, told *Time*. "But I don't think that's true for our generation. We want high energy." And the show was an unquestioned success. It was seen on 175 stations nationwide and reached 95 percent of U.S. television households.

> Hall uses his time and money to help better society. He is the national ambassador for Drug Abuses Resistance Education (DARE) and recently converted a crack house in Los Angeles into a church youth center.

Hall's key was in not trying to outshine Johnny Carson. Hall had a different approach. "What they [Rivers, Thicke, and others whose late-night shows had failed] all had in common is that they tried to out-Johnny Johnny," Hall told *Newsweek*. "I'm not going after Johnny's crowd. I'm going after Johnny's crowd's kids." "The *Tonight* show is an institution," Steve Allen, who launched the talk show format back in 1954, told *Time*. "But with each tick of the clock, its advantage disappears. The *Tonight* show audience is dying every day." Mel Harris, president of Paramount Television, told *Time* that "in the 1960s, Johnny Carson started with a young audience that stuck with him for 20 years. Arsenio's is the new generation."

Brown, Hall's producer, had worked with him on *The Late Show* and told the *New York Times Magazine* that Hall's popularity "comes from this kid, that little boy who is excited dealing with the people he's dealing with." He crossed the color line to become a black entertainer who had a strong appeal to whites. In January 1989, when Hall's show was first pitted against those of Carson, Pat Sajak, and David Letterman, Hall rated fourth in the ratings, but by summer had moved into second place, behind Carson.

The talk show wars begin

Then the late-night world went topsy-turvy, when veteran host Johnny Carson resigned in May 1992. There was a mad scramble to see who would be the next "King" of the talk shows. Jay Leno, the former guest host for the *Tonight Show*, took over Carson's spot and comedian Dennis Miller started his own show. Miller's stay was short-lived, however, and a similar attempt by comedian Chevy Chase quickly failed. The biggest upset in late-night television occurred in September 1993 when David Letterman left NBC and moved to CBS in a time slot that competed directly with the *Tonight Show*.

The sudden influx of new and varied talents began to take their toll on Hall's show. The show also suffered a ratings setback when the controversial Nation of Islam leader, Louis Farrakhan, appeared on the show. Many perceived that Hall was pandering to Farrakhan, and resented the fact that Farrakhan's extreme (some say racist) views were given a receptive platform on national television. As David Letterman's popularity began to increase, Hall's ratings began to dip even further. As quoted in *Time*, Hall made "the most complicated decision of my life" in May 1994 when he decided to terminate his show.

Hall quickly immersed himself in the world of movie production. He recently produced the film *Bopha* (1993), which examines social problems in South Africa and stars Morgan Freeman.

Sources

Entertainment Weekly, January 22, 1993.

Essence, July 1989.

Gentlemen's Quarterly, May 1992.

Jet, November 9, 1987; August 29, 1988; September 19, 1988; April 10, 1989; June 19, 1989; May 4, 1992; May 9, 1994.

Los Angeles Times Magazine, April 16, 1989; November 1992.

Newsweek, April 10, 1989.

New Yorker, June 6, 1994.

New York Times Magazine, October 1, 1989.

Rolling Stone, November 2, 1989.

Time, January 9, 1989; November 13, 1989; May 2, 1994.

TV Guide, September 6, 1989.

Variety, April 25, 1994.

Wall Street Journal, April 19, 1994.

Hammer

Born in 1962
Oakland, California

RAPPER

"I'm on a mission. The music is in me and I have to get it out."

Hailed by *Entertainment Weekly* as "rap's most pervasive, persuasive ambassador," Hammer has a reputation for pursuing his goals with remarkable energy and determination. His first dream in life eluded his grasp, however; if he had achieved it, he would be a professional baseball player today. Instead, Hammer has had to settle for being one of the world's most successful rap artists.

Hammer was born Stanley Kirk Burrell in Oakland, California. He was the youngest of his parents' seven children. "We were definitely poor," he stated in describing his youth to *Rolling Stone* writer Jeffrey Ressner. "Welfare. Government-aided apartment building. Three bedrooms and six children living together at one time." Despite the rough neighborhood he grew up in, Hammer stayed out of trouble by immersing himself in his twin passions, baseball and music.

As a boy he'd be at the Oakland Coliseum to watch the Athletics play as often as possible. If he couldn't see the game, he'd hang around the parking lot hoping for a glimpse of one of his heroes, among them super-star pitcher Vida Blue. When the team was idle Hammer amused himself by copying the dance moves of James Brown, the O'Jays, and others. He showed the first glimmerings of his interest in business when he began writing commercial jingles for his favorite products.

One day his two interests collided in a way that would profoundly influence his life. He was dancing in the Coliseum's parking lot when the Athletics' owner, Charlie Finley, passed by. A comment by Finley on the young dancer's style led to a conversation, and eventually to a job work-ing in the team clubhouse and going on the road as bat boy. Hammer quickly became a sort of mascot for the team. Finley even gave him the honorary title of executive vice-president, while the ball players began calling the former Stanley Burrell "Hammer" because of his striking resemblance to batting great Henry "Hammerin' Hank" Aaron.

Begins music career

After graduating from high school, Hammer tried to break into the world of professional baseball as a player, but to no avail. He briefly pursued a communications degree, but was unsuccessful in that field too. Dejected and at loose ends, Hammer considered getting involved in the lucrative drug trade thriving in his old neighborhood. "I was a sharp businessman and could have joined up with a top dealer," he told Ressner. "I had friends making $5000 to $6000 a week, easy.... I thought about that just like any other entrepreneur would." Hammer turned away from the fast money, however—making a moral choice that reverberates in his current image as a deeply religious, socially conscious performer—and joined the navy for a three-year hitch in Japan. When his stint with the military ended, Hammer applied the discipline he had acquired in the service to launching a career in music. His first musical venture was a rap duo he dubbed the Holy Ghost Boys. Religious rap might seem to have limited commercial appeal, but Hammer talked two record companies into taking a chance on producing a Holy Ghost Boys album. He and his partner went their separate ways before the project could be completed, however.

Two of Hammer's friends from the Oakland A's helped him make his next move. Mike Davis and Dwayne Murphy each invested $20,000 in Bust It Records, Hammer's own company. He hawked his debut single, "Ring 'Em," on the streets. At the same time, he was auditioning and working with musicians, dancers, and his female back-up trio, known as Oaktown's 3-5-7. Striving to put together a more sophisticated act, Ham-mer held rehearsals seven days a week, sometimes for 14 hours at a time.

Shortly after the release of his second single, "Let's Get Started," Hammer teamed with Felton Pilate, a producer and musician from the group Con Funk Shun. The two worked long hours in Pilate's basement studio to bring out Hammer's first full-length album, *Feel My Power*. Produced on a shoestring budget and marketed without the tremendous resources of a major record company, *Feel My Power* nevertheless sold a remarkable 60,000 copies.

Early in 1988 Hammer was catching an act at an Oakland music club when he was spotted by Joy Bailey, an executive at Capitol Records. She didn't know who he was, but his presence and attitude impressed her. She introduced herself and later arranged for him to meet with some of the company's top people at Capitol's Los Angeles headquarters. With his music, dancing, and keen business sense, Hammer convinced Capitol that he was the man who could lead the company successfully into the booming rap music market. He walked away from the meeting with a multialbum contract and a $750,000 advance. The record company didn't have to wait long for proof that they'd made the right decision; a reworked version of *Feel My Power,* titled *Let's Get It Started,* climbed to sales of more than 1.5 million records.

Breaks rap music sales records

Touring and appearing at hip-hop shows around the nation in the company of well-established rap performers Tone-Lōc, N.W.A., and Heavy D and the Boyz didn't keep Hammer from working on his next album—he simply outfitted the back of his tour bus with recording equipment. Such methods enabled him to turn out the single "U Can't Touch This" for about $10,000, roughly the same cost of *Feel My Power*. He predicted to Capitol that the album would break all rap music sales records, and his boast was no idle one. Backed by a unique marketing campaign (which included sending cassettes to 100,000 children, along with personalized letters urging them to request Hammer's music on MTV), "U Can't Touch This" had sold more than 5 million copies by late 1990, easily surpassing the record formerly held by the Beastie Boys' "Licensed to Ill." The song also became the theme song for the Detroit Pistons basketball team during and after their second NBA championship campaign in 1990.

After the release of *Please Hammer Don't Hurt 'Em*, whose immensely popular "U Can't Touch This" was described by *Entertainment Weekly* as "shamelessly copp[ing] its propulsive riff from Rick James' 'Super Freak,'" James took legal action against Hammer. The two entertainers reached an out-of-court settlement, with Hammer paying James for "borrowing"

Hammer won Grammy awards for best rhythm and blues song and for best rap solo in 1990 for "U Can't Touch This." That same year he also won a Grammy for best long-form music video for *Please Hammer Don't Hurt 'Em the Movie.*

James's early 1980s hit song. As reported in *Jet*, Hammer told James, "I felt good using music from a person I idolized. Ya'll used to come out and do a show. Then I'd do my thing at the club to 'Super Freak.'" According to *Jet*, the performers reconciled, with James telling Hammer, "Keep doing it."

In 1992 Hammer released *Too Legit to Quit* which was less successful, but still sold over 5 million copies. Rumors began to circulate, however, that Hammer was in a slump. He suffered some bad press about being in debt due to his excessive lifestyle. In fact, Hammer had turned over some businesses to his family in order to start Roll Wit It Entertainment & Sports Management, which already boasts such clients as Evander Holyfield and Reggie Brooks. Furthermore, in 1994 Hammer released *The Funky Headhunter.* He recreated his image to be less showy and more "street." Wearing baggy jeans and rapping a meaner sound, Hammer is now performing "gangsta rap." Hammer explained in *Ebony:* "A lot of people out there had seen negative stuff in the press. They felt Hammer wasn't going to make any more records—thought I was living in a shack dead broke.... They thought I was down so they kicked dirt at me. You know how they do when they think you are down. So now they see me reappear with 'It's All Good' and 'Pumps and A Bump' [his two hot singles], and they can't understand. It's like, Hammer's back and he's back in a big way."

For now, it looks like Hammer will endure in his present field. As *Entertainment Weekly* phrased it, "Hammer is cultural evolution in fast action, the rapper as wheeler-dealer and sleek entertainer—and the next logical step for a form of music that is quickly becoming part of the fabric of American life."

Sources

Ebony, January 1989; April 1994.

Entertainment Weekly, December 28, 1990.

Jet, November 5, 1990.

New York Times, April 15, 1990.

Rolling Stone, May 17, 1990; July 12, 1990; September 6, 1990; October 23, 1993.

Time, March 7, 1994.

Tom Hanks

Born July 9, 1956
Concord, California

ACTOR

How has Tom Hanks been able to do it? How has the star of such mediocre films as *Volunteers* (1985), *The Man With One Red Shoe* (1985), and *Joe Versus the Volcano* (1990) been able to not only survive but develop into one of Hollywood's most bankable stars? Here, after all, is a leading man who refers to himself as having "a goofy nose and geeky body," but who others have referred to as a modern day Cary Grant. Despite the negative reviews of some of his films, Hanks has usually risen above the criticism by turning in quality performances. And when he delivers a hit film he does it in grand style, pleasing both his fans and the critics with such films as *Big* (1988), *Philadelphia* (1993), and *Forrest Gump* (1994).

"Tom doesn't fit into the molds of the other American icons. It's too easy to find a couple of people that share that same all-Americanness that you can compare him to. But Tom Hanks will always be remembered for being Tom Hanks. He is without peer."—Steven Spielberg

Gets the girl

Hanks's main attraction seems to be an ability to play a role most average people find comfortable to watch. And the looks that he finds "goofy" others find charming. "I don't think I'm ugly," Hanks told *Rolling Stone*, "but I do sometimes look in the mirror and say, 'What is with these lips?'" Nevertheless, in many of his films, it's Hanks who gets the girl. In *Splash* (1984), Hanks falls in love with beautiful mermaid Daryl Hannah; in *Volunteers*, a gorgeous Smith College valedictorian (played by Rita Wilson, whom he later married) falls for him; in *Sleepless in Seattle* (1993) he captivates Meg Ryan, who falls in love with him when she hears him on a radio talk show.

"He has that handsomeness that isn't too beautiful. It's approachable," director Penny Marshall (*Big, A League of Their Own*) told *Rolling Stone*. "I think he's adorable." Oddly enough, one of Hanks's endearing qualities is that he looks unextraordinary. "I guess I have that quality," Hanks told *New York*, "of being like everybody else." And to *Rolling Stone*, he added, "I guess I come off in movies as a guy who you wouldn't mind hanging around with."

But Hanks is being unnecessarily modest. Although he's honed an average-wise-guy persona into a Hollywood commodity, he is anything but average. "There is nothing normal about the guy," Peter Scolari, Hanks's costar in the television sitcom *Bosom Buddies*, told *Rolling Stone*. "He is an imaginative, eccentric individual. He's a very quirky, very unusual young man."

Moves from town to town during childhood

That wasn't obvious from the outset. As a child, Hanks experienced a nomadic, middle-class life with neither ambition nor talent much in evidence. He was born in Concord, California. By the time he was five, his parents had separated. They remarried several times before divorcing for good. His father later married an Asian woman with a large family. "Everybody in my family likes each other," Hanks told *Rolling Stone*. "But there were always about fifty people at the house. I didn't exactly feel like an outsider, but I was sort of outside of it." When his parents divorced, Hanks, his older brother Larry, and his sister went off with their father, a roving cook who rambled through various cities until settling in Oakland when Tom was eight. His younger brother stayed with his mother.

In school Hanks also was unremarkable. "I was a geek, a spaz," he told *Rolling Stone*. "I was horribly, painfully, terribly shy. At the same time, I was the guy who'd yell out funny captions during filmstrips. But I didn't get into trouble. I was always a real good kid and pretty responsible." Although he acted in a few school plays, the names of which he says he can't remember, acting never seemed a real possibility until Hanks transferred from a San Francisco Bay area junior college to California State University at Sacramento. "Acting classes looked like the best place for a guy who liked to make a lot of noise and be rather flamboyant," Hanks told *New York*. "I spent a lot of time going to plays. I wouldn't take dates with me. I'd just drive to a theater, buy myself a ticket, sit in the seat and read the program, and then get into the play completely. I spent a lot of time like that, seeing Bertolt Brecht, Tennessee Williams, Henrik Ibsen and all that."

It was during these acting classes that Hanks met Vincent Dowling, head of the Great Lakes Theater Festival in Cleveland. At Dowling's suggestion, Hanks became an intern at the Festival, which stretched into a three-year experience that covered everything from lighting to set design to stage management. Such a commitment required that Hanks drop out of college. But by the end of the three years he had decided he wanted to become an actor. Part of the bug was due to the Cleveland Critics Circle Award, which he won as best actor for his performance as Proteus in Shakespeare's *Two Gentlemen of Verona*, one of the few times he played a villain.

Lands role in Bosom Buddies

In 1978 he moved to New York, where he married actress-producer Samantha Lewes. Seven years and a son and daughter later they were divorced, but Hanks still sees his children regularly. While in New York, Hanks acted for the Riverside Shakespeare Company. In addition, he made his film debut in a low-budget slasher movie and got a small part in a television movie entitled *Mazes & Monsters*. He continued to audition and finally landed an ABC pilot called *Bosom Buddies*.

"It was flukesville," Hanks told *Newsweek*. Hanks flew to Los Angeles, where he was teamed with Peter Scolari as a pair of young ad men forced to dress as women so they could live in an inexpensive all-female hotel. The series ran for two seasons, and although the ratings were never strong, television critics gave the program high marks. "The first day I saw him on the set," the show's coproducer, Ian Praiser, told *Rolling Stone*, "I thought, 'Too bad he won't be in television for long.' I knew he'd be a movie star in two years." But if Praiser knew it, he wasn't able to convince Hanks. "The television show had come out of nowhere," Hanks's best friend, Tom Lizzio, told *Rolling Stone*. "Then out of nowhere it got canceled. He figured he'd be back to pulling ropes and hanging lights in a theater." But it was *Bosom Buddies* that drew director Ron Howard to con-

Hanks with Robert Loggia in a scene from *Big*, 1988.

tact Hanks. Howard was working on *Splash*, a fantasy/adventure about a mermaid who falls in love with a human. At first, Howard considered Hanks for the role of the main character's wisecracking brother, a role which eventually went to John Candy. Hanks instead got the lead and an incredible career boost from *Splash*, which went on to become a box-office blockbuster, grossing more than $100 million.

Hanks's next three films were weak. But with his role in *Nothing in Common* (1986)—about a young man alienated from his parents who must re-establish a relationship with his father, played by Jackie Gleason—Hanks had begun to establish the credentials of not only a comic actor, but of someone who could carry a serious role. "It changed my desires about working in movies," Hanks told *Rolling Stone*. "Part of it was the nature of the material, what we were trying to say. But besides that, it focused on people's relationships. The story was about a guy and his father, unlike, say, *The Money Pit*, where the story is really about a guy and his house."

Hanks's next two films—*Big* and *Punchline* (1988)—were also successful, not only at the box office but within the industry in establishing

Hanks as a major Hollywood talent. "It's not easy being successful in this town," his friend Scolari told *Rolling Stone*, "particularly for a man of conscience. You get fed a steady diet of adulation. You get fed things that aren't necessarily bad or poisonous or toxic in any way. But they're not really on your meal plan. You have to stop and say, 'Wait a minute—I didn't order this.' You have to take your life by the horns. You have responsibilities that have nothing to do with being an actor. Tom Hanks has dealt with his success. I have never known him to be happier."

In order to appear sickly in *Philadelphia*, Hanks lost 35 pounds and thinned his hair.

Despite this success, Hanks's choice of roles again landed him in trouble with another string of box-office failures. First *The 'Burbs* (1989), then *Joe Versus the Volcano* (1990), and finally the colossal bomb *The Bonfire of the Vanities* (1990), which saw Hanks terribly miscast as a greedy Wall Street type who gets enmeshed in a hit-and-run accident.

Recoups with A League of Their Own

Hanks again climbed back to the top with his endearing portrayal of an unsuccessful baseball manager in *A League of Their Own* (1992). In an interview with *Vanity Fair*, Hanks called the work he's done since *League* his "modern era of moviemaking ... because enough self-discovery has gone on.... My work has become less pretentiously fake."

This "modern era" welcomed in a spectacular 1993 for Hanks, first with *Sleepless in Seattle* and then with *Philadelphia*. The former was a summer smash about a widower who finds true love over the airwaves. Richard Schickel of *Time* called his performance "charming" and most agreed that his portrayal ensured him a place among the premiere romantic-comedy stars of his generation. But it was in the latter film that Hanks truly made his mark. Playing a gay lawyer with AIDS who sues his firm for discrimination, Hanks proved he had the depth and talent to be one of the greats. In a review for *People* Leah Rozen praised Hanks's skill: "Above all, credit for [*Philadelphia's*] success belongs to Hanks, who makes sure he plays a character, not a saint. He is flat-out terrific, giving a deeply felt, carefully nuanced performance that deserves an Oscar." And Hanks's peers agreed, honoring him with the 1994 Academy Award for best actor.

Never one to rest on his laurels, Hanks followed *Philadelphia* with the 1994 summer blockbuster hit *Forrest Gump*. The film is a bittersweet tale of a simple-minded young man who finds himself in the middle of most of the major events of recent history. In the process, the character's very real wisdom shines through and positively affects the lives he touches. In *Vanity Fair* the film's director, Robert Zemeckis, praised Hanks's performance: "[Hanks] brings to this role what any great actor does—and I mean *great* actor—which is a real honesty." In the same article Hanks explained what appealed to him about the script: "When I read the script for *Gump*, I saw it as one of those kind of grand, hopeful movies that the audience can go to and feel ... some hope for their lot and their position in life.... I got that from the movies a hundred million times when I was a kid. I still do."

Hanks's next project reunites him with director Ron Howard in a movie about Apollo 13, in which he plays astronaut James Lovell. In 1970 Apollo 13 was on its way to the moon when an oxygen tank exploded and the spacecraft almost failed to return to Earth. In a *USA Weekend* interview Hanks talked about how he chooses projects: "[Since] *A League of Their Own*, it can't be just another movie for me. It has to get me going somehow.... There has to be some all-encompassing desire or feeling about wanting to do that particular movie. I'd like to assume that I'm willing to go down any avenue in order to do it right."

Sources

Boxoffice, September 1986.

Chicago Tribune, July 27, 1986; May 29, 1988.

Cosmopolitan, July 1985; March 1987.

Entertainment Weekly, December 31, 1993.

Esquire, March 1987.

Film Comment, August 1985.

Harper's Bazaar, December 1985.

Ladies' Home Journal, April 1987.

Life, April 1987.

Maclean's, March 19, 1984.

Mademoiselle, November 1986.

Newsweek, August 26, 1985; August 18, 1986; July 13, 1987; September 26, 1988.

New York, March 12, 1984; July 28, 1986.

New Yorker, November 19, 1984, September 8, 1986.

New York Times, April 26, 1987.

People, April 9, 1984; August 26, 1985; August 11, 1986; August 29, 1988; June 28, 1993; December 20, 1993; December 27, 1993.

Playboy, October 1984.

Rolling Stone, September 25, 1986; June 30, 1988.

Seventeen, August 1985.

Teen, March 1984.

Time, September 9, 1985; June 6, 1988; July 5, 1993.

USA Weekend, July 8-10, 1994.

Vanity Fair, June 1994.

Vogue, August 1985.

Neil Patrick Harris

Born c. 1973

Neil always wanted to make people laugh. Many's the time we had company and had to say, 'Okay, Neil, that's enough.' And he'd say, 'Oh, come one, one more card trick.'
—Ron and Sheila Harris

ACTOR

Neil Patrick Harris is best known for his portrayal of the teenage doctor Doogie Howser on the television series of the same name. He played the role of a child genius who could practice medicine effectively, while still going through adolescent turmoil. He managed to make his character likable and believable, thereby turning *Doogie Howser, M.D.* into a hit series that ran for four years. According to Curtis Pesmen in *Ladies' Home Journal*, "*Doogie Howser, M.D.* is buoyed by Neil's engaging performance as a well-adjusted child prodigy.... While he spouts medical jargon like a pro, he also loves his mom and dad, frets about whether to [sleep] with girlfriend Wanda and tries to keep his constantly [girl-crazy] friend Vinnie under control."

Plays Toto in The Wizard of Oz

Harris's first exposure to acting was in 1979, in Ruidso, New Mexico, when he played the role of Dorothy's dog, Toto, in a school production of *The Wizard of Oz.* He had accompanied his brother Brian (who auditioned for the part of a munchkin), and won the part of Toto because "they needed someone small." Harris discovered then and there that he had a talent and a passion for performing.

In 1987 Harris attended a summer camp that focused on theater and acting for young people. There, Harris met the writer Mark Medoff, who had recently written a screenplay entitled *Clara's Heart.* Medoff thought that Harris would be perfect for the part of the spoiled child in the film and recommended that he do an audition tape. Harris was quickly signed on to the film, in which he costarred with actress Whoopi Goldberg. While the film bombed at the box office, Harris won praise for his performance, and soon other work followed. He appeared in the television movie *Too Good to Be True,* the series *B. L. Stryker,* and the Hallmark Hall of Fame presentation, *Home Fires Burning.*

Stars in Doogie Howser, M.D.

In the winter of 1989, respected television producer Steven Bochco announced plans to do a new series about a child prodigy who scored perfectly on his Standardized Aptitude Test (SAT, a requirement for admission to most colleges), graduated from Princeton University at the age of 10, medical school at 14, and became a resident at a hospital while only 15. Harris auditioned for the lead role, and impressed Bochco and the show's director. The show's casting director, Robert Harbin, told *People,* "We auditioned hundreds of kids from everywhere. It was taking a big gamble no matter whom we chose, because the show wouldn't work if he didn't work in the role. When I first saw Neil, I thought, 'This is our guy,' but we still felt we had to see everyone." Critics laughed at the idea of such an odd premise making a successful television show, yet with Harris as the star, the series proved one of the true hits of the 1989-90 season.

The series had a successful run for four seasons, as fans watched Doogie grow up. While Harris could not quite match the mental aptitude of Doogie Howser, there were other similarities between the two. In 1990 Harris told *People,* "We're both dealing professionally with adults more than kids. We're both involved in jobs that take a lot of our time. And we're both 16, going through the feelings of that age. Sixteen-year-olds tend to have big mood swings that you kind of have to deal with."

Both of Harris's parents are attorneys, but because Harris's schedule became so demanding, the two temporarily stopped working and accompanied their son to Los Angeles, California, where they rented a two-room apartment. There, they acted as managers for Harris, answering his mail and helping him to maintain a balance between his professional and personal life. While working on the show, Harris spent seven hours a day filming and another three hours working with his tutor.

In his spare time Harris likes to perform magic tricks and make video spoofs with his friends. Some video titles include *Amish Death Spree, Amish Death Spree II,* and *Amish Death Spree III,* in which Harris plays a psychotic killer who happens to be Amish. In 1991 he hosted an episode of *Nova* for public television, entitled "So You Want To Be a Doctor." Since the series ended, Harris has worked on a variety of television programs and attends college in California.

Sources

Ladies' Home Journal, May 1990.

People, March 19, 1990.

Seventeen, January 1992.

Video Review, June 1989.

Katharine Hepburn

Born November 9, 1909
Hartford, Connecticut

ACTRESS

Legendary film actress Katharine Hepburn has been a major force in Hollywood for more than 60 years. The first woman to win four Academy awards for best actress, she has played socialites and missionaries, queens and librarians, lawyers and homemakers, all with warmth and dignity. Underneath each role, Hepburn's individual style and strength shine through. Once considered too odd to appeal to mass markets, Hepburn, with her high-society accent, athleticism, sophistication, and distinctive beauty, captured a large and enduring audience.

"Two of an actress's greatest assets are love and pain. A great actress, even a good actress, must have plenty of both in her life."

Hepburn was born on November 9, 1909, the second-oldest of six children, in Hartford, Connecticut. Her father, Thomas, was a doctor with rather progressive ideas and a great belief in the benefits of exercise. One of his favorite sayings was, "Exercise is the surest road to health." As a result of her father's enthusiasm for sports, Hepburn was something of a tomboy who wore short hair and trousers at a time when her peers wore long hair and dresses. From her father, Hepburn learned to believe in her own capabilities and in the importance of perseverance. In her autobiography, *Me: The Stories of My Life*, Hepburn remembered: "Dad once said that he would like to see me run off the diving board and go feet first with toes pointed, arms up, into the water. I tried it and landed flat on my back and was knocked out cold. The important thing was to try."

Hepburn's mother, Katharine, was also a strong presence and great influence on her daughter. As a suffragette, she campaigned for the right of women to vote. She was also an outspoken supporter of birth control at a time when may considered such action immoral and inappropriate for women to discuss, let alone champion. Her daughter flourished in her liberal and open-minded home, fully participating in heated dinner table debates and laying the groundwork for the independent woman she was to become.

Tragedy strikes a happy childhood

With five siblings to play with, Hepburn enjoyed what she has described as "an idyllic, wonderful childhood." In 1920, however, that perfection came to an end with the death of her older brother Tom. She and Tom, who were particularly close, had gone to New York to visit a close family friend, "Aunt" Mary Towle. While there one day, Hepburn went to wake her brother, who had been sleeping in the furnished attic. She found him hanging from a torn piece of sheeting attached to a rafter. Despite several theories, the reason for his apparent suicide remains unknown.

Tom's death had a profound effect on Hepburn. Unable to go back to school and face the sympathetic looks and inevitable questions of her classmates, Hepburn opted for private tutoring. "This incident seemed to sort of separate me from the world as I'd known it," she wrote in her autobiography. "I tried school but it was—well, I should say I was—I felt isolated. I knew something that the girls did not know: tragedy." To fill up her time and lift her spirits, Hepburn created a stage out of an old wooden box and a curtain. There, Hepburn entertained her family with stories she made up. Hepburn continued private tutoring until 1924 when she entered the college her mother had attended, Bryn Mawr.

Hepburn proved an average student who was almost kicked out twice—once for letting her grades slip drastically after a bout with appendicitis and once for smoking on school property, which was against regulations. It was also at Bryn Mawr that Hepburn became involved in college theater productions and consequently decided to become an actress.

Begins career as professional actress

Following graduation, Hepburn defied her parents and went to work with a Baltimore-based stock theater company. She made her professional debut in 1928 as a lady-in-waiting in *The Czarina*. In 1928 she landed a part in the Broadway show *These Days*. While understudying for the star in the Broadway play *Holiday*, Hepburn gave her notice two weeks after the opening and married a prominent socialite, Ludlow Ogden Smith, whom she affectionately referred to as "Luddy." Their marriage was not to be long-lived, however. After some success in New York, Hepburn left for Hollywood in 1932. "It turned out to be the beginning of the end of our marriage," she wrote in her autobiography. A few years later they divorced, though they remained close friends throughout the 1930s, and Smith remained "family" to the Hepburns for the rest of his life.

When Hepburn arrived in Hollywood she presented a number of problems for studio heads. These problems were primarily related to her famous rebelliousness. Hepburn's fiery independence and strong will were almost unknown in the prevailing women stars of the day. Consequently, Hollywood wasn't sure how to publicize her, which type of man to cast opposite her, or what sort of movies to construct around her. It is fitting that one of her 1930s films should be titled *A Woman Rebels*, since rebellion was consistently expressed both by the characters she played and her off-screen image. The rebelliousness could be used, up to a point, to make her as an attractive identification figure for the female viewer. At the same time, many were concerned that her independence could too easily become radical and uncontrollable. Hollywood was quite simply unsure of how to contain her. This gives her career, some would argue, a very special role in relation to feminism. Without ever expressly stating a desire to champion equality—indeed, Hepburn once said she "chose to live as a man"—for women, Hepburn repeatedly challenged a male-dominated social order both on and off the screen.

Many of Hepburn's films in the 1930s were directly concerned with female rebellion against male determination. Films such as *Little Women* and *Stage Door* demonstrate female bonding and mutual support, while a number of her other films question society's definition of masculinity and femininity. It was also in the 1930s that Hepburn worked with an ideal costar—Cary Grant. Perhaps her two finest films in this decade were *Holiday* and *Bringing Up Baby*, in which Grant and Hepburn were allowed to play off each other's pronounced personalities and excellent senses of comic timing.

Films For Which Hepburn Received Best Actress Academy Award Nominations

Morning Glory 1933 (won)
Alice Adams 1935
The Philadelphia Story 1940
Woman of the Year 1942
The African Queen 1951
Summertime 1955
The Rainmaker 1956
Suddenly Last Summer 1959
Long Day's Journey into Night 1962
Guess Who's Coming to Dinner 1967 (won)
The Lion in Winter 1968 (won)
On Golden Pond 1981 (won)

Turns around lagging film career

In 1940 Hepburn's career reached a turning point. After performing in a series of poorly received movies in the late 1930s, a group of movie theater owners banded together to label Hepburn "box-office poison." Her studio, RKO, began to offer lesser and lesser roles to Hepburn, and in her frustration and resentment Hepburn left Hollywood. While vacationing at her family's summer home, Hepburn was approached by friend and playwright Philip Barry to star in his new play *The Philadelphia Story*. Written with Hepburn in mind, the play concerns a cool and detached Philadelphia socialite who is transformed into a warm, vulnerable woman by play's end. Hepburn accepted the role and the production was a great success. When the film version was made, Hepburn—who played opposite Grant and James Stewart—was praised for her vivid and engaging performance, which once again placed her at the top of her profession.

It was also in the 1940s that Hepburn was first teamed with her most famous costar, and a man with whom she fell in love, Spencer Tracy. Hepburn and Tracy made a total of nine films together, beginning in 1942 with *Woman of the Year* and ending in 1967 with *Guess Who's Coming to Dinner*. Tracy's strength and masculinity balanced Hepburn's independence and their on-screen chemistry attracted a large and loyal following. Because Tracy was married and a Catholic, many believe that Tracy's religious beliefs kept him from divorcing his wife to marry Hepburn. As a result, the two had an affair that lasted until Tracy died in 1967. Over the years Hepburn rarely spoke of their relationship and the media was surprisingly discreet in their coverage of the couple. In her autobiography, Hepburn wrote: "I have no idea how Spence felt about me. I can only say I think that if he hadn't liked me he wouldn't have hung around. As simple as that. He wouldn't talk about it and I didn't talk about it. We just passed 27 years together in what was to me absolute bliss. It is called LOVE."

One of Hepburn's unlikeliest, though ultimately most endearing, pairings was with Humphrey Bogart in *The African Queen*. The 1951 film, in which she appears as Rose Sayer, a proper missionary woman who must escape war-torn Africa with a hard-drinking river boatman, is considered one of her lasting triumphs. Hepburn and Bogart, in addition to mastering uncharacteristic roles, endured hostile climatic conditions and the eccentricities of director John Huston to complete a film that has become an American classic.

In her later years, Hepburn continues to perform in both movies and on television. In 1981 she won her fourth Oscar for best actress—an unprecedented achievement—for her role in *On Golden Pond.* Nominated for a total of 12 Academy awards for best actress, Hepburn also won Oscars for *Morning Glory, Guess Who's Coming to Dinner,* and *The Lion in Winter.* Hepburn appeared in *Mrs. Delafield Wants to Marry,* a light made-for-television comedy about a love affair between two senior citizens, in 1987. In 1994 she played a featured role in *Love Affair,* Warren Beatty and Annette Bening's remake of the classic 1957 film *An Affair to Remenber,* which starred Cary Grant and Deborah Kerr.

Sources

Hepburn, Katharine, *The Making of "The African Queen" or How I Went to Africa with Bogart, Bacall and Huston and Almost Lost My Mind,* Knopf, 1987.

Kepburn, Katharine, *Me: Stories of My Life,* Knopf, 1991.

Newsweek, November 10, 1969.

New York Times, October 10, 1962; June 18, 1967; April 27, 1969.

Parish, James Robert, and Ronald L. Bowers, *The MGM Stock Company: The Golden Era,* Arlington House, 1973.

Time, November 16, 1981.

Washington Post, February 10, 1968; September 1, 1969.

Gregory Hines

Born February 14, 1946
New York, New York

ACTOR AND DANCER

"In terms of talent, Gregory is an absolute ticking thermonuclear weapon just waiting to go off."

A show business veteran, Gregory Hines has appeared in films, onstage, and in nightclubs virtually since he could walk. Although he is one of the few black actors who commands star billing and is equally at home in comedic and dramatic roles, Hines is best known for his tap dance artistry. In fact, he has perhaps done more than any other performer to ensure a bright future for that most American of dance styles. As Sally Sommer noted in *Dance* magazine, Hines wants to push tap beyond the expected conventions and clichéd images.... Certainly he is in the right position to initiate such changes, because he is both an enormously popular performer in mainstream entertainment and a radical tap [dancer] who keeps experimenting with the form."

Hines told *Dance:* "I can't ever remember not tapping." He was born in New York City in 1946 and raised in the middle-class, integrated Washington Heights neighborhood. His father, who sold soda and worked as a nightclub bouncer, was the son of dancer Ora Hines, a showgirl at the famous Cotton Club. On his mother's side his ancestors include Portuguese, Jewish, and Irish immigrants. Hines told *People* that he has never felt uncertain about his ethnicity. "When I was a kid," he said, "blacks would say, 'Oh, we have some Irish in us and some Portuguese. We have better quality hair. We're better than other blacks.' I thought it was a load of bull. I always have considered myself a black man. What my mother has on her side is irrelevant. When I go for a role that was written for a white, it means nothing."

Although at age ten Hines ran into a tree stump and was left legally blind in his right eye, the injury did not slow him down or affect his dancing.

Hines's mother had great ambitions for her sons and thus steered both Gregory and his older brother Maurice toward tap dancing. Gregory literally learned his first tap steps as a toddler and was enrolled in dance school at the age of three. Shortly thereafter he and Maurice became professionals with a song-and-dance act known as the Hines Kids. They toured extensively in America and abroad and also played the famous Apollo Theatre in New York. In 1952 they came under the guidance of Broadway choreographer Henry Le Tang; he helped them earn roles in their first musical comedy, *The Girl in Pink Tights*. Gregory in particular rounded out his tap training by watching older tap professionals "Sandman" Sims and Teddy Hale. During breaks in shows these improvisational masters would tutor the youngster, passing on to him a style that might otherwise have been lost in tap's lean years.

In 1963 Maurice Hines, Sr., joined the act as a percussionist and the trio billed themselves as Hines, Hines and Dad. Gregory told *People:* "We weren't ever really successful. We were a very strong opening act, but we never got over the hump." Many would-be entertainers would have been more than satisfied with their level of success, however. Throughout the 1960s Hines, Hines and Dad appeared on the *Tonight Show,* the *Ed Sullivan Show,* and numerous other television programs. They also toured Europe, playing at Eon don's famed Palladium and the Olympia Theatre in Paris. Unfortunately for the Hines family, tap dancing had gone out of vogue by the late 1960s. The trio was reduced to a musical/comedic lounge act, with Maurice as straight man and Gregory as comedian. Slowly the act began to stagnate, and Gregory accordingly revised his ambitions.

In 1973 the Hines brothers disbanded. Almost simultaneously, Gregory's first marriage dissolved. Left to his own resources, he moved to Venice, California, and became "a long-haired hippie," experimenting with the sex, drugs, and rock 'n' roll lifestyle of the West Coast. He worked as a waiter, busboy, and karate instructor during the day and played with a jazz-rock group at night. Today Hines remembers those years in Venice as a turning point in his life. "For the first time in my life, I learned how to take care of myself," he told *Ebony*. "Until that time, I always had somebody—my wife, my manager, my parents taking care of me. There was always somebody between me and what was really happening. I got out to Venice and it was just me and life, and I had to learn how to take care of myself."

Career sizzled with Broadway triumphs

During his sojourn in Venice Hines met his second wife, Pamela Koslow. She returned with him to New York City in 1978 and they were married in 1981. For years Hines thought that he had left tap dancing behind, but upon his return to New York he reconciled with Maurice and auditioned for a Broadway revue. Eventually the Hines brothers teamed again with Le Tang, appearing on Broadway in *Eubie!* in 1978. That show featured Gregory Hines as a tapper and singer and earned him the first of three Tony Award nominations as outstanding featured actor in a musical. After *Eubie!* closed, Gregory starred in two more successful Broadway shows, *Comin' Uptown* and *Sophisticated Ladies*. Both gave Hines the opportunity to shine as a singer, comedian, and dancer, and he again earned Tony nominations for his work.

A national tour of *Sophisticated Ladies* took Hines back to the West Coast; while there he embarked on a film career. In 1981 he earned his first movie roles, appearing in *History of the World, Part I* as a Roman slave and in *Wolfen* as a medical examiner investigating a series of mysterious deaths. Hines absolutely relished film work and aggressively sought further roles. When he heard that producer Robert Evans was casting a major film about the Cotton Club, the dancer-actor "instituted a reign of terror" trying to win a principal role. "I started calling [Evans] everyday and going over to his house telling him how perfect I was for the part," Hines told *Ebony*. In fact, Hines was indeed perfect for the role of "Sandman" Williams, an upwardly mobile Cotton Club dancer. When *The Cotton Club* was released in 1984 many reviewers singled Hines out as the bright spot in an otherwise muddled movie.

The appearance in *The Cotton Club*—and a now-classic performance on the television show *Saturday Night Live*—virtually assured Hines a measure of stardom. Audiences were thrilled with his fast-paced and sexy jazz-tap routines, many of which featured improvisational, arrhythmic flights that pushed far past tap's traditional boundaries. Sommer wrote in *Dance* magazine: "Like a jazz musician who ornaments a well-known melody with improvisational riffs, Hines improvises within the frame of a dance. Among many tappers, improvisation is the most revered art, because it is about creation, demanding that the imagination be turned into choreography instantaneously. Certainly it is the most difficult aspect of tap to master. The tap dancer has to have the brilliant percussive phrases of a composer, the rhythms of a drummer, and the lines of a dancer."

Held his own opposite Baryshnikov

In 1985 Hines faced a daunting challenge when he was cast opposite revered Soviet-born ballet dancer Mikhail Baryshnikov in the dance drama *White Nights.* Hines rose to the occasion, matching the classically trained Baryshnikov step for step in a film that became an impressive box-office draw despite its somewhat stale plot. Hines also turned in several striking dance numbers in the 1988 film *Tap,* a movie that featured three generations of great black tap artists. "Finally," noted Sommer, "the movies have caught up with the real world of dance. Now the moviegoing public will find out what the tap dance audience discovered at least ten years ago—the vital black heritage that shaped the look and sound of American tap dance." No one has been more pivotal than Gregory Hines in bringing that heritage to a mainstream audience.

Hines is also considered a bankable romantic actor. *People* correspondent Mary Vespa wrote: "With his dancer's grace, relaxed wit and bedroom eyes, Hines could move into a realm where no black actor has been before—the hip, sophisticated, romantic-comedy territory staked out by Cary Grant and Fred Astaire." Hines has earned top billing in a variety of roles, from the comic *Running Scared,* where he teamed with Billy Crystal, to the science-fiction adventure *Eve of Destruction,* to the critically well-received big-budget drama *A Rage in Harlem.*

In 1992 Hines won the lead role in the Broadway musical *Jelly's Last Jam.* He played Jelly Roll Morton, a light-skinned Creole musician who rejects his black heritage. Although he found the role taxing, critics have called his performance moving and powerful. In fact, Hines's work was so well regarded that he won the highest praise that Broadway offers—the Tony Award.

Despite the variety of work Hines tackles, he still sees himself first and foremost as a tap dancer. As he settles into middle age, however, Hines has realized that his reflexes are slowing down. "I know I can't dance at this level indefinitely," he told *Ebony.* "Skill diminishes with age; it's just mathematics. Expectations of Hines's decline seem premature, however; he works out regularly and has kept his 5′10″ frame in remarkably sound condition.

Having been in show business for 40-odd years, Hines is used to the frantic pace and months away from home and family. On the rare occasions when he is free, the dancer enjoys spending time with his wife and three children. "My family is very important to my existence," he told *People*. "If there was something beyond the marriage ceremony I could do with [my wife], I would. I have responsibilities as a husband and father that I want to fulfill." With his trademark left earring and drooping eyelids, Hines has an offbeat attractiveness that will undoubtedly sustain him past the age when most dancers retire. Already he has left an indelible mark on the movies by bringing his tough and alluring variety of tap to young audiences. *Dance*'s Sommer concluded that the grand old men of tap, the hoofers of yesteryear, see Gregory Hines as their future, "their immortality, the talented baby of them all, who carries the legacy of their rhythms in the soles of his feet."

Sources

Dance, December 1988.

Ebony, January 1991.

Glamour, December 1985.

People, August 11, 1986.

Dustin Hoffman

Born August 8, 1937
Los Angeles, California

ACTOR

Dustin Hoffman is widely considered one of the best actors of his generation. He is known for his thorough examination of his characters, which leads to realistic and compelling performances. He became an almost overnight sensation after his winning portrayal of a bewildered and endearing college graduate in the 1967 film *The Graduate*. Since that time he has continued to impress the critics and win legions of new fans with such films as *Midnight Cowboy*, *Kramer vs. Kramer*, *Tootsie*, and *Rain Man*.

"I've been a star for 20 years and a human being for 30 years before that. I feel good that I've been a human being longer."

An awkward youth

Hoffman was born on August 8, 1937, in Los Angeles, California. His father worked as a propman at Columbia Pictures. Hoffman remembers being an awkward youth who wore braces and was shorter than the rest of the kids. However, being short helped him win his first dramatic role, as the character of Tiny Tim in a school production of Charles Dickens's *A*

Christmas Carol. Too small for many sports, Hoffman played tennis, lifted weights, and learned to play the piano.

After graduation from high school, Hoffman attended Santa Monica College, where he originally intended to become a music major. He soon discovered that theater was his first love, and he dropped out of school to attend acting classes at the Pasadena Playhouse. He stayed at the Playhouse for two years, and in 1958 left for New York City in order to take further classes and try his luck on Broadway.

Struggles to make a living

Hoffman's first years in New York were difficult. He lived in a small flat with a number of other aspiring actors, among them Gene Hackman. Because acting jobs were few and far between, Hoffman earned money by washing dishes, waiting on tables, and demonstrating toys at Macy's department store. He taught acting at a boys' club and appeared in a number of small parts on television. His fortune began to change in 1966 when he won a role in Ronald Ribman's *The Journey of the Fifth Horse.* For his portrayal of the middle-aged and sarcastic character Zoditch, he won the Obie Award as the best off-Broadway actor of the 1965-66 season. He next appeared in Henry Livings's play *Eh?*, for which he received a Drama Desk-Vernon Rice Award for off-Broadway achievement.

These performances indirectly led to the casting of Hoffman in the 1967 hit film *The Graduate.* The film's director, Mike Nichols, had seen Hoffman off Broadway and immediately thought of him when he began to cast for the role of Benjamin Braddock—the young hero of *The Graduate.* Hoffman flew out to California for a screen test and won the part. The deciding factor for choosing Hoffman was his ability to project a kind of youthful bewilderment that was both genuine and appealing.

The Graduate is based on a novel of the same name by Charles Webb. The story follows Benjamin Braddock, who has recently graduated from a college on the East Coast, and who returns home to Los Angeles, California, uncertain of who he is and what his future holds. The audience begins to see Benjamin mature during the course of the summer. He is enticed into an affair with "Mrs. Robinson," the wife of his father's law partner and a woman old enough to be his mother. The relationship is shallow, and when the Robinsons' daughter, Elaine, returns from college for the summer, Benjamin soon realizes that it is she he truly loves. When the affair between Benjamin and Mrs. Robinson is disclosed, the Robinsons, as well as Elaine, reject Benjamin, and it is up to Benjamin to convince Elaine that they should be together. So Benjamin chases Elaine to a town in California where she is about to be married to the conventional, upper-middle-class man of whom her parents approve. In one of the most famous scenes in all of movie history, just as the bride and groom exchange their vows, Benjamin starts pounding on the windows at the back of the church and shouting "Elaine, Elaine." Elaine realizes that she is only satisfying her parents' expectations and that she would rather be with Benjamin. The two run off and catch a departing bus, safe at last and together as the film's final credits begin to roll. The movie was an immediate and overwhelming success. It spoke to the troubled youth of the late 1960s, who mistrusted anyone over 30 and vowed never to be tempted by the empty materialism they associated with their parents' generation.

Plays antiheroes

After *The Graduate,* Hoffman continued to excel at his craft, making a good number of critical and commercial successes. Many of Hoffman's roles have been termed "antihero," which means that the roles Hoffman tends to play demonstrate traits that are the opposite of what one might expect from a traditional hero. For example, one of his characters might be cowardly or dishonest, instead of brave and truthful. Yet, his characters manage to gain sympathy from the viewers, often because they seem so vulnerable. This is true of his roles in *The Graduate, Midnight Cowboy* (1969), *Marathon Man* (1976), and *Kramer vs. Kramer* (1979). Other times the viewer roots for his characters because, even when they are arrogant (*Lenny* [1974], *All the President's Men* [1976]), or extremely violent (*Straw Dogs* [1971]), they are generally working for a greater political or professional goal. The same is true when Hoffman plays convicts, (*Papillon* [1973], *Straight Time* [1977]); despite their criminal backgrounds, the Hoffman antiheroes of these films still compel audiences to hope for the best outcome.

A number of Hoffman's characters appear neurotic and desperate, a perception heightened by the actor's nasal-voiced, emotionally charged delivery. Indeed, the sight of Hoffman running—for his life in *Marathon Man,* for the life of his son in *Kramer vs. Kramer,* for the woman he loves in *The Graduate*—is a recurring image in his films, reflective of a need to bid goodbye to the tension and conflicts of the American rat race.

A character actor

Few leading men of the American screen are as dependent on their makeup artists as Hoffman. His looks and height (he's five-foot-six) enable him to undergo startling physical transformations on-screen. He played a crippled hustler, Ratso Rizzo, in *Midnight Cowboy*, a 121-year-old man, Jack Crabb, in *Little Big Man* (1970), and a woman, Dorothy Michaels, in *Tootsie* (1982). This chameleon-like skill extended to his acclaimed 1984 Broadway performance as Willy Loman in Arthur Miller's *Death of a Salesman*. Looking as he had never quite looked before, with thinning gray hair, rimless glasses, and circles under his eyes, Hoffman as Willy was simply burnt out and angry, alternately ready for death and anxious to seize the next illusory opportunity that presented itself.

As Hoffman continues to work, he seems increasingly determined to select roles in which he will stretch himself as an actor. Notable among them was his stage performance as Shylock in a London production of William Shakespeare's *The Merchant of Venice*. His recent on-screen roles attest to Hoffman's insistence upon a range of parts in a variety of films: as Raymond Babbit, the autistic savant (autism is a psychological disorder characterized by withdrawal from reality, and a savant is someone gifted with a special intellectual ability) in *Rain Man* (1988); as Vito McMullin, son to Sean Connery and father to Matthew Broderick, in the underrated *Family Business* (1989); as the comic-book gangster Mumbles, for which the actor was made up beyond recognition in a very funny cameo, in *Dick Tracy* (1990); as gangster Dutch Schultz in the screen adaptation of E. L. Doctorow's novel *Billy Bathgate* (1991); and as Captain Hook, to Robin Williams's Peter, in *Hook* (1991)—Steven Spielberg's version of *Peter Pan*.

Whatever the role, Hoffman has proved time and again that he has the range and depth of talent to stand among the great actors of the twentieth century. His skill at vividly creating a wide variety of personalities and his ability to elicit emotion from the audience ensures that he will continue to please and delight his fans as the years go by. Hoffman has won two Academy awards for best actor—one for his performance in *Kramer vs. Kramer* and one for his performance in *Rain Man*.

Sources

Bergan, Ronald, *Dustin Hoffman*, London, 1991.

Lenburg, Jeff, *Dustin Hoffman: Hollywood's Anti-hero*, New York, 1983.

Life, May 1987.

Los Angeles Magazine, March 1994.

Premiere, February 1989.

Rolling Stone, February 3, 1983.

Anthony Hopkins

Born December 31, 1937
Port Talbot, Wales

ACTOR

"I'm still waiting for God to tell me, 'What do you think you're doing? You go back to Port Talbot. This is a mistake. We meant Tomkins, not Hopkins.'"

One night in the fall of 1965, Anthony Hopkins, a 27-year-old actor from Port Talbot, Wales, sat in the gallery of London's Old Vic Theater. Since his ticket was free, Hopkins couldn't complain about his seating, which was "high up ... slightly to the left of the stage," he wrote 24 years later in the *New York Times*, "so I had a diagonal bird's-eye view of the performance." Until that lofty moment in his life, Hopkins had only seen that evening's star performer on-screen. So when Sir Laurence Olivier came onstage as Othello (in Shakespeare's play of the same name), it was "electrifying, terrifying" to Hopkins, "like reading Shakespeare by lightning flashes." The next day, in the main rehearsal room of another famous London stage, Hopkins would audition for the man who ran the National Theater, "a man of medium height, dressed in a gray business suit," who had "thinning gray hair, wore glasses and for all the world looked like a bank manager—Sir Laurence Olivier."

When Hopkins, who today is best known for his Oscar-winning role as the chillingly gruesome Dr. Hannibal "The Cannibal" Lecter in 1991's The Silence of the Lambs, listed the monologues he had chosen for his audition—a piece from the British playwright George Bernard Shaw, a passage from the Russian dramatist Anton Chekhov, and finally, the closing speech from Othello—there was, Hopkins recalled, "a slight pause. Then Olivier said, 'You've got a bloody nerve, haven't you?'" Hopkins was accepted into the National Theater, and his stage performances, which Michael Billington of the New York Times said "exuded a burly strength and suggestion of physical danger," soon convinced the English public that Hopkins was the "next Olivier." Hopkins himself was uneasy with the comparison and hid his own insecurities about his abilities behind a temper that went hand-in-hand with heavy drinking. With his drinking days far behind him now, he seems to have accepted his fierce youth. "I was an awkward customer," he told Anna Brown of Cosmopolitan, "I drank a lot, smashed a lot, worked a lot. And I relished boozing—every hangover, every nosedive into the dirt. It was my weakness and my sustenance."

The "difficult drunk" stories brought on further comparisons, this time to fellow Welsh lush, screen great, and Shakespearean actor Richard Burton. Actually, it was a meeting with Burton that first inspired the 15-year-old Hopkins to pursue acting as a way out of his hometown. He found Port Talbot "closed, parochial, rainy, depressing, impersonal." He realized then, as he told People's Jim Jerome, that he'd "love to get out of this place, out of my own peculiar loneliness. I was so shy, I figured acting would help me devil up the confidence. So I sent a beam into the universe: 'I've got to become something.'"

Born on New Year's Eve

Perhaps this combination of wild drinking and steely resolution should be expected from someone born on New Year's Eve. Hours before 1938, Richard and Muriel Hopkins, who ran a bakery in their working-class town, welcomed into the world their first and only child. Although Anthony drew and played piano as a child, he was, he admitted to John Clark of Premiere, "lousy in school. Real screwed up. A moron. I was antisocial and didn't bother with the other kids. A really bad student. I didn't have any brains. I didn't know what I was doing there. That's why I became an actor."

When he dropped out of high school, Hopkins tried a drama class at the local YMCA. He won a scholarship to Cardiff College of Music and Drama, and after stints in the military and a steel foundry, he went on to

London's Royal Academy of Dramatic Art. To Jim Jerome, Hopkins said of his early years, "I just felt very isolated for years and years, didn't feel I belonged anywhere. It made me depressed and miserable. I've drawn on that melancholia."

But once in London Hopkins's meteoric rise into the constellation of stage stars stopped abruptly when, during a 1972 performance of Macbeth at the Old Vic, he simply walked out. He'd had another abrupt break—a personal one—several years before when he left his first wife, actress Petronella Barker, and their 18-month-old daughter Abigail. He has long since patched things up with his daughter, now in her twenties, but they didn't see each other for seven years. And though his second marriage with Jennifer Lynton, a film production assistant, has endured, (they were married in 1973) it's clear that the early 1970s were a stormy period. "I spent a lot of my personal and professional passion just lashing out," he told Joan Harting of *Harper's Bazaar,* "in a kind of rage, monomania."

In 1974 Hopkins came to the United States and proved essential to the stage success of *Equus,* in which he played a self-doubting psychiatrist. He stayed in the States, disparaging the type of actor that English audiences expected him to be. He told Harting, "I was perceived as a 'respectable' actor, always in tights, carrying spears, and going around to the BBC to do dramas." To *Premiere,* Hopkins said, "Even Shakespeare wanted a bit of fun. Christ must have laughed." Though Hopkins worked continually once he'd crossed the Atlantic, the projects he signed on for varied in quality. He received critical acclaim for his role as the deranged ventriloquist in the 1978 film *Magic,* only to be panned for playing the harrumphing lover of the hot-tub-prone Bo Derek in 1980's *Change of Seasons.* This may have been due, in part, to his status as a Hollywood outsider. "When I first got to Hollywood," he told Michael Billington of the *New York Times,* "I knew all the good scripts were going to Dustin Hoffman and Robert De Niro. They weren't going to come to some limey sitting there on a hill. So I got the castoffs."

Hopkins's work on TV had a similar seesaw quality. He won two Emmys, one for his 1976 portrayal of the Lindbergh baby kidnapper Bruno Hauptmann, the other for the title role in *Hitler,* a 1980 Hallmark Hall of Fame production. But after that, he'd run off to do something like *The Hollywood Wives.* Part of this perverseness sprang from an abiding need to thumb his nose at the British acting establishment. But part of it was surely drink. As the actor told Jim Jerome, "I used to space out and hallucinate. I was a lunatic, very hyper and manic. I was drinking to kill the discomfort of self-contempt. Then it dawned on me: I'm going to kill myself, I'm going to lose my wife, my career. I was destroying everything around me."

Quits ∂rinking

Then one morning Hopkins woke up in Phoenix, Arizona, and he didn't know how he'd gotten there. But he did know the time to change had come. He joined Alcoholics Anonymous and also quit smoking. He returned to the British stage and began to work furiously. He followed his role in David Hare's 1985 production of Pravda with title roles in Shakespeare's *King Lear* and *Antony and Cleopatra.* But during the run of *Antony,* he realized that he'd gone too far again, that he'd been on a "work binge" for years, and was, as he told Anna Brown in *Cosmopolitan,* "knackered, burned out."

To recuperate, he drove across America. "Driving," he told Brown when he described his journey of recovery, "brings out terrible emotions. It engulfs you, takes you over. There's something romantic—dramatic—about driving across huge stretches of empty landscape." Hopkins likes being alone—he avoids the cycle of appearances at parties that is normally expected of the Hollywood elite. He likes to play the piano. He likes Indian food and he likes America. "I'm what you'd call an Amerophile," he told the *New Yorker,* explaining why: "I love hotels and motels. I check in and walk around the streets casing the joints, finding the coffee shops, and watch the dumb TV shows. *Honeymooners* and *Lucy.* I like that. I like to drive around—vast tracts of lost desert, mountains. I drove through Wyoming in a day, crossed over the border into Bozeman, Montana. Did Texas in a day. It was like ... a dream. Took off from Oklahoma City one morning. I said, 'I'll try Dallas.' Thirteen hours I drove. I had the tape machine on [playing] 'The Messiah.' There was smog and great buildings. I was nearly crushed between two trucks.... I crossed over to Baton Rouge, stopped in a run-down motel, watched Lucy. I drove through the Appalachians to Pittsburgh. It was eight at night, I was playing Beethoven's Ninth, going through tunnels. It was like [the film] *Close Encounters [of the Third Kind].*"

And this personal journey from blazing British tantrums to a calm he found wandering alone on miles of U.S. interstate had an effect on Hopkins's acting as well. He discovered after 20 years of pressing that he didn't have to work so hard. He explained in the *New York Times* how he developed the character of the soft-spoken rare-books collector Frank Doel in *84 Charing Cross Road:* "I began way over the top and I'm beginning now to climb down. I have a tendency to go off firing the big guns and I now realize you have to give an audience the chance to listen."

Hopkins is happy to talk about this subtle power he has as an actor, but another force he has been credited with—what Anna Brown called "his powerfully understated sexuality"—makes the normally forthright Hopkins uncomfortable when it's mentioned in interviews. He has suggested it's something all actors have, he's lampooned it, he has spoken about his personal shyness, or his preference for playing the piano—anything to divert the spotlight from this aspect of his attraction. He told Tirzah Lowen, author of a book about the 1987 production of *Antony and Cleopatra*, "I mean, look at me—short, grey haired ... I find it very difficult to go out onstage and lean against the furniture with, you know, the right kind of confidence. It feels ridiculous."

Dr. Hannibal "The Cannibal"

However, this shyness melts away when the topic shifts to his acting roles. Suddenly Hopkins is anxious to talk, and it's clear that he understands the hypnotic effect of his brooding and explosive presence. No role showed this more than his Oscar-winning performance as Dr. Hannibal Lecter in *The Silence of the Lambs*. When he explained his conception of Lecter to *Premiere* he could just as easily have been talking about the mysterious appeal of his own dangerous calm. "Lecter," he said, was "a personification of the Devil. I have always perceived the Devil as very charming, witty, all clever and wise, seductive, sexual—and lethal."

Jodie Foster, who also won an Oscar for her work in *The Silence of the Lambs*, described to *Premiere* how Hopkins-as-Lecter chilled her: "He was in the middle of something, and then he started imitating my accent. The first time he did it, I wanted to cry or smack him. I just was so upset. You're in a scene, so you sort of feel those things, but as an actor, having somebody imitate your accent—it just killed me. It was the perfect thing for Lecter to do, because Clarice has been hiding her rural accent trying to speak better, escape her origins in a certain way. And here's a guy who nails her."

Another 1990s Hopkins role that leaped off the screen was his Henry Wilcox in *Howards End*. As the commanding rubber magnate whose no-nonsense business approach extends to his emotional life, Hopkins showed how complete emotional collapse can hide behind an icy oh-so-British calm. Startling in its economy, Hopkins's performance seemed even more impressive following so closely on the popular success of *The Silence of the Lambs*.

Two of Hopkins's greatest roles followed in 1993 with *The Remains of the Day* and *Shadowlands*. In the former he plays Stevens, a butler whose shyness and extreme dedication to his job keep him from recognizing the

love being offered by the housekeeper with
whom he works. The movie received overwhelming critical praise. Joanne Kaufman of
People commented, "In his utter capacity and
failure to comprehend, the extraordinary
Hopkins, as a butler, is more frightening than even Hannibal Lecter." And
according to Richard Corliss of *Time*, "[With] age and stardom, [Hopkins]
has discovered how to be still. He knows he can do less and be more.
Audiences will study him like a weather-worn statue for hints of dark-
ness, heroism, meaning. Like Stevens, he learned to serve, and to seek
greatness in serving."

In *Shadowlands* Hopkins plays C. S. Lewis, the famous British scholar
and author of the children's classic novel series *The Chronicles of Narnia*.
The film recounts the true story of Lewis's marriage to the feisty American writer Joy Gresham, which is cut short when she succumbs to cancer.
While the film itself received mixed reviews, Hopkins's performance was
uniformly praised. According to *People*, "[It] is Hopkins who steals *Shadowlands*."

Where once Hopkins enjoyed the reputation of an actor who savaged
directors, now he seems more like the funny uncle, startling the script girl
by wishing her "Good moooorning," in his Hannibal-the-Cannibal voice—
an attitude much the opposite from his frighteningly difficult youth. Hopkins was also charming when he strode to the podium to accept his Oscar
for best actor. He seemed both aristocratic and shy, and finished his
remarks with convincing and effusive thanks to his longtime wife, Jennifer. The two of them, by all accounts, live together quietly and happily in
an 1800s townhouse in London. "I've been able to translate my weirdness
into all my work," Hopkins told Jim Jerome. "I wanted to be exactly what
I am now, to live a sane life instead of the lunacy I lived before."

Hopkins has recently finished filming *Legend of the Fall*, an epic span-
ning 200 years, and *The Road to Wellville*, in which he plays Dr. Kellogg,
the health food pioneer who invented the cornflake.

Sources

Cosmopolitan, February 1991.

Harper's Bazaar, February 1982.

Lowen, Tirzah, *Peter Hall Directs Antony and Cleopatra*, Limelight Editions, 1990.

New Yorker, March 16, 1992.

New York Times, July 16, 1989; February 10, 1991.

New York Times Biographical Service, March 1987.

People, February 2, 1981; Spring (special issue) 1991; January 17, 1994; November 8, 1993.

Premiere, March 1991; February 1994.

Time, November 8, 1993; December 27, 1993.

Whitney Houston

Born August 9, 1963
Newark, New Jersey

"I grew up in the church, and gospel music has always been the center of our lives.... At family celebrations, we always end up sitting around the piano and singing. I couldn't get enough of gospel music when I was growing up."

SINGER AND ACTRESS

Since her debut on the music scene in the mid-1980s, Whitney Houston has established herself as an American pop institution. Born into a musical family—her mother, Cissy, is a gospel singer and back-up artist, and the sultry-voiced Dionne Warwick is her cousin—Whitney knew at an early age that she wanted to be a professional singer. After years spent as a back-up vocalist with her mother's acts, she met Arista Records executive Clive Davis, who saw her star potential. Houston's first two albums sold millions, demonstrating her popular appeal to a large and diverse audience.

Houston began her singing career in the basement of her parents' home, belting out Aretha Franklin songs while pretending to perform in Madison Square Garden. By the time she got out of elementary school, she had decided on a career in music, even though her mother wanted her to be a teacher. Cissy Houston conceded to young Whitney's decision, however, and began to personally coach her daughter. "My mom has been my biggest influence," Houston commented in the *New York Times*. "Everything she knows physically and mentally about singing she has passed on to me, and she taught me everything I know about the technology of the recording studio and about the business."

"I would say that gospel music was my greatest influence. It taught me a lot about singing. It gave me emotion and spiritual things, and it helped me to know what I was singing about, because in gospel music the words mean everything. Now, whatever I sing, whether it's gospel or pop or R&B, I *feel* it."

Displayed talent early

Houston began singing with the church choir that her mother conducted. As a high school student, she was singing back-up for her mother and a variety of other artists including Lou Rawls and Chaka Khan. With a pretty face and a slim figure, the hardworking Houston also launched a successful modeling career, appearing in *Vogue, Seventeen,* and *Cosmopolitan.* She wanted to quit high school and devote more time and energy to her career, but her mother advised her to complete her education first. After graduation, Houston signed with a talent management agency and continued to model and sing.

When Houston was 19, she gave a special concert at a Manhattan nightclub to showcase her talents to industry executives. It was there that she met one of the most influential people in her life, Arista Records president Clive Davis. He had significantly boosted the careers of other artists, including Air Supply, Aretha Franklin, and Dionne Warwick. After careful consideration, Houston signed with him. Over the course of two years the shrewd executive showcased Houston at selected venues and carefully selected material for her debut album. This recording, titled *Whitney Houston,* cost Arista an unprecedented $250,000—a very rare expenditure for a first album.

Debut album topped charts

Whitney Houston features songs from some of the top names in the recording industry. After debuting a single in Europe, the album was released in the United States. It contains duets with Jermaine Jackson and Teddy Pendergrass as well as the hit singles "You Give Good Love," "Saving All My Love for You," "How Will I Know," and "The Greatest Love of All." The album remained at the top of the charts for 46 weeks.

"This is infectious, can't-sit-down music," wrote Richard Corliss of the release in *Time.* Other critics were impressed by the catchiness of Whitney's songs and her professional delivery but complained about the lack of originality of her selections. Gary Graff summed up these complaints in the *Detroit Free Press*, noting, "Critics ... uniformly praised her exceptionally trained voice but attacked the unapologetically mainstream approach of her music and her stiff stage performances." Nevertheless, *Whitney Houston* sold over 13 million copies and launched the singer into superstardom almost overnight.

Houston's next album was delayed for half a year because of the resurgence in popularity of her first effort. In 1987, the follow-up LP, *Whitney*, was finally released. "We intentionally sought a waiting period," manager Davis told *Newsweek*. "We didn't want a saturation of the market." *Whitney* was the first album by a female singer to debut on the top of the *Billboard* charts. Corliss reported that "the new album showcases a Whitney Houston who sings bolder, blacker, badder," and added, "Whitney marks graduation day for the prom queen of soul."

Against charges that the album's songs were trite and hackneyed, Whitney became an overnight hit. Part of the reason for this was the singer's popularity with a wide range of listeners. "She can get the kids on the dance floor," said producer Narada Michael Walden in *Time*, "then turn around and reach your grandmother." This was Houston's intention all along. "We wanted that mass appeal," she commented in the *Detroit Free Press*. "I wanted to appeal to everybody—moms, kids, dads.... It's great we achieved that."

Became tabloid target

After the completion of her second album, Houston stepped out of the limelight to assess her career. She established friendships with gospel singers and started a few businesses. By the early 1990s, however, Houston became the victim of rumors about her personal life. She was purported to be involved in a lesbian relationship with her personal assistant, but she was also romantically linked with comedian Eddie Murphy and actor Robert De Niro. Controversy within the music industry also plagued her. Several rhythm and blues enthusiasts suggested that she was "too white" to succeed as a black artist, while the television show *In Living Color* satirized her in a sketch called "Whitney Houston's Rhythmless Nation." (*In Living Color*'s producers apparently felt that Houston's dancing prowess failed to match that of chart-topper Janet Jackson, who showcased her expertise in skillfully choreographed videos from her hit album *Rhythm Nation 1814*.)

Houston, however, bounced back in 1990 with the release of *I'm Your Baby Tonight*. The new album was proclaimed by Davis to be more mature and funky than her previous works. Although Houston's name alone seemed to be enough to sell the album, Davis commented in a *Detroit Free Press* interview: "We don't approach this with any sense of aggressiveness or cockiness. We worked hard to make this ... as great as we can. Hopefully, everyone who liked or loved her before will be happy, and she will also make a giant number of new fans."

Entered new phase

I'm Your Baby Tonight sold over 6 million copies worldwide, which was a slight disappointment compared to sales of her first two albums. Commenting on speculation that the star was losing popularity, Graff suggested: "What's really happening is that, after a sizzling start, Houston's career is cooling down and settling in at a level that's impressive by any standard except when measured against her prior accomplishments."

Houston also scored with U.S. audiences with the release of her stirring rendition of the "Star Spangled Banner," which she belted out at the start of the 1991 Super Bowl. Proceeds from that recording went to the American Red Cross Gulf Crisis Fund. The next year she again grabbed the spotlight with news of her marriage to singer Bobby Brown (her wedding dress reportedly cost $40,000) and her feature film debut opposite Kevin Costner in *The Bodyguard*. The success of *The Bodyguard* was astounding. The film grossed $411 million worldwide, while the soundtrack sold 24 million copies and produced three Top 10 hits. In early 1994 Houston won three Grammy awards, including Record of the Year for the single "I Will Always Love You" from *The Bodyguard*, as well as eight American Music awards.

In 1993 Houston and Brown had a baby girl they named Bobbi Kristina—B. K. for short. Houston considers having a child her greatest accomplishment. In an interview in *Rolling Stone* Houston commented: "Having Bobbi Kristina ... I could never do anything that could top that. There's been nothing more incredible in my life than having her. God knows, I have been in front of millions and millions of people, and that has been incredible, to feel that give-take thing. But, man, when I gave birth to her and when they put her in my arms, I thought : 'This has got to be it. This is the ultimate.' I haven't experienced anything greater."

"Like all of us in the family, Whitney was singing from the moment she came out," Dionne Warwick commented in *Time*. Houston has parlayed this family legacy into an amazingly successful career. And with her breakthrough superstardom, Houston has not only carved a nice niche for herself, but has made it easier for other talented young female singers to get into the business. "Here I come with the right skin, the right voice, the right style, the right everything," commented Houston to Corliss in *Time*. "A little girl makes the crossover and VOOOM! It's a little easier for the others."

Sources

Chicago Tribune, July 1, 1991.

Detroit Free Press, November 5, 1990: June 30, 1991.

Ebony, June 1990; May 1991.

Essence, February 1994.

Greenberg, Keith Elliot, *Whitney Houston*, Lerner Publications, 1988.

Harper's, September 1986.

Jet, June 20, 1988; September 11, 1989; July 16, 1990; February 28, 1994; March 21, 1994.

Ladies' Home Journal, March 1988; March 1989.

Newsweek, July 21, 1986; July 13, 1987.

New York Times, November 11, 1990.

New York Times Biographical Service, October 1985.

People, May 19, 1986; December 22-29, 1986.

Rolling Stone, June 10, 1993.

Vogue, July 13, 1987.

Anjelica Huston

Born c. 1952
Los Angeles, California

ACTRESS

For two decades Anjelica Huston faded in the shadow of her famous family and then her equally famous lover, actor Jack Nicholson. Since 1985, however, she has become a star on her own terms, a respected actress able to breathe vitality into an array of challenging roles. The daughter of director John Huston—and granddaughter of Academy Award-winning actor Walter Huston—Huston underwent several particularly intense periods of self-doubt before finding herself. Today Huston's work "is in high demand," according to James Kaplan in the *New York Times Magazine*, "yet she isn't quite as they say bankable. She seems quite pleased with this state of affairs. John Huston, after all, had commercial and artistic highs and lows, but is remembered as a great artist." The raven-haired actress might be on her way to similar artistic recognition, for she's done some excellent work. Director Nicholas

"The main thing to know about Anjelica is that there's a certain level of sophistication among modern young women in acting, where, frankly, she simply owns the category. There's nobody else that comes near her. And she just gets better. She continues to grow, which is all you can ask of any spectacular person."
—Jack Nicholson

Roeg offered a succinct description of her abilities in the *New York Times Magazine:* "Anjelica's work is so good because she is able to abandon herself and come out unscathed."

A childhood surrounded by the wealthy and famous is no guarantee against stress. In fact, it can present unusual complications of its own, not the least of which is the pressure to "measure up" to the standards of the famous parent. Huston talks freely of her formative years, when she both idolized and feared her father. John Huston was in his mid-forties when Anjelica was born—she was the second child of his fourth wife, ballerina Enrica Soma. Huston had already compiled an impressive list of directing credits, including *The Maltese Falcon, The Treasure of the Sierra Madre* and *Key Largo,* and he was on the verge of winning another Academy Award, for *The African Queen.* This prestigious lifestyle was not lost on Anjelica, even though her father was gone for months at a time while on location filming.

Anjelica's relationship with her father was often strained. In the *New York Times Magazine,* the actress recalled: "My father didn't like weakness. He couldn't abide it in others; and he certainly couldn't tolerate it in himself. He didn't tolerate whining and bad behavior from children. He liked what was adult in children. If you were heard you had to be very careful that you knew your stuff.... He had a cruel streak—made him interesting. He liked his fun. It was certainly sometimes at the expense of others.... But I think that if there were a sin there, it was that he was very much preoccupied with what he wanted to do, which didn't necessarily coincide with his having a wife, or having children." Still, Huston told the *Los Angeles Times Magazine,* when it came time for her father to leave on one of his extended trips, "We would cling to his legs as he was driven to the airport. A sense of magic would be gone from the house, and things would get a little dull again."

Played at estate in Ireland

When Anjelica was still very small, her father bought a large estate, St. Clerans, in County Galway, Ireland. There she grew up in what she has called a "fairy-tale childhood," roaming the countryside, riding horses, and engaging in imaginative games with her brother Tony. The two children used to like to write and perform their own dramas for visiting adults. "Oh, there was a lot of love and magic in St. Clerans!," she told *People* magazine. "I can't imagine why I ever chose to grow up."

The choice to grow up was actually made for the youngster when she was 11 years old. Her parents separated, and her mother took her to live in London, where she attended an exclusive private school. Huston told the *Los Angeles Times Magazine* that life in the city "was very traumatic. I didn't feel particularly attractive at the time and clung to my make up with some persistence. I was very, very skinny—the second-tallest girl in my class. I had knobby knees and this nose, which gave me some tribulation.... It was a difficult period. I was confused, wondering what was happening. My parents' separation wasn't explained to me. I have always been under the erroneous persuasion that if you don't ask, it won't harm you. I preferred to believe everything was all right, that my parents still loved each other."

Adolescence brought new conflicts between Anjelica and her father, culminating in a disastrous film they made together in 1968. Overlooking her lack of experience, Huston cast his daughter in the movie *A Walk With Love and Death,* a love story about teenagers set in medieval France. The 15-year-old Anjelica did not like the part and took her father's direction resentfully. "The making of the movie was uncomfortable," she said. "I didn't communicate well with my father on the set or off the set. I had trouble with my lines. I thought I looked ugly. I felt terribly naked without my makeup." Critical reaction was mostly negative—taking shots at both her performance and her looks. In the end the project only heightened Anjelica's lack of self-esteem.

Mother dies in auto wreck

That blow was compounded by another of even greater severity. In 1969, when she was 16, Huston lost her mother in an automobile accident. Enrica Soma was only 39 when she was killed, and the sudden tragedy took Huston completely by surprise. "My mother's death was a complete overhaul of the world as I knew it," she told the *New York Times Magazine.* "I was in no way prepared for her to die.... It was like losing my best friend, my mother and my sister all in one. Nothing has happened to me before or since to equal the impact of that shock."

Devastated, Huston vowed to quit acting. The reviews of *A Walk With Love and Death,* as well as a break with her father, contributed to the decision. In 1971 she turned to modeling at the insistence of a photographer, Richard Avedon, and shortly thereafter, to quote *People,* she became "the hottest thing on Kodachrome—in one issue *Vogue* devoted 30 pages to Avedon pictures of Anjelica in Ireland." Ironically, the young model still thought of herself as unattractive. Huston was more than ready for a change in 1973, when she attended a party at the home of Jack Nicholson, then an up-and-coming film actor.

Nicholson recalled in *People* that when he first caught a glimpse of Anjelica Huston, he saw "cla-a-a-ss." For her part, Huston fell deeply in love with a man as charismatic—and flirtatious—as her father. Abandoning her modeling, she moved in with Nicholson and devoted herself exclusively to him for three years. Then both partners began to chafe under the restrictions of their relationship. Nicholson's bout of boredom were personal, but Huston's had a professional aspect as well. She wanted to return to acting, but she refused to use "contacts" such as Nicholson to help her land roles. Eventually she enrolled in acting classes with Los Angeles teacher Peggy Feury. In *Film Comment* Huston remembered that Feury "did nothing but reinforce me and give me kindness. She calmed me down a lot, helped me be less demanding of myself, and she was extremely kind—which was what I needed most.... Peggy changed my life. Everyone should have such a guardian angel."

Hit by a drunk driver

Yet another near-tragedy solidified Huston's ambitions to return to performing. In 1982 she was involved in a head-on collision with a drunk driver; her facial injuries required six hours of surgery to correct. She told the *New York Times* that the shock of the crash made her confront "the need not to waste my life." When she recovered she took any work she could find. For a time this consisted of bit parts in television situation comedies and films, but in 1984 she was offered a starring role in a science fiction adventure, *Ice Pirates.*

John Foreman, the producer of *Ice Pirates,* was so impressed with her performance in that film that he cast her first in his next project, *Prizzi's Honor.* Only after Huston had agreed to play Maerose did Foreman hire her father to direct the movie and Nicholson to star in it. Most critics agree that *Prizzi's Honor* created a genuine demand for Huston. She received almost unanimous praise for her portrayal of Maerose, a graceful Mafia princess with a deplorable Brooklyn accent and a penchant for orchestrating violence. Huston won the Academy Award for her portrayal of Maerose, and her father had the distinction of having directed both his father and his daughter in Oscar-winning performances. Nicholson, too, was thrilled for his longtime lover, telling friends that he was more pleased with her victory than he would have been with another of his own.

Since *Prizzi's Honor* was released Huston has not lacked for roles. She played Gretta Conroy in a film adaptation of Irish writer James Joyce's *The Dead* (her father's last directing effort before he died) and an antiwar activist during the Vietnam era in *Gardens of Stone.* She rounded off the

1980s with three very different performances. Her concentration-camp survivor in director Paul Mazursky's *Enemies: A Love Story* was wryly down-to-earth, as she recognized with some bitterness and some compassion that time and suffering had matured her far beyond her husband's reach. In *The Witches* she played the comic-strip villain to the hilt, changing small boys into mice with wicked humor. For director Woody Allen's *Crimes and Misdemeanors* she played a desperate mistress.

"I like women who are survivors. I'm wary in a certain way of what I pull in terms of my life in my work because I find one thing often pulls in the other. I like people who learn something and finally win. Most of all, I like survival stories. And happy endings."

The 1990s have showed no slowing down of Huston's quest for varied and challenging roles. She received widespread praise for *The Grifters.* She played Lilly Dillon, a trashy blonde con artist who manages to destroy anything or anyone that gets in her way. In Woody Allen's *Manhattan Murder Mystery* she played a New York writer. She also played Morticia Addams in two films about the Addams family—a rich and eccentric group of characters, whose idea of mischief is dumping a vat of hot oil on a group of cheery Christmas carolers.

In late 1989 Nicholson and Huston had a very public break-up. It was revealed that Nicholson had fathered the child of actress Rebecca Broussard, while another aspiring starlet was telling bedroom secrets about her affair with Nicholson in *Playboy* magazine. It proved too much for Huston, and she left Nicholson. She rebounded, however, and she met her husband, sculptor Bob Graham, within a year of her split with Nicholson. In 1992, a year and a half after the two met, they were engaged in Ireland and married in Los Angeles. They live in a house on a beach in Venice, California.

Asked whether she sees herself as a character actress or a leading lady, she told the *New York Times Magazine:* "I don't think about that. I think about parts that interest me. It doesn't really matter how big a part is, if it's got juice. I'd much prefer to be on the screen for 5 or 10 impactful moments ... than to meander through a landscape in epic fashion. I like ensemble acting—it's bolstering. I'm more intrigued with playing characters than with playing people closer to myself."

After many years of fighting her image as a Huston and as Nicholson's lover, Huston has acquired a philosophical acceptance of her unique background. "I think Americans particularly, who don't have all that much history, are very pleased to have whatever history they have," she said. "And I think my family's name is strong in the theater and strong in movie history, and I think people like that. It makes me feel good. I feel very much backed by my ancestors." Still, she admitted in *Mademoiselle,* she has been buffeted somewhat by life—and has profited from the hard knocks. "When I look at myself I see the lines in my face, but I have a certain affection for them," she claimed. "You see, I've earned them."

Sources

Commonweal, May 22, 1987.

Cosmopolitan, March 1993.

Esquire, September 1987.

Film Comment, October 1987.

Interview, September 1985; July 1991.

Los Angeles Times Magazine, June 21, 1987.

Mademoiselle, April 1987.

Newsweek, June 17, 1985.

New Yorker, July 1, 1985.

New York Times, June 27, 1985; May 18, 1986.

New York Times Magazine, February 12, 1989.

People, July 8, 1985.

Premiere, November 1993.

Vogue, September 1985; November 1990.

Ice-T

Born c. 1957
Newark, New Jersey

"I try to write about fun/And the good times/But the pen yanks away and explodes/And destroys the rhyme."

RAPPER AND ACTOR

Ice-T appeared on the music scene in 1987 with a new style now known as gangster rap, which offered rhymes about crime and street life in unflinching detail. His tough, groundbreaking records paved the way for the wave of younger gangster-rappers that included Ice Cube and N.W.A. Before Ice-T's arrival on the scene, rappers devoted most of their lyrics to partying. Ice-T, an ex-criminal from south central Los Angeles trying to go straight by way of his music, sang about what he knew: robbery, murder, pimps, hustlers, gangs, and prison.

By the early 1990s, however, Ice-T had reached such a level of success as a recording artist and film star that his gangster image began to give way to that of a teacher. *Newsweek* referred to him as "a foulmouthed moralist." *Entertainment Weekly's* James Bernard declared that "Ice-T has something to teach anyone concerned about the rotting core of America's cities." As his success broadened, Ice-T continued to sing about the street—but with a determination to help black kids escape the ghetto and make white kids understand it. He also considered his financial future a matter of strategy: "The name of the game is capitalism," read a typical Ice-T quote from his publicity packet, "and I aim to win that game, too."

Ice discovers rap music

Ice-T was born Tracey Marrow (some sources cite his surname as Morrow) in the late 1950s—he has refused to release his birthdate—in Newark, New Jersey. By the time he was in the seventh grade both his parents had died, and he went to live with an aunt in Los Angeles. While at Crenshaw High School, he wrote rhymes for local gangs and was soon drawn by his friends into petty crime. At age 17 he left his aunt's home and, in his words, started "hanging out in the 'hood with my friends." By the early 1980s, Ice was also drawn to rap music, thanks to the success of artists like Kurtis Blow. In 1982 he recorded "The Coldest Rap" for an independent label and was paid $20 for it.

Naturally, this kind of money was nothing compared to what he and his friends could make illegally. Although he claimed to have never been a true gang member himself, he was close enough to see that world as a dead end. Eventually his friends started being sent to prison. "Then one of my buddies got life," he told *Musician*. "And they were all calling me from jail, saying, this ain't the place, homes. Stay with that rap. Stay down." He stayed with it, honing his style and landing a part as a rapper in the 1984 movie *Breakin'*.

In addition to the advice and admiration of his friends, Ice relied on his girlfriend Darlene, who stayed with him through the lean years and finally shared his success with him. "Even though we were broke," Ice told Scott Cohen in *Details*, "she knew that I could take five minutes out and go scam $20,000. I needed a girl who was ready to say, 'Don't do it, Ice. It's O.K.'" Darlene added that for a long time they were too broke to go to the movies: "We just lived in one little room and paid rent. We didn't have a car for two years."

Puts L.A. rap on the map

By the mid-1980s rap had grown from an urban phenomenon to a national one, but New York City's rappers had a monopoly on street credentials. California, which had produced the good-natured surf pop of the Beach Boys and psychedelic rock bands like the Grateful Dead, hardly seemed a source of rhymes about urban strife. But Ice-T's 1987 debut, *Rhyme Pays*, put south central Los Angeles on the nation's cultural map with its disturbing stories of inner-city warfare.

This new approach took the music community by storm; it also provoked charges from watchdog organizations like the Parents' Music Resource Center and from critics on the political left and right that Ice glorified violence, theft, and sexism. Subject matter aside, he drew fire—and the first warning sticker placed on a rap record, by his reckoning—for using profanity. "No one has yet been able to explain to me the definition of profanity any how.... I can think of ways to say stuff—saying. Things using legitimate words but in a context—that makes a more profane comment than any ... swear words." The album's rap "6 in the Morning" became particularly well known, telling the story of a handful of gang members escaping the police.

Ice returned in 1988 with *Power*. The cover of the album featured a bikini-clad Darlene pointing a gun at the camera; Ice hadn't softened his approach. The album yielded two hits, "High Rollers" and "I'm Your Pusher." Ice's face began to appear more regularly on MTV, and he contributed the title song to the soundtrack of the 1988 gang film *Colors*. His high-profile gangsterism provoked more attacks from various authorities, particularly when he began speaking to students in schools. In a discussion with Arion Berger in *Creem*, Ice presented his imitation of an FBI agent opposed to his school tours: "He has a record here called, um, 'I'm Your Pusher.' 'Well, have you played it?' Oh, we don't have a phonograph here at the Bureau."

Ice's frustration at attempts to suppress his music motivated a change of direction on his next LP, *The Iceberg/Freedom of Speech ... Just Watch What You Say*, released in 1989. A drawing of his face appeared on the cover with guns held to either side of his head and the barrel of another in his mouth. He enlisted punk politician and former Dead Kennedys lead singer Jello Biafra to deliver an announcement of right-wing martial law over a sampled piece of deathmetal guitar, setting the tone for a relentless counterattack on conservative thinking. Berger called the album Ice-T's "most vicious criminal record so far."

Ice later reflected that the *Iceberg* album was too preoccupied with censorship and free expression. "Sales were good on that album," he told Dennis Hunt of the *Los Angeles Times*, "but [I can see where] some of the raps made some people think I was going soft. I just got caught up in messages—about freedom of speech. People at the record company wanted me to do that and I'm sorry that I listened to them." In the meantime, he added, the rising stars of gangster rap had upped the ante of street-tough rhyming. In 1991, though, he would come roaring to the forefront of the scene once again.

Ice-T landed the role of an undercover cop in the smash 1991 film *New Jack City* and his song "New Jack Hustler" appeared on the film's soundtrack. He received excellent reviews for his acting in the film; Alan Light of *Rolling Stone* called his performance "riveting." "It was scary," Ice told Dave DiMartino of *Entertainment Weekly*. "I didn't know how the actors were gonna react, and in music I'm in my own domain. But when I got there, the first thing I found out was that they were, like, in awe of me—they wanted, like, autographs and stuff." Soon he had signed on to play a drug dealer in another film, *Ricochet*.

Ice's 1991 album O.G.—*Original Gangster* contained 24 tracks of uncompromising and often violent raps. Rather than pursue the anticensorship tack of the *Iceberg* album, O.G. returned to Ice-T's earlier turf with a vengeance. The album's themes are summed up by titles like "Straight Up Nigga," "Prepared to Die," and "Home of the Bodybag." Ice's raps, though laced with the "profanity" of earlier records, had become tougher and leaner; "Mic Contract" likened rap competition to gang warfare and suggested that Ice-T was ready to face off with young gangster-rappers. The album also included a rock and roll song, "Body Count," which was the name of the hardcore band he had assembled. Ice enlisted four different producers to work on the album, and DJ Evil E. provided the eclectic mix of beats and samples.

Reviews of O.G. were mostly very positive. *Entertainment Weekly's* James Bernard gave the album an "A." Even as Jon Pareles of the *New York Times* acknowledged contradictions between Ice's "trigger-happy machismo and his increasing maturity," he remarked that "[O.G.] works to balance the thrills of action and the demands of conscience." "It's his candor that really draws blood," a notice in *Musician* commented, while *Stereo Review* insisted that "Ice-T raps in lightning-quick, no-nonsense rhymes that cut to the bone with lack of pretense or apology." In his *Rolling Stone* review, Mark Coleman noted that "O.G. can be heard as a careening, open-ended discussion. Of course Ice does tend to follow his sharpest points with defiant kiss-offs.... But get past his bluster and this guy is full of forthright, inspiring perceptions."

For its unsparing language and content, O.G. received a parental warning sticker; Coleman claimed that such warnings were "like sticking a Band-Aid on a gunshot wound." Ice-T's response to the sticker, in a quote which appeared in his publicity materials as well as ads for the album, was as follows: "I have a sticker on my record that says 'Parental

Guidance is Suggested.' In my book, parental guidance is always suggested. If you need a sticker to tell you that you need to guide your child, you're a dumb parent anyhow."

In 1994 Ice's book *The Ice Opinion* was published. It's filled with Ice's observations and opinions on such topics as race relations and recent events in the music industry.

Tours with Lollapalooza

Nineteen-ninety-one also saw Ice-T join the ambitious traveling rock festival known as Lollapalooza. Organized by Perry Farrell—whose band, Jane's Addiction, was the headlining attraction—the tour included such divergent acts as Black Rock Coalition founders Living Colour, the industrial dance outfit Nine Inch Nails, and British postpunk veterans Siouxie and the Banshees. As the only rapper on the tour, Ice-T faced Lollapalooza's predominantly white audiences with a positive attitude: "All I want them to do is come out and say 'I like him.' Not get the message, not understand a word I'm saying. Just think, 'Those black guys on the stage I used to be scared of, I like 'em.' I want to come out and say, 'Peace.' If I can do that, that's cool." His participation in Lollapalooza attested to his belief that rap had the same rebellious and unifying quality that rock and roll had when it first appeared: "White kids will continue to get hipper to black culture. With R&B, the kids didn't want to meet us, but this is rock & roll all over again—everybody chillin' together."

Ice-T was again in the middle of controversy when his hardcore band released the album *Body Count* in 1992. One of its singles, "Cop Killer," is about murdering a police officer. Public outcry was so strong that Ice-T and Warner Bros. Records withdrew the song from the album. When Ice-T was ready to release his 1993 album, *Home Invasion,* he did so on his own label because Warner wanted no part of any future uproars.

Ice-T began as a controversial rapper in the late 1980s, throwing around gangster slang and strong language and provoking anxiety in many listeners. By the early 1990s, however, he had matured into a thoughtful, charismatic performer with strong careers in at least two media. Despite his newfound success, though, Ice insisted that he still made a lot of people nervous: "Parents are scared because my record is Number One on the campus charts of Harvard for three months," read a quote in his publicity packet. "These kids are being trained to grow up and become Supreme Court justices and politicians."

Sources

Billboard, June 8, 1991.

Creem, April/May 1991.

Details, July 1991.

Entertainment Weekly, May 24, 1991; May 31, 1991.

GQ, March 1994.

Los Angeles Times, April 21, 1991.

Musician, June 1991; August 1991.

Newsweek, July 1, 1991.

New York Times, May 19, 1991.

Rolling Stone, May 16, 1991; June 13, 1991; September 19, 1991; September 3, 1992; May 27, 1993.

The Source, May 1991.

Spin, May 1991.

Stereo Review, August 1991.

Warner Bros. Media Information, 1991.

Janet Jackson

Born 1966
Gary, Indiana

SINGER AND ACTRESS

Janet Jackson stepped out from the shadow of her famous musical brothers, including superstar Michael Jackson, with the release of her 1986 album, *Control.* Though she had recorded two albums previously, and acted in several television series, she was primarily regarded as Michael's baby sister until two hits from the disc, "What Have You Done for Me Lately?" and "Nasty," began vanishing from record stores, propelling *Control* onto the top of *Billboard's* album charts. Proving that she was no fluke, Jackson handily followed her 1986 success with the critically acclaimed 1989 album *Rhythm Nation 1814,* which featured the popular single "Miss You Much."

"The thing that excites me isn't becoming a bigger star but a better artist, deeper, truer to the things I find exciting.... I hope to be an honest artist'—no more, no less."

Born in Gary, Indiana, Jackson was the last of Joseph and Katherine Jackson's nine children. By the time she was four, five of her brothers had risen to nationwide fame as the Jackson 5; eventually this fame led to the family's move to a suburb of Los Angeles, California. According to Aldore Collier in *Ebony,* Jackson's childhood desire to

JANET JACKSON **347**

become "a horse-racing jockey" was quickly pushed to the side after her father heard her voice on tape. But singing was not the first avenue that brought her to the attention of audiences. When Jackson was nine, a television appearance on one of her brothers' variety specials led to producer Norman Lear's recruiting her for his situation comedy *Good Times*. On the show she played Penny, an abused child adopted by one of the regular characters. Later Jackson portrayed Charlene, the girlfriend of Willis on *Diff'rent Strokes*. And in her late teens, she joined the cast of the syndicated television series *Fame*. As Collier phrased it, Jackson grew up "before the television-viewing public, almost like a slowly blooming rose."

Meanwhile, Jackson released two albums. But they were both, in the words of *People* reporter Suzanne Stevens, "coolly received... co-produced by the Jackson family machine and aimed at the bubble gum set." Jackson made the first break from her wholesome, teen idol image in 1984, however, when she surprised her family by eloping with James DeBarge. A member of another family singing group, DeBarge had been Jackson's friend since she was ten years old. The marriage ended in less than a year. Speculation as to the cause of the breakup included Jackson's youth, but Jackson blamed the heavy demands of both her and her spouse's work. She confided to Collier: "It was really hard and it just couldn't go on that way. You have to really have that free time together."

Shortly after she left DeBarge, Jackson began work on *Control*. According to Stevens the new image that would permeate the album and the accompanying videos was a lot of work: "McClain put Janet on a diet, sent her to voice and dance coaches for three months and shipped her to Minneapolis to record under the tutelage of [singer/songwriter] Prince protégés Jimmy Jam and Terry Lewis." The result, however, was worth it. In addition to quickly selling a million copies, *Control* was labeled "a better album than Diana Ross has made in five years" by *Rolling Stone* reviewer Rob Hoerburger. The record included the hits "What Have You Done for Me Lately?," "Nasty," and the title cut. Though *People* reviewer Ralph Novak complained of what he perceived as the album's excessive production, he did comment that Jackson "can sing with such sweet clarity that it's a puzzle why anyone would insist on burying her." He also concluded that she was "clearly making a strident declaration of independence" with *Control*.

That declaration, however, did not prevent Jackson from moving back to the family home after her marriage ended. She told Collier that she enjoyed early morning conversations with her brother Michael, and she shares his enthusiasm for exotic pets. As of 1990, however, Jackson has been living with her boyfriend, photographer and video director Rene Elizondo.

Though it is difficult to measure up to an album as successful as *Control,* Jackson managed to surpass it with her fourth effort, *Janet Jackson's Rhythm Nation* 1814. In addition to selling phenomenally well, *Rhythm Nation* earned lavish critical praise. The disc is a concept album that takes on the issues of illiteracy, prejudice, homelessness, and other social problems interspersed with mostly dance tunes; Jackson's music and themes on *Rhythm Nation* have evoked comparisons with psychedelic soul group Sly and the Family Stone and the late R&B superstar Marvin Gaye. The record spawned several huge hits, among them "Miss You Much," "Black Cat," "Escapade," and the dance anthem "Rhythm Nation." Jackson's toned physique and dance talent were amply evident in a slew of popular videos. And Jackson believes in what she sings: she supports such causes as the Make-a-Wish Foundation and the United Negro College Fund. Vince Aletti of *Rolling Stone* praised her record's message, its "simplicity and directness," and concluded that "nothing sounds slight, and everything clicks."

Jackson next returned to acting, tackling the lead role in acclaimed director John Singleton's *Poetic Justice.* The much-anticipated film, the follow-up to Singleton's landmark *Boyz N the Hood,* was not well received on its release in 1993. Reviews of Jackson's performance as a poet struggling to overcome grief in a tough urban environment were mixed. Her voice on the soundtrack was more universally admired.

This disappointment, however, was all but forgotten in the wake of Jackson's 1993 album *janet.* Where *Control* marked the singer's embrace of adult responsibilities and *Rhythm Nation* expressed her commitment to education as a way of addressing society's ills, *janet.* was an unabashed tribute to sexuality and relationships. The singles "That's the Way Love Goes," "If," and "Again" kicked off a string of chart-topping songs and Jackson embarked on a world tour that would keep her on the road for two years. As had been the case with *Control* and *Rhythm Nation, janet.* quickly became a multimillion-seller. Jackson raised eyebrows when she appeared topless on the cover of *Rolling Stone,* with only her boyfriend's hands on her breasts for cover. But the controversy seemed only to rule her more popular as *janet.* continued to rule airwaves and video screens throughout 1994.

Sources

Ebony, September 1986.

Newsweek, July 21, 1986.

People, March 24, 1986; July 7, 1986.

Rolling Stone, April 24, 1986; October 19, 1989; February 22, 1990; September 16, 1993.

Michael Jackson

Born August 29, 1956
Gary, Indiana

Michael Jackson is "a stunning live performer, but also a notorious recluse.... He's utterly unlike you and me, with a streak of wildfire that unpredictably lights his eyes."—Jim Miller

SINGER, SONGWRITER, AND
PRODUCER

Michael Jackson is widely recognized as one of the world's top musical entertainers. He has grown from a five-year-old boy-wonder singing with his brothers to a legendary solo artist who dazzles audiences around the globe with his deftness as songwriter, producer, video pioneer, showman, dancer, and vocalist par excellence. With a knack for translating tunes from almost any genre—rhythm and blues, pop, rock, soul—into success, the performer defies all labels. According to Mikal Gilmore in Rolling Stone, Jackson is "a half-mad and extraordinary talent," with the ability to "combine [his] gifts in an electrifying, stunning way ... that has only been equaled in rock history by Elvis Presley."

Born into a working-class family in Gary, Indiana, Jackson was the seventh of nine children, all of whose lives were shaped by their parents' insistence on firm discipline. The Jackson parents, however, were also musical. Joe Jackson, a crane-operator for U.S. Steel, sang and played the guitar with a small-time group known as the Falcons, and Katherine Jackson played the clarinet. Both believed that encouraging their children to pursue their musical interests was a good way to keep them out of trouble.

Had early start in music business

By the time he was five years old, Michael, together with his four older brothers (Jackie, Tito, Jermaine, and Marlon), had formed a rhythm-and-blues act called the Jackson 5. Initially enlisted to play the bongos, Michael revealed himself as such a little dynamo that he soon became the group's leader, even at a young age able to mesmerize audiences with his singing and dancing. The group won their first talent competition in 1963, gave their first paid performance in 1964, and had proven themselves a popular local act by 1967. Although primarily imitative at this stage, with their work rooted in the tradition of such musical greats as the Temptations, Smokey Robinson, and James Brown, they were good enough to cut a couple of singles for Steeltown Records, an Indiana label.

They were also good enough to compete, in 1968, at Harlem's Apollo Theatre, then the most prestigious venue for launching black musicians. Their riveting performance brought them so many national engagements that Joe Jackson left his job to manage his sons' act. It also captured the attention of Motown Records, then in its golden days as the United States' premier black recording label. Before long, the young musicians signed with Motown and moved to California when the label relocated its headquarters there.

Under the strict guidance of the Motown magnates, the Jackson 5 propelled themselves into the public eye with their first Motown single, "I Want You Back." Released in November 1969, the recording reached number one on the charts in early 1970 and eventually sold more than one million copies. It was quickly followed by other hit singles like "ABC," the Grammy-winning pop song of 1970, as well as similarly successful albums. Even a Jackson 5 television cartoon program was created to showcase the group's music. By the time the Jackson 5 took their version of "bubblegum soul," as their music was now called, on worldwide tour in 1972, they were a smashing success, especially among the teenybopper set. Indeed, Michael, "the little prince of soul," was barely a teenager himself and had become not only a millionaire, but an international sex symbol ready to launch his solo career.

The rising star premiered as a solo artist with the 1972 album *Got To Be There*, which earned him a Grammy Award as male vocalist of the year. He followed it with the gold album *Ben,* thus beginning a steady stream of solo recordings. With his first solo tour more than a decade away, however, the young Jackson still directed most of his energy into the group's work. The Jackson 5, in fact, made another breakthrough in 1973 with the single "Dancing Machine." Succeeded by an album of the same name, the sophisticated recording introduced a disco beat that broadened the group's audience.

As members of the Jackson 5 matured, so did their music, and they eventually outgrew the agenda Motown had established for them. They were eager for greater artistic control, and when their contract with Motown expired in 1976 they signed with Epic and renamed themselves the Jacksons (Jermaine dropped out of the group while youngest brother Randy joined it).

Although frustrated by the creative restrictions placed on their first two albums for the label, the Jacksons were finally given control with *Destiny,* an album marking Michael's songwriting debut. The risk proved fruitful both for the recording company and for the artists. Featuring the "funkier" sound the entertaining brothers favored, the 1978 album went platinum, and spun off two hit singles. In 1980 the group duplicated the feat with *Triumph,* written and produced by Michael, Jackie, and Randy, and in the summer of 1981 they embarked on the enormously successful 36-city tour that produced *The Jacksons Live,* the group's last album together.

Michael creates sensation as solo act

As the Jacksons disbanded to pursue individual interests, Michael exploded onto the music scene as an independent artist, outstripping the success of even his own multiaward-winning solo album of 1979, *Off the Wall,* as well as shattering almost every other record in recording history. His landmark album was *Thriller,* unleashed in 1982. It was a sensation that appealed to almost every imaginable musical taste and established Jackson as one of the world's preeminent pop artists. The album went platinum in 15 countries, gold in four, and garnered eight Grammys; its sales exceeded 38 million copies worldwide, earning it a place in the *Guiness Book of World Records* as the largest-selling album in recording history; it spun off an unprecedented seven hit singles, and it enabled Jackson to claim the spotlight as the first recording artist to simultaneously head both the singles and albums charts for both rhythm and blues and pop.

Jackson was riding a wave of popularity known as "Michaelmania." Critics called him "brilliant," a "rock phenomenon," and a "megastar." With this stardom came an ever-increasing lust for information from the public and the press. Although he has been in the limelight since he was five, Jackson has managed to carefully avoid making his private life public. Maclean's once stated that Jackson "has astonished his fans by shedding his lively, button-cute image and transformed himself into a mysterious, other-worldly creature perpetually posing behind a mask."

Jackson revealed in an interview with Oprah Winfrey that he does not artificially lighten his skin. Rather, he has a disease called vitiligo that destroys pigmentation.

Since Jackson rarely gives interviews, he is often the subject of speculation in the supermarket tabloids. Stories have circulated that he has lightened his skin with chemicals and taken female hormones to maintain his falsetto voice. Other rumors question his sexual orientation and suggest that he has extensively remodeled his body with plastic surgery. Jackson has also been criticized in the press for his "weirdness" or "quirkiness." Producer and friend Quincy Jones rose to Jackson's defense in a *People* article by saying "[Michael is] grounded and centered and focused and connected to his creative soul. And he's one of the most normal people I've ever met."

Dissecting the Jackson mystique is a task that even seems to have eluded more serious journalists. Most view him as a paradox. He is both a superstar and a religious man, who—as neither drinker, smoker, nor drug experimenter—has avoided much of the glamorous life for healthy living. Some see him as a man-child living in his own reality—like one of his heroes, Peter Pan, refusing to grow up.

Theories aside, admirers and detractors alike agree, as Gilmore concluded, that Jackson's success is based on his "remarkably intuitive talents as a singer and dancer—talents that are genuine and matchless and not the constructions of mere ambition or hype." It is this talent, coupled with the star's hard work and often touted perfectionism, that has enabled Jackson to cross virtually every music line ever drawn.

Jackson, in fact, has been credited with resuscitating a languishing music industry and with practically eliminating barriers barring blacks from mainstream music venues. More than one critic has referred to his chameleon-like capacity for being all things to all people and thus pleasing everyone.

Faces child molestation charges

Jackson's public image was brought under fire in the summer of 1993, when the father of a 13-year-old boy accused Jackson of molesting his son. Jackson was in Asia on a world tour at the time, but his spokespeople denied all charges of sexual misconduct on Jackson's part. They claimed that the child's father had attempted to extort $20 million from the performer before bringing accusations to the police. Still maintaining his innocence, in February 1994 Jackson paid a sum estimated to exceed $10 million to settle the child molestation suit out of court. Without the child's testimony, it is unlikely that criminal charges will be brought against the singer.

Despite the intense media coverage of this dark chapter in Jackson's life, it seemed practically eclipsed by the news that he had married Lisa Marie Presley, daughter of Elvis Presley, in August 1994. Miraculously recasting himself as a family man—Presley has two children from a previous marriage—Jackson appeared to be rising above his public–image troubles, even receiving a standing ovation when he appeared with his bride at the MTV music video awards show of that year. Within four months of their marriage, however, rumors of an impending breakup were in the news.

Jackson has received a mass of music industry awards and has been honored for working with Lionel Ritchie to produce the song "We Are The World." It was recorded by a score of top artists to benefit the Ethiopian famine relief fund.

Jackson has continued to produce popular tunes and to work closely with top producers and directors in the music video industry. Some say his best work is on the stage, where critics and fans have called him one of the greatest performers of his generation. After so many record-breaking albums, many are wondering how he will be able to surpass his previous endeavors. A greatest-hits album slated for release in late 1994 nonetheless looked like a contender.

Sources

Bego, Mark, *Michael*, Pinnacle Books, 1984.

Brown, Geoff, *Michael Jackson: Body and Soul, an Illustrated Biography,* Beaufort Books, 1984.

Ebony, June 1988.

Essence, July 1988.

George, Nelson, *The Michael Jackson Story,* Dell, 1984.

Jet, May 16, 1988; February, 14, 1994.

Latham, Caroline, *Michael Jackson: Thrill,* Zebra Books, 1984.

Maclean's, July 23, 1984.

Newsweek, July 16, 1987; February 7, 1994.

People, June 11, 1984; July 28, 1984; August 27, 1984; September 14, 1987; October 22, 1987; March 28, 1988; February 7, 1994.

Rolling Stone, March 15, 1984; September 24, 1987; October 22, 1987; May 19, 1988.

Time, July l6, 1984; September 14, 1987.

Robert Joffrey

Born December 24, 1930, Seattle, Washington
Died March 25, 1988, New York, New York

DANCER AND CHOREOGRAPHER

R obert Joffrey began his career as a choreographer of unusual talent; then, of neces-
sity and finally by choice, he abandoned
choreography, and instead focused on his
work as director of the Joffrey Ballet. He was
known for his wide-ranging taste in dance,
and for his youthful dancers and willingness
to experiment. At a time when no traditional
ballet company would think of working with
modern dance choreographers, Joffrey solicit-
ed the work of such choreographers as Alvin
Ailey, Twyla Tharp, Laura Dean, and Mark
Morris. Yet, he also embraced the classical ballet, and revived important works by such
established choreographers as George Balanchine and Anthony Tudor. His own choreography was notably varied, *Gamelan* (1963) used
Eastern movement from the island of Bali and
Astarte (1967) represented the early rock and psychedelic generation of
the sixties, by combining rock music with dreamlike sequences. (In the

*"Robert Joffrey, more than anyone else in
the business I can think of, was an
international figure. Transcending
nationalism, he belonged to the world of
dance, and dance was his entire
universe."—Ronald P. Reagan*

early 1990s, the Joffrey Ballet would again turn to rock music, commissioning music from Prince for the work *Billboards*.) Because of its freshness and originality, *Astarte* was featured on the covers of *Time* and *Life*.

Began dancing to relieve asthma

Joffrey was born Abdullah Jaffa Anver Bey Khan, on December 24, 1930, in Seattle, Washington. He was the only child of an Afghani immigrant father and Italian-born mother. He began dancing while a child on the advice of a doctor, who felt that the breathing exercises would relieve his asthma. His earliest classes were at a studio directly above his father's restaurant. His most important teacher at this time was Mary Ann Wells. It was she who encouraged him to experiment with all forms of dance— modern, tap, Spanish. His willingness to embrace a wide array of dance styles was her legacy to him. At age 18 he left Seattle for New York to study under Gertrude Shurr and Mary O'Donnell at the School of American Ballet. Even at this time, however, while Joffrey was performing with O'Donnell's troupe and Roland Petit's Ballet de Paris, the dancer had ideas of forming his own company. An injury he sustained while dancing with Petit resulted in his retirement as a dancer in the early 1950s.

The Robert Joffrey Ballet Concert launched its first tour in 1956 with six dancers, among them Joffrey's longtime friend and the company's cofounder and associate director, Gerald Arpino. Arpino became the company's leading dancer for the next ten years. The troupe traveled to 23 cities in a borrowed station wagon while Joffrey remained in New York, funding the tour with the money he was earning as a teacher at New York's High School of Performing Arts. Because they traveled to many small towns, the company reached an audience that had previously been unexposed to ballet, and began to gain grassroots support for their work. By the early 1960s the troupe had grown to 32 dancers and was sponsored by Rebekah Harkness Kean and the Rebekah Harkness Foundation. The company began to receive international attention after its tour of the Middle East, India, and Pakistan. In 1964, however, after the Ballet's successful tour of the Soviet Union, Joffrey refused Rebekah Harkness's demand that the company change its name to Harkness, and she dropped her funding. After a short time, during which Joffrey scrambled to secure financing from the Ford Foundation and others, the re-christened Joffrey Ballet made its debut performance in Chicago in 1965. In 1966 the company became the official dance company of New York's City Center. In 1982,

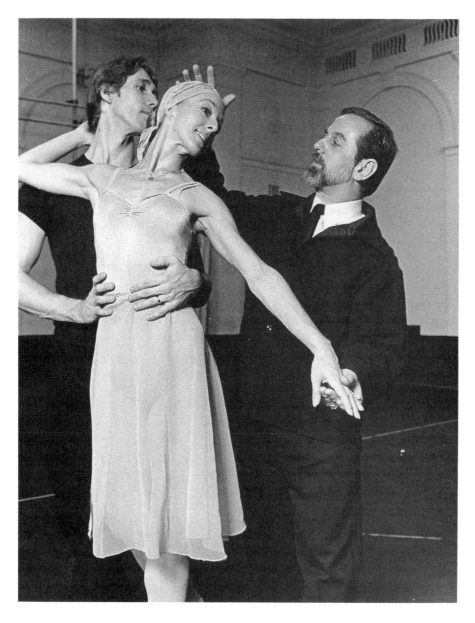

Joffrey with Joffrey Ballet dancers Ross Skelton and Denise Jackson in a rehearsal for *Postcards*, October 20, 1980.

in an attempt to gain further financial security, the Joffrey Ballet was the first company to become "bicoastal," with home bases in both Los Angeles, California, and New York City.

The Joffrey Ballet

In keeping with Robert Joffrey's view that ballet is an evolving, theatrical art, the Joffrey Ballet became known for its vitality, athleticism, and a willingness to experiment with new choreographers and new ideas. When Joffrey first began choreographing, most of his ballets were designed around specific occasions and dancers. His last ballets reflected a sense of longing for a more romantic and wittier time. For example, his final production (which he planned and oversaw, but was too weak to choreograph) was a *Nutcracker* stressing nineteenth-century American warmth. The last program Joffrey planned was a tribute to the famous early-twentieth-century dancer Vaslav Nijinsky, and featured the dances *L'Apres-midi d'un faune*, *Le Sacre du printemps*, and *Les Noces*. All three pieces are considered twentieth-century masterpieces.

The resilience that enabled him to rebuild a company and a repertoire after the Harkness disaster won him the respect and the support of the dance community. According to Richard Philp of *Dance Magazine*, "[Joffrey] was sustained by a persistent, almost childlike innocence in his certainty that anything is possible if you believe hard enough. Joffrey believed. Joffrey enthused. Joffrey prevailed." The support continued as Joffrey struggled to keep the company afloat during difficult financial times, and especially as he worked to plan the company's future when death was near. He suffered from physical deterioration, which was complicated by his asthma. He died on March 25, 1988, in New York, New York, of liver and kidney ailments and respiratory arrest. He was 57.

Joffrey's teaching stressed clarity and understanding of tradition, while also acknowledging the athleticism of American modern dance. As a result, his dancers were able to dance in a wide variety of styles. This balancing of the up-to-date with the timeless was also reflected in his concern for promoting young dancers through workshops, regional festivals, and international competitions. He also trained a "junior" company (Joffrey II) and had an interest in dance scholarship. Joffrey's teaching always attracted many leading dancers but, although offering dancing on a high level, his companies had a "no star" policy putting the emphasis on the ballet rather than the personality of the performer. Many former company members and students have gone on to become teachers or company directors, thus passing on the traditions that Joffrey learned from his own teachers, as well as those he established through his emphasis on developing an American style within the framework of academic classicism. This, together with the company that he shaped and the repertory that he gathered, remains his legacy.

Ronald P. Reagan, the son of former president Ronald Reagan, used to dance with the Joffrey. In a tribute he wrote for the *National Review,* he recalled some advice Joffrey once gave him: 'Remember,' [Joffrey] said, 'when you leave the stage you want to leave an impression of continuity, a lasting feeling. Don't stop at the edge of the stage. Carry the movement all the way into the wings.' So he did."

Sources

Chicago Tribune, March 26, 1988.

Coe, Robert, *Dance in America,* New York, 1985.

Dance Magazine, March 1964; October 1970; November 1975; June 1988.

Los Angeles Times, March 26, 1988.

National Review, April 29, 1988.

Washington Post, March 26, 1988.

Raul Julia

Born March 9, 1940, San Juan, Puerto Rico
Died October 24, 1994, Manhasset, New York

Julia was "a performer with a social conscience, but also with a sense of fun."
—Scott Rudin

ACTOR

R aul Julia was a versatile and distinguished actor who was equally at home on the stage playing in a Shakespearean tragedy such as *Othello* as he was on the screen in a zany comedy such as *The Addams Family*. Whatever he took on, he studied carefully to understand his character's background, feelings, and beliefs. What was most important for Julia was the testing of his own acting abilities. "I love diversity in acting," he explained to Phoebe Hoban in *New York* magazine. "Trying to do things I'm not sure I can do."

Raúl Rafael Carlos Julia y Arcelay was born in San Juan, Puerto Rico, in 1940, the oldest of four children of Raul and Olga Julia. Before Julia was born, his father studied electrical engineering in the United States. After returning to San Juan, the elder Julia opened a gas station, then a chicken and pizza restaurant. Both of his parents wanted the young Julia to grow up to become a lawyer, but he had a different idea early in life.

Julia had his first role on the stage at the age of five, playing the devil in a school play. From that moment on he was hooked. While attending parochial schools in San Juan, he performed in every school play that was staged. After he graduated from high school, he enrolled at the University of Puerto Rico, eventually earning a bachelor of arts degree. He then moved to New York City in the mid-1960s to study acting. At the beginning, he lived on money his parents sent to him. After he won his first role in the Spanish play *Life Is a Dream*, he supported himself, but times remained tough.

For a while Julia and his roommate were so poor that they survived by eating chicken backs—four of them cost only 25 cents.

Brings Shakespeare to Hispanic neighborhoods

To save money, Julia shared a small apartment with another actor. Because he could not get work in the theater, he often performed in small plays on the street. More than once he was hit with eggs and bottles by rude, unappreciative audiences. In 1967 he landed a role in a Spanish mobile-theater production of Shakespeare's *Macbeth*. He traveled through New York neighborhoods in a truck that turned into a stage. Julia was happy not only to have work but to bring theater to people who didn't have the time or the money to see plays.

This role led to others, but Julia still had a hard time earning money. For a while he tried to sell magazines and pens, but his heart wasn't in it. He then worked as a house manager for the New York Shakespeare Festival. He was happy to do anything connected with theater. Occasionally he was even allowed to play a small role in the Festival's productions.

Julia's big break came in 1971 when he played the role of Proteus in Shakespeare's *Two Gentlemen of Verona*. The drama, which originally played in New York City's Central Park, became a hit after it moved to Broadway. Julia's performance caught the attention of theater critics, and he was nominated for a Tony Award. Over the next decade, he played larger and larger roles in such theatrical productions as Shakespeare's *Hamlet* and Kurt Weill's *Threepenny Opera*. His work brought three more Tony award nominations.

Researches his roles thoroughly

During this time Julia began branching out into roles on television and in motion pictures. For a while, his work in movies was limited to small roles that did not attract much attention. In 1985, however, he achieved stardom for his portrayal of a South American political prisoner in the film *Kiss of the Spider Woman,* which also starred William Hurt. To prepare for the role, Julia talked to Brazilians who had been in prison or tortured for their political beliefs. He explained to Hoban the reason for his research: "I needed to know what the feelings and emotions were of a person who had gone through that. You feel humiliated. You feel anger. And you cannot express it."

Similarly, he had immersed himself in the feelings of other serious characters he's played. When he portrayed a lawyer in *Presumed Innocent,* he spent days in court with a criminal lawyer to become familiar with the legal system, courtroom manners, and the behavior of lawyers. For his role as Archbishop Oscar Romero of El Salvador in the film *Romero,* he listened to the priest's actual taped sermons and diaries.

Julia's in-depth research often changed his outlook, something he carried with him even after the cameras have stopped rolling. For example, Julia was raised a Catholic, but had drifted away from Catholicism as he grew older. His research for *Romero* required him to delve back into the religion of his childhood. It brought about a renewal of faith. After filming was completed, Julia became a practicing Catholic once again.

Julia was married to his second wife, Merel Poloway, and they had two sons, Raul Sigmund and Benjamin Rafael. When he was not acting, Julia did work for Project Hunger, a group devoted to finding ways to end world hunger by the year 2000. With each new role on the stage, on television, and on film, he continued to receive acclaim.He died suddenly in October 1994 from complications of a stroke at the height of his acting powers.

Sources

America, February 25, 1989.

New York, November 25, 1991.

New York Times, October 25, 1994.

Stefoff, Rebecca, *Raul Julia: Puerto Rican Actor,* Chelsea House, 1994.

Michael Keaton

Born September 9, 1951
Pittsburgh, Pennsylvania

ACTOR

L ong before the film *Batman* opened in thousands of theaters in the summer of 1989, the casting of Michael Keaton as the Caped Crusader had already sparked a firestorm of controversy. A legion of Batman fans—by some estimates more than 50,000—had written to Warner Bros. studios complaining that Keaton was a terrible choice for the Bruce Wayne/Batman role. After all, Keaton was a jokester, a clown. He had made a name for himself as the high-strung, manic attendant in *Night Shift* who turned a morgue into a brothel. His later roles gave little indication that Keaton could bring anything but a buffoon

"I was kind of a wild kid, and I was the ring leader in the sense that I was funny and I could make the guys laugh."

approach to playing Batman. In such films as *Gung Ho* and *Mr. Mom*, Keaton had parlayed a wisecracking persona into major motion picture stardom. Then there was the down period, with such duds as *Johnny Dangerously, Touch and Go,* and the atrocious *The Squeeze* which sent his career into a seemingly irreversible tailspin. Yet despite a comeback that included the highly successful offbeat comedy *Beetlejuice* and the critically acclaimed drama *Clean and Sober*, Batman fans were aghast at the thought that some wiseguy would play their brooding, vigilante hero. After all, Keaton admitted he only occasionally watched the campy television series, never read the comics as a kid, knew virtually nothing about the superhero and didn't intend to research the role before shooting the movie.

Besides, it wasn't his idea to star in *Batman* in the first place. In fact, when director Tim Burton suggested the role he turned it down. "When Tim first came to me with the script, I read it out of politeness," Keaton told *Rolling Stone*. "All the while I'm thinking there's no way I'd do this. It just wasn't me. My name doesn't spring to my mind when somebody says, 'Batman.' But I read it and thought, 'This guy's fascinating!' I saw him as essentially depressed. I told that to Tim, thinking he wouldn't agree, but he said, 'That's exactly what I see.' The choice was to play Batman honestly. So I started thinking, 'What kind of person would wear these clothes?' The answer seemed pretty disturbing. This is a guy in pain."

For their part, Warner Bros. welcomed the controversy and the free publicity it generated. Burton, meanwhile, never wavered from his decision. "It's his eyes," he told *Rolling Stone*. "Eyes are the windows into the soul. You can see in Michael's eyes that the guy has something going on. And Bruce Wayne is somebody who's definitely got too much going on in his mind. It's funny. Getting Michael wasn't my idea. One of the producers, Peter Gruber, I think, said to me, 'What about Michael Keaton?' I said. 'Whoaaa.' I actually had to think about it. The more I did, the more it made sense. I met with some very good square-jawed actors, but I had real trouble seeing them put on the outfit. Physical presence didn't seem to be enough. I was looking for the unknown." It took Keaton a while to graduate from the unknown.

The class clown

Keaton grew up in Forest Grove, near Pittsburgh, Pennsylvania, the youngest of seven children. His father was a civil engineer whose education came through a correspondence course. At home Keaton fooled around entertaining his large family with jokes and Elvis impressions. In school he learned to make friends by being the class clown. "I was kind of a wild kid," he told the *Los Angeles Times*, "and I was the ring leader in the sense that I was funny and could make the guys laugh."

For two years he majored in speech at Kent State University before dropping out. Then he returned to Pittsburgh to drive an ice cream truck. He also sold silk-screened T-shirts while working on his first comedy skit, about a folk-singer who rushes to his gig and then realizes he's forgotten his guitar. In 1972, when he was 21, Keaton got a job as an engineer at WQED, Pittsburgh's public education station. It was about this time that he and a station coworker began working up a routine in which Keaton would pretend to be the ventriloquist and his buddy would be the dummy. While at WQED, Keaton sometimes worked on *Mister Rogers' Neighborhood,* running the trolley or Picture-Picture.

It wasn't long, however, before Keaton left the station for Los Angeles. He had $500 and the name of a producer who earlier worked at the television station with him. To get by, Keaton got a job as a singing bus boy. It lasted two nights. In the daytime he parked cars; at night he waited on tables and would perform at the local comedy club during open mike nights. His Hollywood contact, who had a job as a story editor on the *Maude* program, landed him a one-shot audition as a reporter on the show. Norman Lear liked him and wrote Keaton into the short-lived *All's Fair* show.

Has a hit with Night Shift

That was one of several television roles Keaton had during the next five years, each connected to the other by how unmemorable they were. He auditioned often for movie roles but received few offers. And he was almost fired from his first real movie role, the manic morgue attendant in *Night Shift.* Warner Bros. studio executives had doubts about Keaton's performance. But the critics loved it, praising him as much if not more than they did the movie's star, Henry Winkler.

For his second movie, *Mr. Mom,* Keaton made $300,000, five times his salary for *Night Shift.* After his third movie, *Johnny Dangerously,* 20th Century-Fox offered him a four-picture contract. Things couldn't have looked better. Even Woody Allen was on the phone, seeking him out for the lead in *The Purple Rose of Cairo.* But things weren't as good as they looked. Allen was unsatisfied with Keaton's performance. After three days of shooting, Allen told him it wasn't working and fired him. It was around this time that Keaton also made several business decisions that later proved to be devastating. He had turned down a role in the highly successful *Splash* for the marginally popular *Johnny Dangerously.* Worse still, he thumbed his nose at *Stakeout* for the horrible *The Squeeze,* a movie so bad that the phones just stopped ringing. "Life is short in Hollywood," Keaton's partner and business manager Harry Colomby told the *Los Angeles Times.* "You're either in a buy position or you're in a sell position. A half year ago we were in a sell position."

That's about the time Keaton decided to take some risks. Before then, he had always played the good-hearted, sarcastic, wiseguy, the kind of character he called the "approachable Everyman." With *Beetlejuice* Keaton broke that mold. Like he did with *Batman*, Keaton at first balked at *Beetlejuice*. "I turned down the role because I didn't quite get it," he told *Rolling Stone*. "I went home and I thought, 'Okay, if I would do this role, how would I do it?' It turns out the character creates his own reality. I gave myself some sort of voice, some sort of look based on the words. Then I started thinking about my hair: I wanted my hair to stand out like I was wired and plugged in, and once I started gettin' that, I actually made myself laugh. And I thought, 'Well, this is a good sign, this is kind of funny.' Then I got the attitude. And once I got the basic attitude, it really started to roll."

Drew critical praise with Clean and Sober

Most critics praised Keaton for his portrayal of a "bio-exorcist" demon. And they liked even more his turnabout in *Clean and Sober,* in which Keaton played Daryl Poynter, a successful real estate agent addicted to drugs. 'These last two movies were choices that were real risky and absolutely right,' Keaton told the *Los Angeles Times*. "At a time when I should have been playing it as safe as I possibly could, I said, 'These parts are just what I want to do.' What was my next movie going to be—another script that starts, 'He's young and handsome in an offbeat way?' Two of those make me bored."

Considering the outcry Batman fans raised at just the mention of Keaton playing their favorite hero, that film provided yet another set of risks. Suppose he could not pull off the schizophrenic elements that cause a wealthy playboy to don body armor and a cape at night to fight the underworld? Suppose up against an actor like Jack Nicholson, who had been tapped to play Batman's nemesis, the Joker, Keaton came off looking like a second fiddle? Suppose the comic-book fans who lobbied Warner Bros. so hard against him were right? "Risk really works for me," Keaton told *USA Today*. "I like my back against the wall. I love it when people count me out. It's my favorite thing."

Judging from the box-office returns in the summer of 1989, Keaton had little to worry about. In a summer of blockbuster movies, *Batman* jumped out its first weekend to a commanding box-office lead. Already, even before its first weekend was through, there was talk of a *Batman II* and *Batman III.* Indeed, after all the second guessing and controversy that surrounded the casting of Michael Keaton as Batman, he was able to prove them wrong.

"This is what will happen," he told *Rolling Stone*. "I'm gonna do four or five of these movies, and it's going to become my career. I'll have to keep expanding the bat suit, because I get fatter every year. I'll be bankrupt. I'll have a couple lawsuits going. I'll be out opening shopping malls, going from appearance to appearance in a cheesy van. I'll kind of turn into the King, into this bloated Elvis, smoking and drinking a lot. I'll invent a little metal attachment, like a stool, for my hip, where kids can sit, because my back can't take their weight. I can hear myself already—'Just climb right up there, li'l pardner. Is that yer mom over there? Heh-heh-heh. Go tell her ol' Batman would like to have a drink with her a little bit later.'"

Only part of Keaton's prediction has come true. He did go on to star in *Batman Returns* in 1992. The movie boasted a stellar cast, with Michelle Pfeiffer playing Catwoman and Danny DeVito playing the Penguin. Once again directed by Tim Burton, the film was criticized for relying too heavily on special effects and gadgets, and not concentrating enough on plot. Despite the mixed critical reaction, Keaton was often singled out for his performance and fans flocked to see it. A reviewer for *Rolling Stone* wrote that "Michael Keaton's manic-depressive hero remains a remarkably rich creation."

There will be no third Batman film for Keaton, however. First the director was changed from Tim Burton to Joel Schumacher, then Robin Williams was dropped from consideration to play the Riddler. In July 1994 negotiations finally broke down between Keaton and Warner Bros. and it was announced that Val Kilmer, not Keaton, would play the caped crusader in *Batman Forever*. The exact reasons for his departure are unknown. Some sources report that Warner Bros. shied away from his asking price of $15 million, while still others suggest he was afraid of being overshadowed by the villainous characters.

In addition to his work as Batman, Keaton has continued to play a variety of roles. These include an evil scam artist in *Pacific Heights* (1990); a police detective who adopts the three daughters of his killed partner in *One Good Cop*; an executive dying of cancer in *My Life* (1993); and an editor for a New York City tabloid in *The Paper* (1994). While none of these movies matched the success of the Batman films, Keaton drew favorable notices in all of them.

Sources

American Film, July-August 1983.

Boxoffice, May 1986; November 1986; February 1987.

Chicago Tribune, March 9, 1986.

Detroit Free Press, June 18, 1989; July 12, 1994.

Los Angeles Times, March 30, 1986; August 9, 1988.

Maclean's, March 31, 1986.

Newsweek, August 29, 1988.

People, March 31, 1986; November 22, 1993; March 21, 1994.

Playboy, July 1983.

Premiere, July 1989.

Rolling Stone, June 2, 1988; July 9, 1992.

Time, March 31, 1986; June 19, 1989; November 22, 1993; March 21, 1994.

Us, May 5, 1986.

USA Today, August 10, 1988.

Video, November 1988.

Vogue, June 1989.

Gene Kelly

Born August 23, 1912
Pittsburgh, Pennsylvania

DANCER, ACTOR, AND SINGER

According to John Updike in the *New Yorker*, "[Gene Kelly] had plenty of ginger but no Ginger [Rogers]: although he danced affectingly with Leslie Caron, amusingly with Debbie Reynolds, snappily with Judy Garland, bouncily with Rita Hayworth, broodily with Vera-Ellen, and respectfully with statuesque, stony-faced Cyd Charisse, we think of Gene Kelly as a guy in loafers and a tight T-shirt tap-dancing up a storm all by his lonesome." As opposed to the grace of the lithesome Fred Astaire, to whom he is often compared, Kelly became famous for his masculine and energetic solo numbers. He never wanted to play the part of a privileged socialite, opting instead to portray the "average Joe" who needs only his girl and his home to make him happy. While Kelly originally began working as a dancer, he quickly became involved in choreography, and he established an excellent reputation for combining film technique with dance, thereby producing original and exciting dance sequences.

"As a depression kid who went to school in very bad years, I didn't want to move or dance like a rich man. I wanted to do the dance of the proletariat, the movements of the people. I wanted to dress in a sailor suit or a pair of jeans. It was part of my social outlook."

Grew up an athlete

Kelly was born in Pittsburgh, Pennsylvania, in 1912, and was the middle son of five children. His father was Canadian-born and loved sports, especially hockey. Every winter Kelly, Sr., would flood their backyard and make an ice rink for hockey. As quoted in the *New Yorker,* Kelly remembered how the sport would later influence his dancing: "I played ice hockey as a boy and some of my steps come right out of the game— wide open and close to the ground." At 15 Kelly was playing with a semi-professional ice hockey team. Yet, he was also influenced by his mother's love of the theater. In fact it was she who sent him to dancing lessons.

In 1929 Kelly left for Pennsylvania State college, but because of the Great Depression, his family lost their money, and Kelly had to move back home and attend the University of Pittsburgh in order to save the cost of room and board. Eventually, all five children would graduate from that school. While at Pitt, Kelly worked at a variety of odd jobs to pay his tuition: ditchdigger, soda jerk, gas pumper. Kelly's mother began to work as a receptionist at a local dance school, and she came up with the idea of the family running its own dance studio. They did and the studio was a big success.

After graduation from the University of Pittsburgh, Kelly attended law school. After only a month, he decided that law was not the career for him and he quit and continued to teach dance for another six years. In 1937 he left for New York, and was confident enough of his talent to believe that he would find work. He was right. He landed a job his first week in New York. Kelly's big break came in 1940 when he was cast as the lead in the Rodgers and Hart musical *Pal Joey.* He played the part of an Irish nightclub singer who was a good-for-nothing loner.

Goes to Hollywood

The show was a hit and Kelly attracted the attention of producer-songwriter Arthur Freed, who convinced his boss, Hollywood studio executive Louis B. Mayer, to see the show. Mayer liked what he saw and told Kelly that he would like to have him under contract for the MGM studio. But it was Mayer's nephew, David O. Selznick, who signed Kelly to a contract in 1942. After six months, Kelly's contract was sold to MGM and he worked for MGM for the next 16 years.

His first Hollywood film was *For Me and My Gal,* in which he starred opposite Judy Garland. Garland was only 20, but she had begun working in films at the age of 16. It was she who insisted that Kelly have the role,

Kelly dancing on a lamppost in *Singin' in the Rain,* 1952.

and she tutored him in how to act for the wide screen. "I knew nothing about playing to the camera," Kelly told *Architectural Digest*. "It was Judy who pulled me through." He learned quickly, however. After a couple of years doing stock musicals, Kelly made a breakthrough with *Cover Girl* (1944). Of his work in *Cover Girl*, Kelly told *Interview*: "[That's] when I began to see that you could make dances for cinema that weren't just photographed stage dancing. That was my big insight into Hollywood, and Hollywood's big insight into me."

Experiments with film

Gene Kelly established his reputation as an actor and dancer, but his contribution to the Hollywood musical includes choreography and direction. His experiments with dance and with film technique include combining the two, as demonstrated in such films as *Anchors Aweigh* (1945) and *Invitation to the Dance* (1956). He also made use of special effects, as in the "Alter-Ego" number in *Cover Girl* (1944), where he danced with his reflection, or in the split-screen dance of *It's Always Fair Weather* (1957). His first attempts at film choreography relied on the established formulas of the film musical, but subsequently he developed a flexible system of choreography for the camera that took into account camera setups, movement, and editing.

Kelly consciously integrated dance into film in order to help the audience gain insight into the types of characters he played. For example, the song-and-dance man of *For Me and My Gal* (1942) is a common, unpretentious character, and his principal dances are tap routines—the kind of dance accessible to the general public of the era. The sailor of the "A Day in New York" sequence from *On the Town* is introspective and his dance is therefore more lyrical and balletic. The swashbuckler of the dream dances in *Anchors Aweigh* and *The Pirate* (1948) is an athletic performer, combining the forceful turns of ballet with acrobatic stunts.

Kelly often played a guy who feels that the best way to get what he wants is to impress people. He almost always realizes, however, that his brashness offends people, and that he will more easily succeed by being himself. The worldly wise sailor trying to impress Vera-Ellen in *On the Town* is really just a boy from Meadowville, Indiana. In *The Pirate* the actor Serafin pretends he is a treacherous pirate in order to win Judy Garland's heart, but it is the lowly actor that she really wants. In *An American in Paris* (1951) Kelly plays an aggressive painter, and in *It's Always Fair Weather* he portrays a cool and sophisticated New Yorker. Yet, underneath each of these characters' masks are the charming and clever "true" selves, which are expressed wittily through song and dance.

Though Kelly's characters are naturally high-spirited, they also have a somewhat sad aspect and tend to brood about their loneliness at key moments in the films. Kelly expresses the loneliness in dances that are almost meditations on the characters' feelings. After Gaby has lost Miss Turnstiles for the second time in *On the Town,* he dreams the ballet "A Day in New York." The isolation of his character is emphasized by the anonymity of the other dancers as well as the disappearance of Vera-Ellen. The ballet in *An American in Paris* serves a similar thematic purpose. The "Alter-Ego" dance in *Cover Girl* expresses Kelly's anxiety over losing his girlfriend, and the squeaky-board dance number in *Summer Stock* (1950) is a rumination on his new feeling for Judy Garland's character.

Kelly's performances left the impression that anyone—sailors, soldiers, ball players—could sing and dance. As he matured his characters took on greater dimension, responding to the anxiety of city living, falling in love, and being lonely by distilling such experiences into dance.

And while most of his audiences were not really aware of Kelly's sophisticated techniques—thus the magic—virtually all found him uniquely appealing as a leading man. Nowhere was he more engaging than in 1952's *Singin' in the Rain.* One of the all-time great movie musicals, and perhaps the film most associated with Kelly, this comedy illustrates the late–1920s transition from silent pictures to "talkies." *Singin' in the Rain* showcased the considerable acting, singing, and dancing gifts of Debbie Reynolds and Donald O'Connor, but it is Kelly who dances away with the movie. His rendition of the title song has become an icon of American entertainment; Kelly makes a driving rain his partner, communicating the joy in movement at the heart of all his performances.

Gene Kelly will always be remembered for his incredible contribution—through dance performance, choreography, and photography—to the genre of the movie musical. While he had some success in nonmusical films—*Christmas Holiday, Marjorie Morningstar, Inherit the Wind*—his legacy lies in dance.

Sources

Architectural Digest, April 1992.

Interview, May 1994.

Kobal, John, *Gotta Sing, Gotta Dance,* New York, 1970.

New Yorker, March 21, 1994.

Thomas, Tony, *That's Dancing,* New York, 1985.

k. d. lang

Born in 1961
Consort, Alberta, Canada

"I would like to be global instead of local. As everything—as an artist, a spiritualist, a cook, a singer."

SINGER AND SONGWRITER

Her music has been called cow-punk, new wave country, and, more recently, "post-nuclear cabaret." Canadian singer k. d. lang transcends easy labeling but one thing is certain: her expressive voice and wild stage shows brought a whole new generation of listeners back to country music. With the release of her third album, *Shadowland,* lang joined young singers like Dwight Yoakam and Randy Travis as new stars in the country music firmament. But unlike Yoakam, a country purist who rejects Nashville "schmaltz," lang embraces both the old, the new, and the different. In her constant quest for change, lang even reached beyond country to mainstream pop and won tremendous acclaim for her 1992 album *Ingenue.*

Kathy Dawn Lang, who likes to go by k. d., seems to have a broad appeal. She has garnered standing ovations everywhere from Vancouver punk clubs to the Grand Ole Opry itself. The *Nashville Banner* called her "one of the most exciting new artists to come around in a while." At the same time, *Rolling Stone* applauded her already "legendary" live performances. Among her many influences, lang lists country legend Patsy Cline and gender-bending pop singer Boy George. This unique selection has its drawbacks. Edmonton, Alberta, music director Larry Donohue summed up the problem in *Western Report:* "A lot of her stuff isn't country enough to go country, and it isn't pop enough to go pop." And Robert K. Oermann, music critic for the *Tennessean,* explained, "She is in some kind of weird place between artsy new wave and country."

Lang's focus, however, seems to be narrowing as her music matures. She has discarded some of her props, like the horn-rimmed glasses and the rhinestone-studded cowboy skirts. She says she doesn't want to become known simply as an "act" like Bette Midler's Divine Miss M. Her concern may be warranted. The *Nashville Banner* once referred to her as a singer with "Patsy Cline's sublime power ... inside Pee Wee Herman's mind."

Lang has country roots. She was born in 1961 in the tiny town of Consort (population 672), Alberta. Her father ran the local drugstore and her mother was the second grade schoolteacher. As a teenager, lang earned summer money driving a three-ton grain truck for local farmers. But despite her rural surroundings, lang's early musical influences were not country. She trained on classical piano and listened to her older sister's rock music collection. "I grew up not liking country music," she told Jay Scott in *Chatelaine.* "I was brought up in a family that studied classical music, at the piano. We also listened to Broadway shows. And I listened to Janis Joplin and the Allman Brothers." Besides music, the young Kathy Dawn was interested in athletics. She was able on the volleyball court, and she claims her first professional ambition was to be a roller derby queen. Later, in college, she dabbled in performance art. She played in productions that ranged from a seven-hour reenactment of Barney Clark's landmark artificial-heart transplant to filling up an art gallery with garbage.

Discovers country music

But music remained her first love. As a teenager, lang was a would-be professional, doing numbers like "Midnight Blue" and the "Circle Game" on her acoustic guitar at weddings and other functions. At college, she discovered the music of Patsy Cline, whose emotional approach drew lang back to the golden age of country, when singers like Johnny Horton and Hank Williams sang simple tributes to the everyday life of ordinary people.

In 1982 lang answered an ad in an Edmonton newspaper for a singer for a Texas swing fiddle band. Her future manager, Larry Wanagas, was at the audition. He knew immediately that a unique talent was ready to be developed. "The first show she did," he told Perry Stern in *Canadian Musician* magazine, "surprised herself as well as me. I knew she could sing, but what she brought to the stage was this undeniable presence."

For the next two years, lang and her band, the Reclines, toured throughout Canada. They played country, college, and rock bars. lang would stomp out wearing ugly, rhinestone-studded glasses (without lenses) and cowboy boots with the tops sawn off. She would fling herself to the stage in the middle of her version of the 1960s girl-pop classic "Johnny Get Angry." But no matter how contorted her hijinks, her voice rang deep and melodious. She was clearly capable of vocal gymnastics, tumbling from a full-throated alto line one moment to a yelping yodel the next. It didn't take long for the word to spread—this weird-looking woman from the plains of Alberta was singing country tunes like they had never been sung before.

Lang's first album, *A Truly Western Experience,* was recorded during this period on an independent Edmonton label. It showed that her voice could be transposed successfully to vinyl, but it didn't sell well. Then, in the spring of 1985, after playing a gig at New York's Bottom Line club, the head of Sire Records signed her to his label. Seymour Stein was already recording Talking Heads, Madonna, the Pretenders, and the Ramones. After witnessing her Bottom Line show, he decided she was ready for big-time exposure. "You are what should have happened to country music 30 years ago," he told her at the time.

Lang's star was on the rise. In November she was named Canada's "most promising female vocalist." But in 1986, lang disappeared from the concert circuit. When she reappeared, she had abandoned the persona that had won her headlines. A restrained, new lang emerged, without the cat's-eye glasses and the studied attempts to make herself ugly. "The reason I've tempered my style is because I'm taking my music more seriously," lang told *Western Report.* "I'm tired of being written about as some zany, crazy kid. I think the gap between K.D. and Kathy has lessened to the point where I'm almost completely Kathy on stage now." lang clearly sought to defy the critics who doubted her artistic commitment.

Lang's second album, but first major release, *Angel With a Lariat,* was the product of lang's new devotion to her music. It was a complex collection of lang's own pieces and country classics, like Patsy Cline's heartbreaker "Three Cigarettes in an Ashtray." Produced in England by rocker

Dave Edmunds, it featured the spontaneity of a live performance. And at the same time, it strove to recapture the honesty and purity that lang found lacking in contemporary country music. The reviews were generous. The *Toronto Globe and Mail*, for example, called the production "a breathlessly paced, musically adventurous album that's unlike anything in contemporary or rock music."

Makes appearances on U.S. television

With the release of her first major commercial effort, lang began to look south of the Canadian border. In May 1987 she made her television debut on *The Tonight Show*. Johnny Carson was so impressed that he invited her back three times. She quickly became a television regular, appearing on the Smothers Brothers' program, *Late Night with David Letterman, Hee Haw,* and on pay TV alongside Bruce Springsteen and Elvis Costello. She also teamed up with music legend Roy Orbison to record a stirring version of the rock veteran's classic ballad "Crying." Their coproduction sold more than 50,000 copies in the United States. Nonetheless, major radio airplay still seemed to elude lang.

Angel With a Lariat did not climb the charts as expected. Journalist Liam Lacey told *Chatelaine* the album failed to showcase lang's voice as much as it could have. And it lacked a hit song that would have ensured regular radio play.

In the summer of 1988, lang released the album that was to feature her vocal talents in a way that *Angel With a Lariat* never did. *Shadowland* was produced by country legend Owen Bradley, the man who developed Patsy Cline's talents. Indeed, *Shadowland* seems to be a coming-to-terms of lang's longtime obsession with her role model. None of the songs on the album are her own. Instead, they are nostalgic, sincere interpretations of emotional ballads—known in the country music business as "weepers." There is no wacky sarcasm in these songs; one track, "Honky Tonk Angels' Medley," features country stars Kitty Wells, Loretta Lynn, and Brenda Lee, former Bradley protegées and contemporaries of Cline.

The album did well, garnering respectable sales and laudatory reviews. *Rolling Stone* called it a celebration of country music, and *Maclean's* suggested the collection of Nashville classics was "richly nostalgic" and "a major turning point." A single from the album, Patsy Cline's "I'm Down to My Last Cigarette," climbed both the country and pop charts. And it has been credited with sparking a revival of interest in Cline's work. Her label, MCA Records, has re-released Cline's greatest hits

Country legend Owen Bradley produced *Shadowland* while recovering from a heart attack. He later said: "After working with K.D. for a while, I didn't need to take my pills. She was medicine, invigorating therapy."

collection and has issued two previously unreleased recordings.

lang's 1989 release, *Absolute Torch and Twang*, "splits the difference between the unbridled high spirits ... of *Angel With a Lariat* and the more studied, Patsy Cline-influenced studioscapes crafted by legendary country producer Owen Bradley on *Shadowland*," noted Holly Gleason in a *Rolling Stone* review. "There are more obvious records lang could have made, Gleason continued, "ones designed to make her a queen. Instead, she opted for songs that challenge her abilities and make a case for artistic vision.... This album isn't gonna win her any points with the Nashville Network or country-radio programmers, but it shows what country music, when intelligently done, can be."

The year 1992 was one of turmoil and change for lang. She switched labels and released *Ingenue*, an album of more-traditional pop standards. The result was a crossover smash hit and the album went platinum, selling one million copies. According to *Rolling Stone*, with *Ingenue* "Lang has established herself as a major vocal technician of [Barbara] Streisandian proportions." The album earned several Grammy nominations and she won the award for Best Female Pop Vocal for the single "Constant Craving." This same year lang infuriated those country music fans with ties to the meat industry because of her vocal anti-meat stance. Hot on the heels of "cattlegate," lang created an additional furor by "coming out" as a lesbian. In general lang has found coming out to be a freeing experience. She told *Rolling Stone* that it "was positive, totally positive. Like an emotional veil had been taken away."

Most recently lang has completed the soundtrack for the film adaptation of Tom Robbins's novel *Even Cowgirls Get the Blues.* lang continues to defy the easy labels. As she told *Maclean's:* "Change is the essence of growth. You must take a look at where you came from, but keep moving ahead." Her growing legion of fans, suffice it to say, will probably go along for the ride.

Sources

Calgary Herald, February 14, 1987.

Canadian Composer, December 1985; November 1987.

Canadian Musician, April 1987.

Chatelaine, January 1988.

Entertainment Weekly, December 31, 1993.

Interview, December 1992.

Maclean's, July 6, 1987; August 3, 1987; May 30, 1988.

Rolling Stone, June 16, 1988; July 13, 1989; August 5, 1993.

Vancouver Sun, March 15, 1986.

Vanity Fair, August 1993.

Western Report, March 2, 1987; September 28, 1987.

Winnipeg Free Press, April 12, 1986.

Brandon Lee

Born in 1965, California
Died March 31, 1993, Wilmington, North Carolina

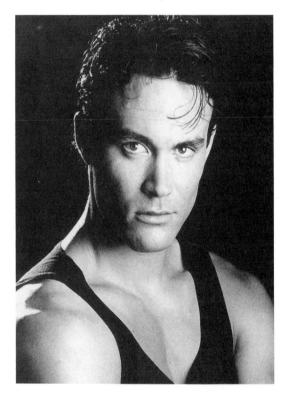

"You know for years I was in my father's shadow, and I resented it. I wanted to be an actor, not do martial arts films. But it finally dawned on me—I am who I am, and I might as well accept it. Once I realized that, doors started to open for me. I'll go in and do what they ask of me, and I'll use it to get the kind of movies that I want to make."

ACTOR

Brandon Lee, like his father Bruce Lee, is known for his martial arts skill and the bizarre circumstances under which he died. The number of coincidences between the two performers is astounding. Both died young—Brandon was 28 and Bruce was 32—and both died while filming their sixth film. In the posthumous movie *Game of Death*, the elder Lee played an actor who is killed after gangsters substitute a real bullet for a fake one on a movie set. Fourteen years after the release of *Game of Death*, the younger Lee was killed on a movie set by a prop gun that should have been harmless, but held live ammunition.

Learns martial arts from his father

Born in California in 1965, Brandon Lee was only an infant when his parents took him to

Hong Kong. It was the hope of the young Bruce Lee that he might find fame and fortune in his native land. At the age of two, Brandon began to learn the martial art of Jeet Kune Do from his father. Jeet Kune Do was a style of martial arts developed by Bruce Lee after years of studying and teaching. As a child, Brandon learned to speak both Cantonese and English fluently.

In 1973 Bruce Lee died without warning from a swelling of the brain, caused by an allergic reaction to a painkiller. He was filming a movie in Hong Kong at the time. His death devastated his family—his wife, Linda, daughter Shannon, then three years old, and Brandon, who was eight years old. Brandon Lee told *People,* "Like everyone, I was real respectful toward my Dad. He was quite a hero." Yet over the years, each family member made their own peace with the death. The excellence of Lee's work, his untimely death, and the mysterious circumstances surrounding it made him a cult figure on the order of James Dean and Elvis Presley.

After the elder Lee's death, Linda moved her family first to Seattle, then to the exclusive community of Rolling Hills, California. There, Brandon was constantly challenged to prove himself because of his father's reputation as an unbeatable fighter. He told *People,* "I always had a pretty good knack for raising hell." Lee was in and out of trouble during his school years, and was kicked out of two high schools. He finally quit his third high school during his senior year.

Decides to pursue acting

Lee had dreamed of becoming an actor from the time he was a little boy. After high school, he left for Boston where he studied drama at Emerson College. Within a few years he was taking acting classes in New York City and performing in various off-Broadway productions. In 1985, at the age of 20, Lee headed for Hollywood. He had difficulty finding work, however, and had to work as a script reader in order to earn money. Despite his desire to avoid being stereotyped as "Bruce Lee's son," Lee's television debut made use of his martial arts background. He starred with actor David Carradine in *Kung Fu: The Next Generation.*

Lee, like his father, found it necessary to return to Hong Kong to try to break into major motion pictures. There he starred in the Cantonese martial arts film *Legacy of Rage* in 1987. In 1989 he made *Laser Mission,* and in 1991 he costarred with American actor Dolph Lundgren in *Showdown in Little Tokyo.* While *Showdown in Little Tokyo* was not a huge hit, it did serve to increase Lee's exposure.

In 1990 Brandon Lee surprised a burglar who had broken into his home. Lee told the intruder to put down the knife he was holding, but the burglar refused and instead lunged at Lee. Lee's left arm was cut, but he quickly used his martial arts expertise to dislocate the robber's shoulder and break his arm.

Wins first starring role

In 1992 Lee returned to the United States to film *Rapid Fire,* in which he had his first starring role. In the film, Lee played a college student battling mobsters. Just as Bruce Lee had choreographed all his own fight scenes, so too did his son. The film's producer, Robert Lawrence, told *People,* "His father had a burning intensity onscreen; Brandon's more fun. He's free-wheeling, hip, and tongue-in-cheek."

Lee's next major project was the film *The Crow,* which concerned a rock star who returns from the dead to avenge his and his girlfriend's murder. Lee was originally intrigued by the film because it was different from the standard martial-arts films he was usually offered. The producer had wanted the actor Christian Slater for the lead, but when Slater turned down the role the part was offered to Lee.

Troubles on the set

Filmed in North Carolina, the film was riddled with problems from the start. The crew was constantly tired because they had to put in 12- to 14-hour days. "They wanted to make a $30 million movie but they only wanted to spend $12 million in it," complained one former crew member to *Premiere.* On the first day of shooting a carpenter was almost electrocuted. Soon after, a stuntman fell and broke his ribs, and a prop person drove a screwdriver threw the palm of his hand. The mood on the set was worsened because the cast and crew were working, often at night, in the midst of winter storms, which caused the set to be dark, wet, and gloomy.

On March 30, Lee arrived on the set ready to film the scene in which his character is murdered. He was supposed to enter his apartment door and find his girlfriend about to be raped by a band of punks, who shoot and kill him. The revolver used in the scene should have been filled with blanks, but by some tragic mistake, a live bullet was in the gun. (One report explained that a closeup had been shot in which a bullet was shown being loaded into the gun, apparently a fragment of the shell was left behind when the real bullet was removed and replaced by a blank. Criminal charges were not pursued in the matter.) Lee was shot in the abdomen and the bullet settled near his spine. He was whisked to the hospital and operated on, but the doctors were unable to stop the bleeding and at 1:04 p.m., on March 31, Lee died with his fiancée, Eliza Hutton, by his side. The two were to have been married on April 17, after *The Crow* had finished shooting. Instead, on April 3, Lee's family and friends gathered in Seattle to see Lee buried next to his father at Lake View Cemetery.

It was uncertain for a time whether *The Crow* would be released. Roughly six weeks after the tragedy, the shaken cast and crew had managed to use special effects and a modified script in order to finish the film without Lee's presence. In May 1994, the film opened in New York and Los Angeles, and was soon released to theaters across the country. Reviews were generally mixed, and critics and viewers alike were unsure of how to separate the film's hero from the actor Brandon Lee. But many observers saw a charisma in Lee that could well have propelled him to stardom.

And so, in death as in life, the memory of the two Lees will always remain interlocked in the minds of their fans. Some comfort can be taken from the joy and exuberance that Brandon Lee exhibited during his short lifetime; he lived life to the fullest. As the younger Lee told *People*: "My dad said time was the most valuable thing a person had. That really struck me. I've made a conscious effort not to waste it."

Sources

Entertainment Weekly, May 13, 1994.

People, September 7, 1992; April 12, 1993; April 19, 1993.

Premiere, July 1993.

Spike Lee

Born March 20, 1957
Atlanta, Georgia

FILMMAKER AND ACTOR

"You can take an unknown, all-black cast and put them in a story that comes from a black experience, and all kinds of people will come to see it if it's a good film."

"**F**ight the Power," the theme song to his 1989 film *Do the Right Thing,* could easily be Spike Lee's personal motto. From his earliest days as a student filmmaker to his $33 million epic *Malcolm X,* Lee has shown a willingness to tackle prickly issues of relevance to the black community—and has savored every ounce of controversy his films invariably produce. "Spike loves to fight," the filmmaker's friend and business associate Nelson George told *Vanity Fair.* "There's a gleeful look he gets, a certain kind of excitement in his eyes when [things are] being stirred up." "I guess you could call me an instigator," Lee admitted in an interview with *Vogue.*

Once the bane of Hollywood executives, Lee has proven through his creativity and resolve that films by and about African Americans can be both profitable and universally appealing. And almost singlehandedly, he has generated an industry-wide awareness of a neglected market niche, the black moviegoing public. Following the unforeseen box-office success of Lee's earliest films, Hollywood's gates have opened to a new generation of young African American filmmakers. "Spike put this trend in vogue," Warner Bros. executive vice president Mark Canton told *Time.* "His talent opened the door for others." Lee relishes his role as path-paver. "Every time there is a success," he explained to *Ebony,* "it makes it easier for other blacks. The industry is more receptive than it has ever been for black films and black actors. We have so many stories to tell, but we can't do them all. We just need more black filmmakers."

Shelton Jackson Lee was born in Atlanta, Georgia, on the eve of the civil rights era. He grew up in Brooklyn, New York, an area that figures largely in his work as a mature filmmaker. Lee's awareness of his African American identity was established at an early age. His mother, Jacquelyn, instilled in her children with a schoolteacher's enthusiasm for black art and literature. "I was forced to read Langston Hughes, that kind of stuff," Lee told *Vanity Fair.* "And I'm glad my mother made me do that." His father, Bill, an accomplished jazz musician, introduced him to African American jazz and folk legends like Miles Davis and Odetta, respectively.

By the time he was old enough to attend school, the already independent Lee had earned the nickname his mother had given him as an infant, Spike—an allusion to his toughness. When he and his siblings were offered the option of attending the predominantly white private school where his mother taught, Lee opted instead to go the public route, where he would be assured of the companionship of black peers. "Spike used to point out the differences in our friends," recalled his sister Joie, who was a private school student. "By the time I was a senior," she told *Mother Jones,* "I was being channeled into white colleges." Lee chose to go to his father and grandfather's all-black alma mater, Morehouse College, where he majored in mass communication.

Pursued film career

It was at Morehouse that Lee found his calling. Following the unexpected death of Jacquelyn in 1977, Lee's friends tried to cheer him with frequent trips to the movies. He quickly became a fan of directors Bernardo Bertolucci, Martin Scorsese, and Akira Kurosawa. But it wasn't until he had seen Michael Cimino's *The Deer Hunter* that Lee knew the die was cast. His friend John Wilson recalled their conversation on the ride home from the film in an interview with *Vanity Fair.* "John, I know what I want to do," Lee had said. "I want to make films." But not just any films: Lee wanted to make films that would capture the black experience, and he was willing to do so by whatever means necessary. "Spike didn't just want to get in the door of the house," Wilson explained. "He wanted to get in, rearrange the furniture—then go back and publicize the password."

He pursued his passion at New York University, where he enrolled in the Tisch School of Arts graduate film program. One of only a handful of African American students, he wasted no time incurring the wrath of his instructors with his affinity for "rearranging the furniture." As his first-year project, Lee produced a ten-minute short, *The Answer,* in which a black screenwriter is assigned to remake D. W. Griffith's classic film *The Birth of a Nation. The Answer* was panned. Although the film program's director, Eleanor Hamerow, told the *New York Times,* "It's hard to redo *Birth of a Nation* in ten minutes," Lee suspected that his critics were offended by his digs at the legendary director's stereotypical portrayals of black characters. "I was told I was whiskers away from being kicked out," he told *Mother Jones.* "They really didn't like me saying anything bad about D.W. Griffith, for sure."

Hardly deterred, Lee went on to produce a 45-minute film that won him the 1983 Motion Picture Arts and Sciences' Student Academy Award, *Joe's Bed-Stuy Barbershop: We Cut Heads.* Although the honor enhanced his credibility as a director, it didn't pay the bills. Faced with the reality of survival, Lee worked for a movie distribution house while hustling funds for a semiautobiographical film, *The Messenger.*

A coming-of-age story about a young bicycle messenger, *The Messenger* was aborted prematurely when sufficient funding failed to materialize. "We were in pre-production the entire summer of 1984, waiting on this money to come, and it never did," Lee told *Vanity Fair.* "Then, finally, I pulled the plug. I let a lot of people down, crew members and actors that turned down work. I wasn't the most popular person. We were devastated." But all was not lost; Lee had learned his lesson. "I saw I made the classic mistakes of a young filmmaker, to be overly ambitious, do something beyond my means and capabilities," he said. "Going through the fire just made me more hungry, more determined that I couldn't fail again."

Scored a surprise hit with She's Gotta Have It

When he filmed *She's Gotta Have It* a year later, Lee's determination paid off. Made on a shoestring $175,000 budget in just 12 days, the black-and-white picture was shot on one location with a limited cast and edited on a rented machine in Lee's apartment. By the time it was completed, Lee was so deeply in debt that the processing lab he'd used threatened to auction off the film's negative.

After Island Pictures agreed to distribute it, *She's Gotta Have It* finally opened in 1986. A light comedy centering on artist Nola Darling and her relationships with three men, the film pokes fun at gender relations and offers an insightful spin on stereotypically macho male roles. It packed houses not only with the black audience Lee had anticipated, but also with a crossover, art-house crowd. Grossing over $7 million, the low-budget film was a surprise hit.

With the success of *She's Gotta Have It,* Lee became known in cinematic circles not only as a director, but also as a comic actor. Mars Blackmon— one of Nola's lovers, played by Lee—won an instant following with his now-famous line, "Please baby, please baby, please baby, baby, baby, please." "After *She's Gotta Have It,* Spike could've gone a long way with Mars Blackmon," the film's co-producer Monty Ross told *Mother Jones.* "He could've done *Mars Blackmon the Sequel, Mars Blackmon Part 5.*" Not anxious to be typecast, though, Lee "said to the studios 'Mars Blackmon is dead.'"

School Daze: *more than a picture of black campus life*

With a major hit under his belt and the backing of Island Pictures, Lee had more latitude with his next film, a musical called *School Daze.* An exposé of color discrimination within the black community, *School Daze* draws on Lee's years at Morehouse. "The people with the money, " he told the *New York Times,* "most of them have light skin. They have the Porsches, the B.M.W.'s, the quote good hair unquote. The others, the kids from the rural south, have bad, kinky hair. When I was in school, we saw all this going on." This black caste system, Lee explained to *Newsweek,* was not a limited phenomenon. "I used the black college as a microcosm of black life."

School Daze created a brouhaha in the black community: while many applauded Lee's efforts to explore a complex social problem, others were offended by his willingness to "air dirty laundry." Everyone agreed that the film was controversial. When production costs reached $4 million, Island Pictures got cold feet and pulled out. Within two days, Lee had arranged a deal with Columbia Pictures that included an additional $2 million in production funds. But Columbia, then under the direction of David Puttnam, apparently misunderstood the film's true nature. "They saw music, they saw dancing, they saw comedy," Lee told *Mother Jones.* By the time *School Daze* was released in 1988, Puttnam had been ousted.

Despite the fact that the studio's new management failed to promote it, the film grossed $15 million.

Explored racial tensions in Do the Right Thing

School Daze established Lee's reputation as a director ready to seize heady issues by the horns. *Do the Right Thing,* released in 1989, confirmed it. The story of simmering racial tension between Italian and African Americans in the Bedford-Stuyvesant section of Brooklyn, the film becomes a call to arms when violence erupts in response to the killing of a black man by white police officers. It ends on a note of apparent uncertainty with two opposing quotes: Martin Luther King's "The old law of an eye for an eye leaves everyone blind," followed by Malcolm X's "I am not against violence in self defense. I don't even call it violence when it's self-defense. I call it intelligence."

The meaning of "the right thing," Lee told *People,* is not vague. "Black America is tired of having their brothers and sisters murdered by the police for no reason other than being black." "I'm not advocating violence," he continued. "I'm saying I can understand it. If the people are frustrated and feel oppressed and feel this is the only way they can act, I understand."

Critical response to the film was both enthusiastic and wary. Media critic Roger Ebert called it "the most honest, complex and unblinking film I have ever seen about the subject of racism." Others voiced warnings of possible violence. *New York* magazine said, "Lee appears to be endorsing the outcome, and if some audiences go wild he's partly responsible."

Striking a balance: Mo' Better Blues

Despite the fact that *Do the Right Thing* failed to inspire the predicted violence, Lee chose a lighter topic for his next film—a romance. The saga of a self-centered jazz trumpeter, Bleek Gilliam, whose personal life plays second fiddle to his music, "*Mo' Better Blues* is about relationships," Lee explained to *Ebony.* "It's not only about man-woman relationships, but about relationships in general—Bleek's relationship to his father and his manager, and his relationship with two female friends. Bleek's true love is music, and he is trying to find the right balance."

Bleek's character was inspired by Lee's jazz-musician father, Bill Lee, who wrote the film's score. "Bleek is my father's nickname," Lee told *People.* The character's dilemma—the need to temper the obsessive nature of the creative act—however, has universal relevance. That theme, *Newsweek* suggested, is one with which the director himself can readily identify.

Although recognized for its technical mastery and snappy score—partially the result of a $10 million budget—*Mo' Better Blues* received lukewarm reviews. "The movie is all notions and no shape," said the *New Yorker*, "hard, fierce blowing rather than real music." And more than one critic took offense at Lee's shallow treatment of female characters and ethnic stereotyping of Jewish jazz club owners Moe and Josh Flatbush.

Examined interracial love in Jungle Fever

In his next film, *Jungle Fever*, Lee explored the theme of romance further—but this time, from a more provocative slant. Inspired by the 1989 murder of black teenager Yusuf Hawkins by a mob of Italian American youths, *Jungle Fever* examines interracial romance. "Yusuf was killed because they thought he was the black boyfriend of one of the girls in the neighborhood," Lee told *Newsweek*.

Jungle Fever looks at issues of race, class, and gender by focusing on community response to the office affair of a married, black architect and his Italian American secretary. Lee concludes that interracial relationships are fueled by culturally based, stereotypical expectations. "You were curious about black ... I was curious about white," the architect explains when the couple parts ways. But Lee insisted in an interview with *Newsweek* that the film does not advocate separatism. The characters aren't meant "to represent every interracial couple. This is just one couple that came together because of sexual mythology." Although it received mixed reviews, *Jungle Fever* succeeded in whetting the appetite of Lee fans for further controversy. *Malcolm X*, Lee's pièce de résistance, satisfied even the most hungry.

Malcolm X

The making of *Malcolm X*, a movie that sparked controversy from the moment of its inception, became a personal mission for Lee, who had long been an admirer of the legendary black leader. Vowing to cut no corners, Lee planned a biographical film of epic proportions that required months of research, numerous interviews, and even an unprecedented trip to Saudi Arabia for authentic-looking footage of Malcolm's pilgrimage to the holy city of Mecca. Taken shortly before his assassination in 1965, this journey caused a significant change in Malcolm's political and religious outlook.

The final product, a three-hour-and-21-minute production, traces Malcolm X's development from his impoverished, rural roots to his final years as an electrifying speaker and leader. "I knew this was going to be the toughest thing I ever did," Lee told *Time*. "The film is huge in the canvas we had to cover and in the complexity of Malcolm X."

Lee fought tooth and nail to win the right to direct the film and to defend his vision of Malcolm X from the start. When he learned of plans by Warner Bros. to make *Malcolm X*, Norman Jewison had already been chosen as its director. After Lee told the *New York Times* that he had a "big problem" with a white man directing the film, Jewison agreed to bow out.

Lee, however, faced considerable resistance to his role as director of the film. Led by poet and activist Amiri Baraka (formerly LeRoi Jones), a focus group that called itself the United Front to Preserve the Memory of Malcolm X and the Cultural Revolution voiced its opposition to Lee's direction in an open letter. "Our distress about Spike's making a film on Malcolm is based on our analysis of the [exploitative] films he has already made," *Ebony* quoted the group as saying.

But Lee's spat with Baraka was only a momentary setback. He still had to deal with reworking an unsatisfactory script, which had been started by African American novelist James Baldwin shortly before his death and completed by writer Amold Perl. And when Lee first locked horns with Warner Bros. over *Malcolm X*'s budget, he was bracing for another prolonged battle.

Initially, the director had requested $40 million for the film—an amount that was necessary, he claimed, in order to accurately portray all of the phases of his subject's life. The studio countered with a $20 million offer, prompting Lee to raise an additional $8.5 million by selling foreign rights to the film, kicking in a portion of his $3 million salary, and, to make up the difference, acquiring the backing of a host of black celebrities, including Bill Cosby, Oprah Winfrey, Michael Jordan, Janet Jackson, and Prince—much to the studio's embarrassment. "It didn't look good for Warner Bros. that Spike had to go to prominent African Americans to finish the movie," noted *Entertainment Weekly*. When the film was completed, Barry Reardon, the studio's president of distribution, conceded, "Spike did a fabulous job. He knows theaters, he's very smart. This is Oscars all the way."

Although *Malcolm X* received no Oscars, the film played a significant role in the elevation of the black leader to mythic status; it also spawned a cultural phenomenon often referred to as "Malcolm-mania." By the time the movie was released, its logo, a bold "X," was pasted on everything from baseball caps to posters, postcards, and T-shirts. What's more, a wealth of spin-off products were born, ranging from serious scholarly studies to a plastic Malcolm X doll, complete with podium and audio cassette. Promotional merchandise for the film was marketed by Lee himself through Spike's Joint, a chain of stores that comprise a portion of the director's growing business empire.

Lee is quick to defend himself against charges of commercialism. In fact, he says, Malcolm X's philosophy—that African Americans need to build their own economic base—is the motivation for his business investments. "I think we've done more to hold ourselves back than anybody," Lee told *Esquire*. "If anybody's seen all my films, I put most of the blame on our shoulders and say, 'Look, we're gonna have to do for ourselves.'... I feel we really have to address our financial base as a people."

Lee's innate ability to "do for himself," his father suggested in an interview with *Mother Jones*, is the key to his success as a filmmaker. "Spike was kind of chosen," he explained. "I think there was something spiritual about it. He inherited it from his family. [The ability] to make a statement." Fellow filmmaker John Singleton, writing in *Essence*, said of Lee, "No other Black contemporary entertainer can claim to enlighten so many young Black people." But, as he stated in the *New York Times*, Lee wants even more to prove "that an all-black film directed by a black person can still be universal."

In mid-1993 Lee began shooting his seventh feature film, *Crooklyn*, a comic tribute to his childhood memories of life in Brooklyn in the 1970s. He managed to take a break from filming, however, in order to marry Linette Lewis. Lewis, a lawyer, had been romantically linked to Lee for the year prior to their wedding. *Crooklyn* was released in 1994 to mixed reviews and a tepid reception at the box office.

Sources

America, August 19, 1989; September 15, 1990; August 10, 1991.

American Film, July/August 1989; September 1989.

Ann Arbor News, October 30, 1992; November 18, 1992.

Commonweal, November 8, 1991.

Detroit News, January 26, 1992.

Ebony, November 1991.

Emerge, November 1991.

Entertainment Weekly, November 27, 1992.

Esquire, August 1991.

Essence, November 1991.

Film Comment, July/August 1989.

Jet, June 10, 1991; October 18, 1993.

Lee, Spike, *By Any Means Necessary: The Trials and Tribulations of Making Malcolm X,* Hyperion, 1992.

Lee, Spike, *Do the Right Thing: The New Spike Lee Joint,* Simon & Schuster, 1989.

Lee, Spike, *Mo' Better Blues,* Simon & Schuster, 1990.

Lee, Spike, *Spike Lee's Gotta Have It: Inside Guerrilla Filmmaking,* Simon & Schuster, 1987.

Lee, Spike, and Lisa Jones, *Uplift the Race: The Construction of "School Daze,"* Simon & Schuster, 1988.

Maclean's, February 17, 1992.

Mother Jones, September 1989.

Ms., September/October 1991.

Newsweek, February 15, 1988; August 6, 1990; June 10, 1991; February 3, 1992; November 16, 1992.

New York, June 17, 1991.

New Yorker, August 13, 1990; June 17, 1991; October 12, 1992.

New York Times, August 9, 1987; November 15, 1992; November 29, 1992; December 6, 1992.

People, July 10, 1989; March 5, 1990; August 13, 1990; June 22, 1992; October 18, 1993.

Rolling Stone, November 26, 1992.

Time, June 17, 1991; March 16, 1992.

Upscale, October/November 1992.

Vanity Fair, June 1991.

Video, February 1990; February 1991.

Vogue, August 1990.

David Letterman

Born April 12, 1947
Indianapolis, Indiana

TELEVISION TALK SHOW HOST

"*W*hen I think about television and show business, it grinds my stomach. I want to say to people, 'Don't you understand this is just bull ... driven by egos, and that's all it is?' I mean, nothing makes me madder than to be sitting there, watching somebody who's just the winner of the genetic crapshoot, and there they are, big stuff on the air, a star." This opinion comes not from a scholar or a critic, but from a figure who has in his own career conducted on-air elevator races, presided over "Stupid Pet Tricks," and thrown himself against a Velcro wall. David Letterman, speaking to *Rolling Stone* reporter Peter W. Kaplan, continued: "There's nothing I love more than getting hot over what's really bad."

"I used to have a paper route, and now I have three floors of a theater building on Broadway in New York City. I'm the luckiest man alive."

Letterman has himself become a star by pointing out to a receptive America the wretched excesses of Hollywood-style showbiz. The former TV weatherman and announcer has parlayed his success as a stand–up comic into three talk shows. While the first was a flop, the second, *Late*

Night with David Letterman on NBC, all but redefined the traditional talk show. And the third, *The Late Show with David Letterman* on CBS, continues to provide the kind of subversive, cranky and hip humor that originally made *Late Night* a success. "Consider this Great Moment in *Late Night* history," offered *Newsweek*'s Bill Barol in a Letterman cover story. "The guest was Don King, who is probably as well known for his mile-high electrified Afro as for his career in boxing promotion. As King launched into his usual bombastic spiel, Letterman listened politely. But the first time King paused for breath Letterman leaned over and said: 'Let me ask you something. What's the deal with your hair?' [That exchange] violated every single rule of talk-show politesse. And it got a big laugh besides."

Though Johnny Carson took pains to point out that his own *Tonight Show* was a comedy program, not a talk show, Letterman appears more literal-minded about his show. "I think it is a talk show," he told Tom Shales in an *Esquire* cover story. "It has exactly the structure of Merv and Johnny and, all the others. I sit at a desk and guests come out." Other conventions of traditional talk show structure prevail as well, including the obligatory bandleader/comic foil, personified by self-styled hipster musician Paul Shaffer.

The comic, often described in the press as boyish and gap-toothed, follows another tradition of TV hosts—he seems nonthreatening. As Shales put it, talk-show stars "have to be mellow boys next door—after all, you'll be spending many hours of your life with them. Letterman is the mellowest and most neighborly yet.

Sometimes offends guests

On the other hand, Letterman has cultivated such a strong reputation as a harsh interviewer that some celebrities have resisted invitations to appear with Letterman for fear of being publicly skewered. One such instance affected Letterman personally. "I've always been a big fan of [1960s talk show phenom] Jack Paar's," he told *Time*'s Richard Zoglin, "and he had invited me to his home a couple of times. I had always found him to be really interesting and still very energetic and dynamic, and I had wanted to get him on the show. But the response was that he had been advised by friends not to go on our show because we would make fun of him. I was saddened by that."

Responding to Zoglin's charge that he has been perceived as "condescending, smug, even mean," Letterman acknowledged: "I suppose I am all of those things, but we never invite somebody on to demonstrate condescension—or condensation. If somebody comes on and is a bonehead and is loafing through an interview, I resent that, and maybe I will then go after them. But if you come on and are polite and well groomed and behave yourself, then you've got nothing to worry about. I'm stunned at the number of people in show business who come on and don't seem to get that what we want from them is a performance."

Nonetheless, Letterman's satiric edge "can be rough," wrote Glenn Collins in a *New York Times* article, especially on non-celebrity "civilians" who sometimes bear the brunt of his jokes. The columnist cited the host's "unrehearsed phone calls to unsuspecting people or [his] on-camera forays to places like the General Electric building in Manhattan, where a hapless security official doing his job was made to look foolish preventing Mr. Letterman's entry. Some people have written the network to say they won't watch because of the show's cruelties." In his defense, Letterman offered Collins his opinion that his humor may border on cruelty, "but I'm not malicious. I don't want to get a laugh at the expense of others.... Then again, if I see an opening, I go for it."

Though on-air stunts and remote segments are as old as the talk-show itself, what distinguishes Letterman's show is its approach to the genre. "The talk show is ideal television because of its shriveled minimalism," explained Shales. "Two people talking to each other, the director cutting back and forth between them, really has enough movement and visual substance to occupy this small and imprecise electronic canvas.... [Big-budget film producer] David Wolper can put three thousand extras on that screen and not generate anything a whit more kinetic than David Letterman talking to [actress] Teri Garr and making her laugh."

It's only television

In his own way, Letterman has helped redefine the public's attitude toward television. "Talk to [the comic] and his staff about the mass of TV, and the phrase 'it's only television' comes up again and again," noted Barol. "They're well aware that the sense of wonder that suffused the medium in the early days, when wild men like Steve Allen ruled, has given way to a snoozy familiarity. Among the [Letterman] staff, it's literally true that familiarity has bred contempt. What they have done in response is energize the talk-show format by melting it down and recasting it in Letterman's own odd image."

Some of that image is based on a youthful ideal of what makes good comedy. As Collins wrote, many of the show's popular mainstays—"like crushing things as disparate as bowling balls and a six-pack in a hydraulic press—seem to work because they use the awesome power of the television medium to evoke a silly sense of wonder."

Though Letterman keeps a low profile concerning his personal life (he has talked more of his beloved dogs, Stan and Bob, than he has about his early marriage, which ended in divorce, and his long liaison with former *Late Night* writer Merrill Markoe), he's faced some controversies that can only be called Lettermanesque. In one instance, the comedian was hit with a multimillion-dollar suit by a woman whose poodle, Benji, appeared on *Late Night* performing a Stupid Pet Trick. It seems Letterman was unimpressed by Benji's talent for walking around on his hind legs, and told a Boston television station that he was sure the owner had "performed some sort of unethical and intricate spinal surgery on the dog, and that's illegal and she'll end up doing time," as *American Film* critic Peter Exline quoted. The suit contended that Letterman's remarks caused the owner "to suffer contempt and scorn and have impaired her standing in the eyes of a considerable class of the community." The defendant's lawyers stated only that the woman should have known that Letterman was just kidding.

In another, more serious incident, a 36-year-old woman repeatedly broke into Letterman's vacated Connecticut home. Identifying herself as Mrs. Letterman, the woman and her three-year-old son lived on the premises for days, even driving Letterman's Porsche. When the woman, who had a history of mental problems, was finally discovered and arrested, the comedian, "his heart as big as the gap between his teeth, declined to press charges," as a *People* reporter wrote. "This may have been a tactical error, though, because five days later [the woman] was back in the house.... This time Dave decided to prosecute."

Letterman's reticence to reveal his inner self stems from a larger sense of modesty noted by Barol in the *Newsweek* piece: "At a Bruce Springsteen concert [one summer], he was astounded to hear Springsteen mention *Late Night,* and to hear 'a significant number of people in the audience not boo.'" "I like talking about things that happen in my life if I think I can make me the butt of the joke," Letterman told Zoglin. "But I'm not crazy about actually talking about real things in my life.... If something funny happens in the supermarket, I like trying to talk about that.... But I don't want to start explaining in great detail what makes me happy, what makes me sad, that kind of crap."

Leaves NBC

When NBC announced that after Carson's retirement in 1992 comedian and fill-in host Jay Leno would replace him on the *Tonight Show,* it was reported that Letterman felt hurt and betrayed. NBC had been home to Letterman since he began *Late Night* in 1982, and he had always felt that he would be that natural replacement for Carson. So when Letterman's contract came up in 1993, it came as no big surprise that he defected to CBS for a cool $14 million and a time slot opposite Leno. The surprise came when Letterman succeeded in trouncing his competition in what came to be called the Great Late Night War of 1993. During the fall of 1993 *The Late Show with David Letterman* premiered, as did a new show featuring comedian Chevy Chase on the Fox network. (NBC replaced Letterman's show with a new one featuring the then-unknown television producer Conan O'Brien.) Both Leno and late-night host Arsenio Hall felt the competition and attempted to increase their visibility. Chase and Hall would be out of the picture by late 1994.

Letterman has a clear-cut policy of never letting industry VIPs receive tickets in any way other than those available to the general public. So while other talk shows always hold a few choice seats for the network hotshots, Letterman's show instructs those hotshots to write away for their tickets.

The big question was whether Letterman's offbeat, often caustic style would translate well in an earlier time slot (11:30 p.m. versus the 1:00 a.m. of *Late Night*). By December Letterman was the clear-cut winner. An article in *People* explained: "To the surprise of many, the mainstream late-night audience, long inured to Johnny Carson's comfort food, proved ready to embrace Letterman, who had previously appealed ... to a younger, hipper crowd. More surprisingly, perhaps, Letterman proved ready to embrace the mainstream. That's not to say that Dave has lost his edge, but rather he's leavened it with a newfound amiability."

Sources

American Film, June 1987.

Chicago Tribune Magazine, January 6, 1980.

Cosmopolitan, June 1994.

Esquire, November 1986.

Latham, Caroline, *The David Letterman Story,* Franklin Watts, 1987.

Newsweek, July 7, 1980; February 3, 1986.

New York Times, July 27, 1986.

People, February 4, 1980; March 21, 1988; June 13, 1988; October 4, 1993; December 27, 1993.

Rolling Stone, November 3, 1988.

Time, February 6, 1989; August 30, 1993; March 14, 1994.

U.S. News & World Report, June 23, 1986.

Vanity Fair, February 1989.

Vogue, January 1994.

Washington Post Magazine, April 21, 1980.

Los Lobos

ROCK BAND

"Los Lobos have brought their rich musical hybrid ... into the mainstream with a vengeance."—Gene Santoro

The four original members of Los Lobos, David Hidaigo, Cesar Rosas, Louie Perez, and Conrad Lozano (Steve Berlin joined around 1983), have known each other since their high school days and grew up in practically the same neighborhood. Up until 1973, they had all played in various Top 40 bands. Realizing that just replaying current popular songs was not what any of them wanted to do, they decided to explore their Mexican roots and learn the folk songs they were raised on but had never paid much attention to. "We were just rock and roll musicians, and we discovered this stuff," Perez told *Guitar Player*. "All of a sudden it was like we lifted a rock and there was this incredible life that was teeming under it."

When the roots-rock revival of the early 1980s appeared, Los Lobos (which means "The Wolves" in Spanish) would probably have been picked as the least likely to succeed. While bands like the Stray Cats and the Fabulous Thunderbirds stuck mainly to one genre, Los Lobos took on a bigger challenge by combining country, swing, rock and roll, Mexican nortena, rhythm and blues, and the blues. It may sound like an impossible repertoire to pull off, but the five-piece unit from East Los Angeles shifts among their various influences effortlessly.

Los Lobos began by collecting as many of the old recordings as they could find and then dissecting each one in order to play it properly. Their

skills were tested on many instruments that they had never even played before as they gathered in backyards to learn tunes by artists like Miguel Aveces Mejia from the late 1950s. They started playing at parties, weddings, and other small events before landing their first full-time gig in 1978 at an Orange County Mexican restaurant. "

For their first eight years, Los Lobos was an all-acoustic group playing only traditional music. They had accumulated over 30 different instruments but it took a University of California at Los Angeles student, Art Gerst, who was a fanatic for Mexican music, to set them straight on the proper and authentic techniques to use. "He told us he liked the spirit we had in our playing," Hidaigo told Harold Steinblatt in *Guitar World.* "Unfortunately, he also said that we were playing completely incorrectly." After that was straightened out, the band began to incorporate some Tex-Mex instruments, like the accordion, and songs from Flaco Jimenez, Jacito Gartito, Los Piuquenes del Norte, and Los Alegres de Tiran. As their influences broadened, so did their arsenal of equipment and before long they were pulling out their electric guitars and amplifiers. Their two-year stint at the restaurant ended when the owner complained about their loudness. That incident was repeated shortly thereafter at another restaurant when they played Cream's version of the old blues number "Crossroads."

They had earlier recorded an album, *Just Another Band From East L.A.*, on a very limited budget, but it got them nowhere. With so many different influences among them, they decided to try and put together some originals. "We started writing songs to satisfy our need to play something in between, something that belonged to us," Perez stated in *Down Beat*. They sent a tape of songs to Phil Alvin, leader of another roots band that was gaining notoriety in L.A., the Blasters. Alvin was impressed enough to have Los Lobos open for them at the Whisky nightclub in Hollywood and convinced his own label, Slash, to sign them. Suddenly, with a record contract under their belts, what had started out as a hobby and a labor of love was now much more serious. "We never thought that we might get gigs out of this, we just enjoyed what we were doing," Lozano told *Musician*. "But then we started getting TV coverage, and Chicano awareness began happening, and suddenly it turned out we had a lot of input, a lot of influence over people because of this music."

Win Grammy Award for "Anselma"

They released a seven-song EP, ... *And A Time To Dance*, in 1983 to critical raves. Produced by T-Bone Burnette and Blasters saxman Steve Berlin, the record was just the beginning of Los Lobos' muscle flexing. Dan Forte wrote in *Guitar Player* that the group "displayed almost an overabundance of confidence." Their Grammy Award for Best Mexican-American song for "Anselma" convinced anyone who doubted their authenticity.

Their range of musicianship was astonishing. Instead of hiring additional musicians for the different instruments, the four members split the chores among themselves. Perez, who along with Hidalgo is the group's chief songwriter, had begun playing drums only years after he joined the group. He was originally a guitarist, picking up the instrument when he was 12 and continuing to play throughout his stints with various rock bands. In his mid-twenties he was elected band drummer when Los Lobos began to go electric. "We couldn't see bringing anybody new into the band. And when we got into the Tex-Mex format, which had drums, I just sort of fell into that," he explained to *Guitar Player*. He continues, however, to add acoustic guitar for their recordings and in concert.

Bassist Lozano began playing Beatles and Rolling Stones-style British Invasion rock and roll when he was 16. Before joining Los Lobos, he played in another L.A. band, Tierra, which had a hit single with "Together." After juggling his time between the two bands, Lozano decided to become a full-time member of Los Lobos in 1973, about six weeks after the group had formed. He plays both the electric and acoustic bass in addition to the guitarron and tackles vocal chores.

Rosas is from Sonora, Mexico, and immigrated to L.A. with his family when he was seven. Although he had dabbled in the guitar previously, it wasn't until high school that he began to get serious. Basically self-taught, Rosas took some lessons early on in order to learn a bit about theory and chord work. With influences like Jimi Hendrix, Eric Clapton, and the blues Kings (Albert, B. B., and Freddie), Rosas provides the "crunch" for Los Lobos. In addition to guitar, he also plays the bajo sexto, mandolin, and the vihuela, and his vocals offer a distinctly rough contrast to Hidalgos.

"You have to understand, the band does work and evolve around David," Lozano said of Hidalgo in *Musician*. "His playing is so strong; his talent is still being tapped." A musician's musician, Hidalgo began his musical career as a drummer in the early 1970s, playing in a Christian rock band. He had already been playing guitar since he was 11, growing up on standard rock influences like Chuck Berry and the Ventures. However, Hidalgo expanded into more sophisticated areas and began to absorb the work of guitarists like Les Paul, Hank Williams, and the Hawaiian lap-steel players. His capabilities extend from guitar and violin to accordion and drums. "There are certain things you can only do on certain instruments," he told *Guitar Player*. "It's just that I wanted to hear those sounds, and nobody in the group played them, so I figured I'd try." In addition, Hidalgo's compelling vocals provide the central contours Los Lobos' sound and create great depth along with Rosas's. "I don't think it's an overstatement to say that their voices are as important to the impact of this music as Lennon's and McCartney's were to the Beatles," declared Jim Roberts in *Down Beat*.

Steve Berlin joined the group after working on their EP. His full tenor and baritone saxes add another dimension to Los Lobos' sound, as evidenced on the 1950s-styled party tune "I Got Loaded." "It got silly trying to do both the Blasters and Los Lobos, and since I got to play so much more with Los Lobos, it was more fulfilling," he told *Down Beat*.

Berlin also coproduced their first LP, *How Will The Wolf Survive?* Every song covered different territory, from Tex-Mex polkas to New Orleans rhythm and blues, and as Perez pointed out in *Guitar Player*, the group defied categorization. "As far as this band is concerned, coming from a diverse background and diverse musicianship, I think it would be unfair to stick us under one label." *Rolling Stone* would later name *How Will The Wolf Survive?* one of the 100 best albums of the 1980s.

Their follow-up LP, *By the Light of the Moon*, showed them expanding even more. Not only was the musicianship superb, but the songwriting also belonged in a class of its own, moving beyond previous lyrical limitations into social commentary. "The portraits that emerge ... are arresting as much for their diversity as for the appalling waste of human potential they illustrate time and again," wrote Gene Santoro in *Down Beat.*

Won larger audience with soundtrack to La Bamba

In 1987 Los Lobos was the centerpiece of the soundtrack to the movie *La Bamba.* They were able to recreate, and sometimes outdo, the original recordings of the late Richie Valens. Their version of the title track reached the Top 10 and helped to secure an even larger audience for the group. With record sales beyond the wildest expectations of both Los Lobos and Slash, the band now had the clout to do what only a few artists (such as Bruce Springsteen) are capable of accomplishing.

In 1989 the group released *La Pistola y El Corazon,* an album consisting solely of the type of folk songs that they began with some 15 years earlier. "We talked about doing something like this since the day we signed a deal with the company, to take this music and record it properly," said Hidalgo in *Guitar World.* In 1992 they released *Kiko and the Lavender Moon,* as well as the soundtrack for the movie *The Mambo Kings.* In 1993 Los Lobos released *Just Another Band From East L.A.: A Collection.* The release contained over 41 songs on two CDs, and it commemorates the band's twentieth anniversary. Ron Givens of *People* praised the new project: Los Lobos makes music that defies time and geography. If this is 'just another band from East L.A.,' I want to hear all the rest. Now.

In the fall of 1994 it was reported that Los Lobos would contribute a song and the instrumental score to *El Mariachi II,* a film by hot young director Robert Rodriguez. They were also finishing up a children's album at the time and had begun writing material for a new record, production of which was slated to begin at the end of the year.

Sources

Down Beat, May 1984; February 1985; April 1985; April 1987.

Guitar Player, March 1984; May 1984; January 1985; February 1987; October 1987; December 1988; November 1992.

Guitar World, September 1986; February 1989.

Los Angeles Times Calendar, October 9, 1994.

Musician, April 1987.

People, December 6, 1993.

Yo-Yo Ma

Born October 7, 1955
Paris, France

"What people call my exuberance comes from wanting to share what I've gained from a piece with my listeners. I hope I'll always do that."

CELLIST

Yo-Yo Ma is a world-famous cellist whose performances draw sellout crowds. Since his early childhood, Ma has had an affinity for the cello that earned him prodigy status, and he matured into a talented interpreter of solo and ensemble works for cello. He has appeared with major orchestras throughout the world and recorded most of the solo cello repertoire. Ma's popularity rests not only on his technical mastery of the cello and superb musicianship, but also on his ability to communicate to the audience his love of the music he performs.

Discovers the cello

Born into an upper-class Chinese family living in Paris, Yo-Yo was the youngest of two musically talented children. Ma's affinity for music came as no surprise as his mother, Marina, was a mezzo-soprano and his father, Hiao-Tsiun, was a violinist, composer, and musicologist who specialized in the education of gifted children. The Ma children were schooled at home in the traditional Chinese fashion, with lessons in the Chinese language, literature, and calligraphy. Ma's first musical training was on the violin, but because his sister, Yeou-Cheng, also played that instrument, Ma wanted to, in his words, "play something bigger." Ma began to study the cello at age four with his father, who, when he could not find a small enough cello,

> "Never lose your idealism, the passion you have for music. It's easy to get cynical, bogged down.... It's important to find the point of the music—what does it say? You have to be within a piece of music, and then things become really exciting. You have to open yourself up to the audience."

gave his son a viola to which he had attached an end pin. Ma's father taught using a method that involved practicing for only a half hour each day and memorizing several bars of a Bach suite for unaccompanied cello. In this way, the young cellist learned three such suites by the time he was five years old and performed one of them at his first public recital at the Institute of Art and Archeology at the University of Paris. Despite his astounding ability, Ma was not pressured by his parents to go on tour as a child prodigy.

When Ma was seven years old his family moved to New York City, where his father taught at a school for musically gifted children, including the children of the virtuoso violinist Isaac Stern. One day Stern heard the young Ma play and recommended that he study with Leonard Rose at the Juilliard School of Music. Ma auditioned for Rose and as a student in the college preparatory division became the youngest pupil ever of the distinguished cellist. Ma credits Rose with much of his success for, as he told Stephen Wigler of the *Baltimore Sun*, Rose taught him "everything I know about the cello." Remembering those lessons, Ma told Thor Eckert, Jr., a *Christian Science Monitor* reporter, "It was quite intense, and from the start Rose taught me that to play the cello you must have an absolute physical relationship with your instrument. When you play you must feel as though the instrument is a part of your body, the strings are your voice, and the cello is your lungs." For his part, Rose described the student's technical and interpretative ability: "He was very small and already quite extraordinary.... When he was about seventeen, he gave a performance of Schubert's *Arpeggione*, which is a holy terror for cellists, and it was so gorgeous I was moved to tears," he told a writer for *Time*.

As a teenager, Ma attended New York City's Professional Children's School. He skipped two grades and graduated at age 15. That same year he made his New York debut at Carnegie Hall and was asked by the famous conductor/composer Leonard Bernstein to perform on national television for a fund-raising event for the Kennedy Center for the Performing Arts in Washington, D.C. Ma then attended Juilliard's college division for a year and the following summer attended the Meadowmount music camp, where, freed from the discipline of his home, he rebelled with irresponsible behavior. At the end of the summer, his rebellion against the narrowly defined focus of conservatory courses continued in his decision to attend Columbia University instead. Yet after a semester, Ma was also dissatisfied with the academic life at Columbia, and in 1972 he transferred to Harvard University, from which he graduated with a Bachelor of Arts degree in humanities in 1976. While at Harvard, Ma took courses in music history, theory, and appreciation and he played in student ensembles. He also began his professional music career by performing on weekends at local venues.

Begins full-time performance career

Ma began his full-time performance career in 1976 and in 1978 it was given a critical boost when Ma won the prestigious Avery Fisher Prize. The purpose of this award is to give talented young instrumentalists opportunities to perform with major orchestras, and Ma benefited directly through performances with the New York Philharmonic, and other ensembles. After being forced into a one-year hiatus from performing because of surgery to correct a curvature of the spine, Ma resumed a busy schedule of appearances that range to 125 per year.

When Ma plays the cello, the tone he produces is not always as powerful as those of other famous cellists, but it is silky and he is undoubtedly a master of technique and expressivity. Ma performs and has recorded works from many eras and styles, ranging from Bach concerti to the Britten *Symphony for Cello*. Since he likes to learn several new pieces each year, early in his career Ma nearly exhausted the somewhat limited repertoire of works for solo cello and began to commission new works from such composers as Leon Kirchner, one of his teachers at Harvard, and Oliver Knussen. Not only does Ma perform as a soloist, but since he is committed to chamber music, he appears and records with his own piano trio, string quartet, and string trio.

Sources

Baltimore Sun, May 25, 1986; March 21, 1988.

Christian Science Monitor, May 26, 1978.

Diapason-Harmonie, June 1988.

Kansas City Star, September 15, 1985.

New York Daily News, March 24, 1987.

Stereo Review, April 1990.

Time, January 19, 1981.

Tuscon Citizen, March 16, 1988.

Madonna

Born August 16, 1958
Bay City, Michigan

SINGER, SONGWRITER, AND ACTRESS

The reigning queen of pop music is Madonna Louise Veronica Ciccone, a sultry singer-dancer born in Bay City, Michigan. Madonna has been virtually unrivalled on the concert scene, the pop charts, and the music-video airwaves since 1985. Her engaging blends of hip dance music and suggestive, sometimes campy lyrics have attracted vast listening audiences and have made her one of the wealthiest active performers in the world. She is also one of the most controversial.

Madonna's music videos and live concert performances have featured some of the most sexy dancing and posing ever seen in the music industry. Some feminists have been quick to complain that the singer perpetuates the "woman as sexual plaything" stereotype, with her lingerie costumes and "boy toy" belt buckle. Madonna herself couldn't disagree more. She told *Rolling Stone:* "People have this idea that if you're sexual and beautiful and provocative, then there's nothing else you could possibly offer. People have always had that

"The fascinating thing about Madonna is that she is all-real and all-fake—in other words, pure show biz."
—Richard Corliss

Madonna kept herself in a college preparation program all through high school. She was often on the honor roll, scored well on the SAT tests, and scored in the top 10 percent on a verbal intelligence test. Her counselor's recommendation on a scholarship application to the University of Michigan described her as having an "extremely talented, dedicated, motivated, sparkling personality."

image about women. And while it might have seemed like I was behaving in a stereotypical way, at the same time, I was also masterminding it. I was in control of everything I was doing, and I think that when people realized that, it confused them.... You can be sexy and strong at the same time."

Madonna was born August 16, 1958, and was named after her mother, who was also Madonna Ciccone. The singer had a very abbreviated childhood—when she was five, her mother died of cancer after a long and painful illness. At first Madonna and her five siblings were shuttled among relatives, then they were placed under the care of a housekeeper who eventually married their father. Remembering her days at home with a new parent, Madonna told *People:* "I felt like Cinderella with a wicked stepmother. I couldn't wait to escape." Madonna was tapped for child care and babysitting chores to such an extent that she had little time to be a child herself. She also attended Catholic school, where she earned top grades despite a tendency to decorate her dull uniforms and cavort in class.

In junior high Madonna discovered the world of drama and dance. She began taking private ballet lessons with Christopher Flynn, a teacher who encouraged her to dream of fame. During her high school years at Rochester Adams High in suburban Detroit, Madonna was able to make the honor roll and be a cheerleader while still pursuing dance with great seriousness. Even then she had the determination to succeed, an attitude that she took no pains to hide. She graduated early and won a full scholarship to the University of Michigan.

Heads for New York City

After only two years at Michigan, Madonna left for New York City with the clothes on her back and less than $100 in pocket money. She worked for some months as an artist's model and even posed for some nude pictures while waiting for a break into the entertainment business. Her first professional work came with the Alvin Ailey Dance Theater, where she earned a spot in the third company. She left that troupe and studied briefly with Pearl Lang, but she soon became convinced that dancing alone would not provide her an avenue to fame.

Madonna gravitated toward music, especially the new wave sounds of the Pretenders and the Police. Between 1979 and 1982—with a brief hiatus in Paris as a back-up singer to disco star Patrick Hernandez—she performed with a number of post-punk groups, including the Breakfast Club, Emmy, and the Millionaires. She soon tired of back-up role, and with a former Michigan boyfriend, Steve Bray, she formed a band with herself as lead singer. This group, simply called Madonna, caught the eye of Camille Barbone, who became Madonna's manager in 1981.

From new wave Madonna moved to funky, rap-influenced dance music, which she performed in New York's thriving dance clubs with great success. This shift from rock to funk alienated her first manager, but it won her the attention of Mark Kamins, a deejay with wide contacts in the industry. Through Kamins, Madonna signed with Sire Records, a division of Warner Bros. She cut her first album, *Madonna,* early in 1983 and engaged the services of Freddie DeMann, Michael Jackson's manager.

Sales of Madonna's debut album were hardly brisk at first, but she found powerful allies in the dance clubs. Eventually the exposure led to more radio coverage of her first singles, "Holiday," "Lucky Star," and "Borderline." The latter two songs finally began to inch up the pop charts until both made it into the top 20 in 1984. While stuffy critics predicted that she would be just another flash in the pan, the energetic performer set out to win the world—and she did just that in 1985.

Like A Virgin *goes platinum*

Like a Virgin, Madonna's second album, was released early in 1985 and quickly went platinum in sales, with more than one million records sold. Madonna had the rare treat of seeing two of her singles, "Material Girl" and "Crazy for You," in the top five simultaneously, while her funky tune "Into the Groove" became the rage in the dance clubs. Her fame was sealed, however, by the music videos she released with *Like a Virgin*—and with the white-hot performance she delivered in the film *Desperately Seeking Susan.* The "Like a Virgin" video featured the singer flirting in a lace wedding gown, and the even campier "Material Girl" offered a tongue-in-cheek tribute to Marilyn Monroe's rendition of the title song from her film *Diamonds Are a Girl's Best Friend.* The "Like a Virgin" tour began in 3,000-seat halls, but quickly moved to the largest arenas as shows sold out in a matter of hours.

International fame brought with it the usual troubles. Critics accused Madonna of releasing only the blandest pop. The news media hounded the star, making a mockery of her short marriage to actor Sean Penn. Still, Madonna conducted herself with dignity, eventually winning over some of the hardest-to-please rock writers. Her album *True Blue* was the first to earn critical acclaim, for its message song "Papa Don't Preach," about unwanted pregnancy, and its lovely ballad "Live To Tell." As she confronted her marital difficulties and disappointments, the so-called "Material Girl" began to write and sing about deeper subjects—much to the dismay of those who accused her of pandering to mediocrity.

In 1989 Madonna released *Like a Prayer,* an album containing brutally frank music about her childhood, her marriage, and her Catholic upbringing. The music video of the title track caused the a huge sensation, with its sly mixture of religious and sexual symbolism. Behind the sensationalism, though, was some serious music, as J. D. Considine noted in his *Rolling Stone* review. The songs on *Like a Prayer,* Considine wrote, are "stunning in their breadth and achievement.... as close to art as pop music gets." The often critical reviewer added: *"Like a Prayer* is proof not only that Madonna should be taken seriously as an artist but that hers is one of the most compelling voices."

Madonna's 1990 album, *I'm Breathless,* marked a return to the funky dance-and-flirt style that made the performer famous. Having put her marriage behind her without answering the sensational press reports, the singer was ready to have fun again. The star had an extremely successful 1990 road outing that was tagged the "Blond Ambition" tour. That tour and Madonna's backstage exploits were detailed in the highly successful 1991 documentary *Truth or Dare.* Madonna also won critical and popular kudos for her performance in the 1991 movie *A League of Their Own.* She was one in an ensemble cast of women who played female baseball players who became professional during World War II when the lack of male players made a female league necessary.

The year 1992 was another extremely busy one for Madonna. She recorded an album entitled *Erotica,* published a book of erotic photographs entitled *Sex,* and filmed the sexually explicit movie *Body of Evidence.* These three ventures, however, met with less than the usual acclaim that accompanies Madonna's work. *Body of Evidence,* in which Madonna plays a woman accused of killing her lover, earned only $14 million and *Erotica* has sold only around 2 million copies in the U.S., 5 million fewer than *Like a Virgin. Sex* was panned by the press, but the media hype helped to create an early sensation and sales of the book reached 500,000 copies. The sensation soon ended, however, and the book is now found on sale racks.

Madonna bounced back in 1993 with the "Girlie Show" tour, which sold out in almost every city it played. David Hildebrand of *People* called it "a surprisingly sophisticated show, with great stage design and costumes, provocative choreography and fresh musical arrangements." And Richard Corliss in *Time* praised Madonna's sense of theater: "The fascinating thing about Madonna is that she is all-real and all-fake—in other words, pure show biz. Girlie Show—at once a movie retrospective, a Ziegfeld revue, a living video, and an R-rated takeoff on Cirque de Soleil [Circus of the Sun]—opens with Smokey Robinson's 'Tears of a Clown' and closes with Cole Porter's 'Be a Clown' ... the calliope music announces that this is a three-ring circus of clowning around. And Madonna, once the Harlow harlot and now a perky harlequin, is the greatest show-off on earth." In the fall of 1994 Madonna released a collection of rhythm and blues-styled material called *Bedtime Stories*. Its initial run on the charts promised further success for the singer.

All the hype surrounding her career notwithstanding, Madonna does have enormous talents upon which to draw. She is an able songwriter who has contributed original material to every album she has released, she is a fine dancer who can set trends, and she covers a somewhat thin voice with sophisticated but never dominating instrumentation. It is not surprising, then, that she complained to *Rolling Stone:* "There are still those people who, no matter what I do, will always think of me as a little disco tart." *Rolling Stone* contributor Mikal Gilmore concluded that Madonna need offer no apologies for her hard-won fame. "Madonna will still have her detractors," the critic wrote, "but somehow little girls across the world seem to recognize a genuine hero when they see one."

Sources

Mademoiselle, December 1983.

New Republic, August 26, 1985.

Newsweek, March 4, 1985; November 2, 1992.

New Yorker, April 22, 1985.

New York Times, April 14, 1985.

People, March 11, 1985; September 2, 1985; December 23, 1985; December 14, 1987; December 28, 1992; November 22, 1993.

Playboy, September 1985.

Record, March 1985.

Rolling Stone, November 22, 1984; May 9, 1985; May 23, 1985; December 19, 1985; June 5, 1986; September 10, 1987.

Spin, May 1985.

Time, March 4, 1985; May 27, 1985; April 6, 1989; October, 25, 1993.

Vanity Fair, August 1985.

Village Voice, June 18, 1985.

Vogue, May 1989.

Washington Post, May 26, 1985; November 25, 1985.

Marky Mark

Born June 5, 1971
Dorchester, Massachusetts

RAPPER

Rap star Marky Mark (born Mark Wahlberg) became as well known for his bulging muscles as his music. At one point in his career, fans could catch either his musical routine on MTV or his highly publicized appearances in Boston courtrooms on assault charges. He may travel by limousine to concerts and engagements, but he hasn't lost the tough edge he honed in the rough streets of his hometown, Dorchester (near Boston), Massachusetts.

"I think I'm different now, in how I think about life, think about people, how I think people think about people. Nobody's really doing anything about these kids, kids like me. I didn't care about going to school. I cared where I was gonna get mine."

Learned from big brother

Mark's rise began on the shirttail of his big brother, Donnie Wahlberg, one of the members of the pop group New Kids on the Block. After a brief stint with the New Kids, he quit, but made his comeback in 1990 as Marky Mark and the Funky Bunch to concentrate on issue-oriented rap music. Donnie still keeps tabs on his youngest brother by offering advice, helping to produce Mark's albums, and even writing much of his younger brother's music. "Everything that I do, I always talk to my brother about, and the same with him," Mark told *YM*. "With him and me, it's cool."

While the New Kids on the Block's style and product were mostly wholesome, squeaky-clean, boy-next-door stuff, the younger Wahlberg's image reflects the mean streets of his youth. His raps touch on a life scratched out around the perils of gang violence, the drug scene, and day-to-day survival of the fittest. His first album, *Music for the People*, went platinum (one million copies sold), with three dance-tune rap singles hitting *Billboard*'s Top 10: "Good Vibrations," "Wildside," and "I Need Money." "I'm a positive person," Mark told *TV Guide*, "and if I can give a positive outlook to people who, like me, grew up without many opportunities, then that's a great accomplishment."

Less success with second album

Album number two, *You Gotta Believe*, offered more message and less dance music. It wasn't as successful as its predecessor, but Mark considers it a necessary step in his self-expression. "*You Gotta Believe* just deals with all of the accusations and the misconceptions of Marky Mark, you know," he told *Teen Machine*. "A lot of people say, 'Well, the single's not doing that well,' but its a hit to me because it's out there and people who normally wouldn't have heard a 'Good Vibrations' type of record are hearing Marky Mark and they're hearing where I'm coming from. And, you know, if I have to slow things down for a few months to make my point, then I will."

In order to promote *You Gotta Believe*, Mark did a whirlwind tour of Japan, France, New York, London and San Francisco. The media hounded him and hordes of fans lined up to get his autograph on his photo-biography, *Marky Mark*. Fans love his concerts. The highlight of his high-energy performance comes when he rips off his shirt and drops his pants to reveal boxer shorts and his pumped-up body.

Works out

Mark started bodybuilding when he quit smoking, in 1991. He makes a point of scheduling workouts even when he's touring. "If I don't go to the gym, I'll be crazy all day," he told *People*. "Weight lifting is the only time to let my frustrations out. And the cuties love it!" The "cuties" include teenage girls, older women, and gay men. This may seem a tough line to walk, but Mark is trying. He's made his own heterosexual preference plain, but has begun to accept engagements in gay clubs. In his trademark fashion statement, Mark wears oversized beltless jeans which dip strategically to reveal his briefs.

Mark's public presence has turned controversial on occasion, and detractors point out his "positive outlook" has been somewhat selective. In 1986 he was in trouble for taunting and throwing rocks at black elementary school children, and in 1988 he spent 45 days in jail for assaulting two Vietnamese men while attempting to steal their case of beer. In 1992 he broke the jaw of a security guard in a fight at a public tennis court near his old Dorchester neighborhood, and in February of 1993 he defended a British television show in which reggae singer Shabba Ranks made anti-gay statements. The rapper was deluged with criticism from the committee Against Anti-Asian Violence, and the Gay & Lesbian Alliance against Defamation. Mark responded by agreeing to appear in public service advertisements against bias crimes and issued a public statement, "I denounce racial violence of all kinds." The public service announcement was put in jeopardy, however, after an incident in Hollywood in July of 1993. Reportedly, Mark had a confrontation with pop star Madonna after he called one of her group "a homo." After the two stars exchanged insults, the argument spilled outside and Mark allegedly hit a nightclub manager in the nose. A representative of the Gay & Lesbian Alliance told *People* that Mark's announcement was "on hold until we verify what happened."

> Mark described the racial situation in his neighborhood for *People:* "I think in a way, see, we never really took it as a racial thing because everybody was really against everybody, you know what I mean? People say, 'Marky Mark hates everybody but himself. He hates blacks, he hates whites, he hates gays, he hates Vietnamese, he hates Japanese....' Until I shined the light I did hate everybody—not for what they were, but because of who I was."

Wants GED

Mark quit school at 16 and admits that hanging out on the street led to his legal troubles. Now he is working for his high school equivalency diploma with typical intensity. "I've learned a lot in the past year, but school is still a priority for me," he told *YM,* "and that's why I'm going back to get my GED [General Equivalency Diploma]. I got all my tests done except science. Science, boy, I'm terrified of science but I will pass, because I want it, and I'll work hard for it , you know what I'm saying? Then, when I need to learn more about business and the real world, I can go and take a course."

Of his future, he told *Entertainment Weekly,* "I hope maybe that I'll be able to do other things. Maybe do educational films. I'm lookin' at possibly doin' something' that can be helpful. Somethin' that would suit me.

Somethin' that fits or that deals with somethin' I can really relate to. I think that would be cool." In the summer of 1994 Mark branched out by appearing in a featured role in the Danny DeVito comedy *Renaissance Man*.

Sources

Entertainment Weekly, January 15, 1993.

Mademoiselle, June, 1993.

New York Times, February 18, 1993.

People, July 27, 1992; March 1, 1993; August 15, 1993.

Super Stars, May 1993.

Teen Machine, May 1993.

TV Guide, March 28, 1992.

Wall Street Journal, January 15, 1993.

YM, February 1993.

Bob Marley

Born February 6, 1945, Nine Miles, Saint Ann, Jamaica
Died May 11, 1981, Miami, Florida

REGGAE SINGER, SONGWRITER, AND
GUITARIST

In his brief life, Bob Marley rose from poverty and obscurity to the status of an international superstar—the first Third World artist to be acclaimed to such a degree. Were it not for his charisma and ambition, reggae music might still be confined to Jamaica's ghettos where it originated. Loved by millions for his musical genius, Marley was also a heroic figure to poor and oppressed people everywhere because of his passionate musical portrayals of their plight and his relentless calls for political change. As Jay Cocks wrote in *Time*, "His music could challenge the conscience, soothe the spirit and stir the soul all at once."

"Marley was an inspiration for black freedom fighters the world over.... When his death was announced, the degree of devastation felt ... was incalculable."
—*Timothy White*

Robert Nesta Marley was born to Cedella Malcolm when she was barely 19 years old. The child was the result of her secret affair with Norval Marley, the local overseer of crown lands in the rural parish where she lived. Captain Marley, a white man more than twice Cedella's age, married the girl to make the birth legitimate, but he left the countryside the day after his impromptu wedding in order to accept a post in the city of Kingston. He had virtually no contact with his wife and son for several years, and Bob grew up as part of his grandfather Malcolm's large clan. He was known as a serious child and had a reputation for clairvoyance.

When Bob was about five years old, Cedella received a letter from her estranged husband, who asked that his child be sent to Kingston in order to attend school. Bob's mother reluctantly agreed and put her young son on the bus to Jamaica's largest city. Captain Marley met the child, but, for reasons unknown, he took him to the home of an elderly, invalid woman and abandoned him there. Bob was left to fend almost entirely for himself in Kingston's ghettos, generally considered some of the world's most dangerous. Months passed before Cedella managed to track down her child and bring him back to his country home. Before long, however, mother and child had returned to Kingston, where Cedella believed she had a greater chance of improving her life. She and Bob were joined by Bob's closest friend, Bunny Livingston, and Bunny's father, Thaddeus.

Jamaican society held very few opportunities for blacks at that time. Bob and Bunny grew up in an environment where violent crime was glorified by many young people as one of the few ways of getting ahead. Music was seen as another means of escape. Like most of their contemporaries, the two boys dreamed of becoming recording stars, and they spent their days coming up with songs and practicing them to the accompaniment of makeshift guitars, fashioned from bamboo, sardine cans, and electrical wire. By 1963, Marley's dream had come true—he'd released his first single, "Judge Not." Soon he and Bunny teamed with another singer, Peter Macintosh (later known as Peter Tosh), to form a group known as the Wailers. Through talent shows, gigs at small clubs, and recordings, the Wailers became one of the most popular groups in Jamaica.

Their early success was based on popular dance hits in the "ska" music style. As time passed, they added social commentary to their lyrics and were instrumental in transforming the light, quick ska beat into the slower, bass-heavy reggae sound. The three men also came under the influence of Rastafarianism. This complex set of mystical beliefs holds that the now-deceased Emperor Haile Selassie I of Ethiopia (whose given name was Ras Tafari) was the living God who would lead blacks out of oppression and into an African homeland. It was once considered the religion of outcasts and lunatics in Jamaica, but in the 1960s it came to represent an alternative to violence for many ghetto dwellers. Rastafarianism lent dignity to their suffering and offered them the hope of eventual relief. Rejecting the standards of the white world that led many blacks to straighten their hair, Rastas let theirs mat up into long, ropy "dreadlocks."

They follow strict dietary rules and abhor alcohol and most drugs, but revere "ganja" (marijuana) as a holy herb that brings enlightenment to users. The Wailers soothed ghetto tensions with lyrical messages of peace and love, but at the same time, they warned the ruling class of "imminent dread judgment on the downpressors."

Wailers gained worldwide popularity

For all their acclaim in Jamaica, the Wailers saw few profits from their early recording career, as unscrupulous producers repeatedly cheated them out of royalties and even the rights to their own songs. That situation changed in the early 1970s, after Marley sought an alliance with Chris Blackwell, a wealthy white Jamaican whose record company, Island, was the label of many major rock stars. At the time, reggae was still considered unsophisticated slum music that could never be appreciated by non-Jamaican audiences. Blackwell had a deep interest in the music, however, and because he felt that the Wailers were the one group capable of popularizing reggae internationally, he offered them a contract. He handled the marketing of their first Island album, *Catch a Fire*, just as he would have handled any rock band's product, complete with slick promotional efforts and tours of Britain and the United States. Slowly, the Wailers' sound began to catch on beyond the borders of Jamaica. An important catalyst to their popularity at this time was Eric Clapton's cover of Marley's composition "I Shot the Sheriff," from the Wailers' 1973 album *Burnin'*. Clapton's version became a worldwide hit, leading many of his fans to discover the Wailers' music.

As their popularity increased, the original Wailers drew closer to a parting of the ways. Bunny Livingston (who had taken the name Bunny Wailer) disliked leaving Jamaica for extended tours, and Peter Tosh resented Chris Blackwell's efforts to make Marley the focus of the group. Each launched solo careers in the mid-1970s, while Marley released *Natty Dread* in 1974, which was hailed by *Rolling Stone* reviewer Stephen Davis as "the culmination of Marley's political art to this point." The reviewer continued: "With every album he's been rocking a little harder and reaching further out to produce the stunning effect of a successful spell. *Natty Dread* deals with rebellion and personal liberation.... The artist lays his soul so bare that the careful listener is satiated and exhausted in the end." *Rastaman Vibration* was released in 1976 to even more enthusiastic reviews. It was full of acid commentary on the worsening political situation in Jamaica, including a denouncement of the CIA's alleged involvement in island politics—a bold statement that brought Marley under the surveillance of the CIA and other U.S. intelligence organizations. His prominence in Jamaica reached messianic proportions, causing one *Time* reporter to exclaim, "He rivals the government as a political force."

Assassination attempt followed by exile

Marley regarded all politicians with skepticism, considering them to be part of what Rastafarians call "Babylon," or the corrupt Western world. In the election for prime minister of Jamaica, however, he was known to favor Michael Manley of the People's National Party—a socialist group—over Edward Seaga, candidate of the right-wing Jamaican Labour Party. When Manley asked Bob Marley to give a "Smile Jamaica" concert to reduce tensions between the warring gangs associated with the two parties, the singer readily agreed.

Shortly before the concert was to take place on December 3, 1976, Marley's home was stormed by seven gunmen, suspected henchmen of the Jamaican Labour Party. Marley, his wife, Rita, and their manager Don Taylor were all injured in the ensuing gunfire. Yet despite the assassination attempt, the concert went on as scheduled. An audience of 80,000 people was electrified when Marley, bandaged and unable to strum his guitar, climbed to the stage to begin a blistering 90-minute set. "At the close of his performance, Bob began a ritualistic dance, acting out aspects of the ambush that had almost taken his life," reported Timothy White in *Catch a Fire: The Life of Bob Marley.* "The last [the audience] saw before the reigning King of Reggae disappeared back into the hills was the image of the man mimicking the two-pistoled fast draw of a frontier gunslinger, his locks thrown back in triumphant laughter."

Immediately after the "Smile Jamaica" concert, Marley left the country, beginning a long term of self-imposed exile. After a period of recuperation, he toured the United States, Europe, and Africa. Reviewing his 1977 release, *Exodus,* Ray Coleman wrote in *Melody Maker:* "This is a mesmerizing album ... more accessible, melodically richer, delivered with more directness than ever.... After an attempt on his life, Marley has a right to celebrate his existence, and that's how the album sounds: a celebration." But *Village Voice* reviewer Roger Trilling found that *Exodus* was "underscored by deep personal melancholy, a musical echo of the rootless wanderings that followed [Marley's] self-exile from Jamaica."

In 1978 Marley injured his foot during an informal soccer game. The painful wound was slow to heal and finally forced the singer to seek medical help. Doctors informed him that he was in the early stages of cancer and advised amputation of his damaged toe. He refused, because such treatment was not in keeping with Rasta beliefs. Despite worsening health, Marley continued to write and perform until September 1980, when he collapsed while jogging in New York's Central Park during the U.S. leg of a world tour. Doctors determined that tumors were spreading throughout his lungs and brain. He underwent radiation therapy and a controversial holistic treatment in the Bavarian Alps, but to no avail. After his death on May 11, 1981, he was given a state funeral in Jamaica, which was attended by more than 100,000 people. Prime Minister Edward Seaga remembered Marley as "a native son ... a beloved and departed friend." "He was a man with deep religious and political sentiments who rose from destitution to become one of the most influential music figures in the last twenty years," eulogized White in *Rolling Stone.*

Marley was awarded a special citation on behalf of Third World nations from the United Nations in 1979. He also received Jamaica's Order of Merit in 1981. May 11 is Bob Marley Day in Toronto, Ontario.

Legal battles over estate

Throughout his life, Marley had always remained a man of the street. Even after earning millions of dollars, he would frequently return to the neighborhood where he grew up, leaving his BMW automobile unlocked at the curb while he visited old friends. His casual disregard for money and material possessions endeared him to the masses but gave rise to a monumental legal tangle after his death. Though his estate was worth an estimated $30 million at the time he passed away, he had scoffed at the idea of a will, believing that such a document showed an inappropriate concern with earthly matters.

Under Jamaican law, half of the estate of a man who dies without a will goes to his widow, while the remainder is divided equally among his children. When the court advertised for heirs, hundreds stepped forth claiming to be Marley's offspring. Marley's widow, Rita, became locked in a ten-year battle with the court-appointed administrator of the estate, a conservative lawyer who had not liked Marley when he was alive and who, after the singer's death, sometimes seemed bent on taking as much as possible from those who had been closest to the deceased. The administrator attempted to evict Marley's mother from a house her son had given her—on the grounds that the title had never been legally transferred; in a similar fashion, he tried to have property seized from Rita and accused her of illegally diverting royalty money that should have become part of the contested estate.

That royalty money represented a considerable sum. At the time of his death, Marley had sold about $190 million worth of albums and had an average annual royalty income of $200,000. Posthumous releases of his work were ranked high on *Billboard*'s music charts ten years and more after his death, pushing the annual royalty income to $2.5 million and leading many industry experts to rank Marley as one of the largest-selling recording artists of all time. Control of the rights to his music was as hotly disputed as the division of his estate, with rival record companies trying to wrest control from Rita Marley and Island Records.

Eventually, Rita Marley admitted in court that she had forged her husband's signature on backdated documents that transferred ownership of some of his companies to her. Showing a disregard for legalities similar to her husband's, she calmly told a *Newsweek* reporter that she had been acting on her lawyers' advice. Firm in her belief that Marley would have wanted her to protect herself and his rightful heirs—which were eventually determined to include his and Rita's four children, as well as seven other offspring with various women—she asked, "How can I steal from myself?" She was dismissed as an executor of the estate for this transgression but charged with no crime. The battle over Marley's fortune was finally settled late in 1991. The Jamaican Supreme Court ruled in favor of Rita Marley and Chris Blackwell's Island Logic Ltd., a company that had controlled the estate since 1989. Under the terms of the court ruling, the estate would be managed by Island Logic for ten more years before passing into the hands of Marley's widow and his 11 legally recognized children.

Enduring cultural and musical legacy

Bob Marley's artistic output was so great that previously unreleased work of his has continued to appear on the market years after his death. In 1992 a 78-song package entitled *Songs of Freedom* was released, tracing his career from his first single, "Judge Not," to a version of his haunting "Redemption Song" recorded at his final concert in 1980. The tenth anniversary of his death was marked by several days of commemorative celebrations in Kingston, and *New York Times* writer Howard W. French noted that "whereas Marley's long-haired, ganja-smoking Rastafarian sect was long seen by the staid Establishment [in Jamaica] as an embarrassing threat to tourism, the Jamaica Tourist Board sponsored the memorial [events]." Once shunned, Marley is now acknowledged as the person who, more than any other, has generated lasting interest in his native country.

Marley's musical legacy can be seen in the continuing popularity of reggae and its pervasive influence on mainstream music. The musical group the Melody Makers was formed by Marley himself years ago; its members are his children, led by his oldest son, Ziggy. The September 13, 1993 issue of *Time* magazine reported that hits by reggae acts Shaggy, Shaw, and Inner Circle appeared on the pop charts, and that a reissue of Bob Marley's hits was breaking records previously held by Pink Floyd and the Beatles for number of weeks on the *Billboard* charts. By the mid-1990s, "dancehall"—a Jamaican hybrid of hip-hop and reggae—was also making inroads into mainstream popular music.

Yet no one, not even his son, has been able to touch Bob Marley's position as the undisputed "king of reggae." David Fricke summarized in *Rolling Stone:* "Since Jamaica's favorite musical son succumbed to the ravages of cancer, the search for a worthy successor—a 'new Marley' with comparable vision, personality and musical nerve, not to mention the magic crossover touch—has yielded only flawed contenders.... But looking for a new Marley is as pointless as looking for a new [Bob] Dylan or [Jimi] Hendrix. Bob Marley, like those other two originals, revolutionized pop music in his own singular image, transforming a regional mutant product of Caribbean rhythm, American R & B and African mysticism into a personalized vehicle for spiritual communion, social argument and musical daring."

Sources

Blackbook: International Reference Guide, 1993 Edition, National Publications, 1993.

Black Stars, July 1979.

Crawdaddy, July 1976; August 1977; May 1978.

Creem, August 1976.

Davis, Stephen, *Bob Marley,* Doubleday, 1985.

Davis, Stephen, *Reggae Bloodlines: In Search of the Music and Culture of Jamaica,* Anchor Press, 1979.

Down Beat, September 9, 1976; September 8, 1977.

Encore, January 1980.

Essence, January 1976.

First World, Number 2, 1979.

Gig, June-July 1978.

Goldman, Vivian, *Bob Marley: Soul-Rebel—Natural Mystic,* St. Martin's, 1981.

Guitar Player, May 1991.

Interview, August 1978.

Jet, May 28, 1981; December 30, 1992; January 10, 1994; February 7, 1994.

Los Angeles Times, May 5, 1990; July 16, 1991.

Maclean's, December 28, 1981.

Melody Maker, May 1, 1976; May 14, 1977; November 18, 1978; September 29, 1979.

Mother Jones, July 1985; December 1986.

Newsweek, May 25, 1981; April 8, 1991.

New York Times, May 12, 1981; May 21, 1981; May 13, 1991; September 3, 1992; December 13, 1992.

New York Times Magazine, August 14, 1977.

People, April 26, 1976; December 21, 1992.

Playboy, January 1981.

Rolling Stone, April 24, 1975; June 1, 1978; June 15, 1978; December 28, 1978; January 11, 1979; May 28, 1981; June 25, 1981; March 18, 1982; May 27, 1982; June 4, 1987; March 7, 1991.

Sepia, March 1979.

Spin, June 1991.

Stereo Review, July 1975; September 1977; February 1982.

Time, March 22, 1976; December 20, 1976; May 25, 1981; October 19, 1992; September 13, 1993.

Variety, May 20, 1981.

Village Voice, June 27, 1977; April 17, 1978; November 5, 1979.

Washington Post, August 25, 1991.

White, Timothy, *Catch a Fire: The Life of Bob Marley,* Holt, 1983.

Whitney, Malika Lee, *Bob Marley, Reggae King of the World,* Dutton, 1984.

Steve Martin

Born in 1945
Waco, Texas

ACTOR AND COMEDIAN

For years the very name Steve Martin conjured up the image of a daffy comic wearing rabbit ears, bellowing "Well, excuuuuuuse me!" and cavorting as a "Wild and Crazy Guy." Those days are behind him now, and Martin has retired his old routines in order to embark on a film career of equal, if not greater, renown. The star of such hit movies as *The Jerk, All of Me, Roxanne, Parenthood,* and *Father of the Bride,* Martin has tapped a deeper comic vein, one that often combines both frolic and pathos in a single performance.

Miami Herald correspondent Ryan Murphy described Martin as "the Fred Astaire of comics, a performer who has evolved into opting for the quiet, bittersweet stumble over the broad guffaw almost every time." Martin's brand of humor has indeed changed dramatically, but the work he is doing now more closely resembles the man he is privately—and is thus a source of pride for him.

"I think it's apparent that you can't continue to act stupid into your forties. I feel real confident of my potential in movies in the future. I can play a pretty good range."

Martin quit stand-up comedy at the very height of his career because he realized he had exhausted his material. He turned to writing screenplays and starring in movies—a daring decision that might have spelled the end of his career. After a string of film failures, including *Pennies from Heaven, The Man with Two Brains, Dead Men Don't Wear Plaid,* and *The Lonely Guy,* his stardom indeed seemed doomed. He rebounded with the touching and popular *Roxanne,* the physically demanding *All of Me,* and *Planes, Trains, and Automobiles,* his first outing as straight man to another comic. Subsequently he has become one of Hollywood's hardest-working actors, appearing in as many as two or three films each year.

"Martin may be the most all-American of comedians because of his nose-to-the-sawdust work ethic and his ambition," wrote *Gentlemen's Quarterly* correspondent Elvis Mitchell. "From his first starring role, in *The Jerk,* in which he threw a saddle over his stage shtick and rode it to box office-champeen status, to *All of Me,* in which he married pinpoint concentration to a grown-up movie star's performance, to *Parenthood,* in which he fully entered the adult world, you can see Martin steadily working his way through level after level of accomplishment."

In interviews, Steve Martin is reluctant to talk about his past or his private life. He told one reporter that he finds such anecdotes boring and often beside the point. Asked about his childhood and his family relations, he told *Time* magazine: "We were not close-knit—not a lot of hugging and kissing, not vocal or loud. We were middle class. When frozen food came in, we were right in there buying frozen food."

Discovers Disneyland

Martin was born in 1945 in Waco, Texas. He describes his youth there as "ordinary." The pivotal moment for young Steve Martin came in 1955, when his family pulled up stakes and moved to Garden Grove, California. Suddenly the star-struck boy found himself living just two miles from Disneyland. "I just loved the idea of Disneyland," the comic told *Time.* Martin promptly sought work in the theme park despite his tender age, and he was hired to sell guidebooks at the entrance. "The norm was about 50 books a day," he told *Time.* "One day I sold 625. I think it was a record."

An interest in magic earned him a performing job in Merlin's Magic Shop when he was only 15. He proved so popular there that he began accepting engagements at parties and Kiwanis Club banquets. At 18 he was a regular at the Bird Cage Theater at Knott's Berry Farm, performing four shows a day, five days a week. "Basic training," he called it in *Time.*

Martin added: "I was aiming for show business from early days, and magic was the poor man's way of getting in." Martin also taught himself to play the banjo, bluegrass-style, and he incorporated the instrument into his stage act.

Never an enthusiastic student in school, Martin was not planning to attend college. Stormie Sherk, a fellow performer at Knott's, persuaded him to change his mind. She gave Martin novels to read and introduced him to philosophical ideas that he found intriguing. Martin enrolled at California State University at Long Beach with a major in philosophy. "I was romanticized by philosophy," he told *Time*. "I thought it was the highest thing you could study. At one point I wanted to teach it."

Turns to comedy

The academic honeymoon came to an end when Martin read the works of Ludwig Wittgenstein, a philosopher who redefined and reduced the scope of the discipline. "As I studied the history of philosophy, the quest for ultimate truth became less important to me, and by the time I got to Wittgenstein it seemed pointless," the comic told *Time*. "I realized that in the arts you don't have to discover meaning, you create it. There are no rules, no true and false, no right and wrong." Martin returned to his first love—comedy, and began to pursue the career with more ambition.

In 1967 Martin enrolled in a television writing course at the University of California at Los Angeles. He was also doing stand-up work at the time, but his audiences often were not responsive to his act. He was more successful finding work writing for other performers. By 1968 he had won a shared Emmy for comedy writing for the controversial *Smothers Brothers Comedy Hour,* and he went on to produce material for such varied entertainers as Glen Campbell, John Denver, Sonny and Cher, and Dick Van Dyke.

Writing for others never satisfied Martin. He was still possessed by the idea of stage success on his own terms. In 1973 he left Los Angeles, based himself in Aspen, Colorado, and took his act on the road. "I was in my middle years and just needed some freshness," Martin said in the *Los Angeles Times*. "I needed to get out. It was a good thing, as it turned out, because my career started happening out of [Los Angeles] ... in San Francisco and Miami—the [famed] Coconut Grove, of all places. In Hollywood, I was regarded as just another act."

About the same time, Martin sensed a mood change in the nation at large, and he restructured his act to fit the new mood. He gave up the conventional stand-up act of one-liners and honed sheer stupidity into an art form. "I developed a philosophy of never admitting to the audience that what I was doing wasn't working, never admitting that I wasn't the greatest thing in the world," he noted in *Rolling Stone*. "The usual theory in comedy is that setting up a joke creates tension, and telling the punch line breaks the tension. My theory was, 'Let 'em break their own tension,' the idea being that after wondering, 'What ... is this guy doing?' everyone starts to laugh because they're nervous."

He pulled out the rabbit ears and the fake arrow-through-the-head. He skidded across the stage on "happy feet." He gave the 1970s its mantra with "Well, excuuuuuse me." The audiences loved it. By 1976, television had found him.

Martin hosted *Saturday Night Live* for the first time in the fall of 1976. He was invited back numerous times thereafter, so often in fact that he and Dan Aykroyd developed a series of running skits featuring two "Wild and Crazy Guys," based on a pair of Eastern European immigrants. During the same period, Martin also hosted *The Tonight Show* frequently, and he recorded several best-selling albums of his live concerts. He even had a Top Ten hit single with the novelty song "King Tut."

By 1980 Martin was packing the largest concert halls in the nation and starring in prime-time network television specials. He was also beginning to feel a strain. His routines were becoming tired and predictable, he was running out of new material, and he was especially annoyed by fans who expected him to be silly in public. Late in 1981 he gave up live comedy forever. "I was tired," he told *Rolling Stone*. "I didn't feel I had a choice about giving up the stage; it was just over."

Starts movie career

It was not an end for Steve Martin, but a new beginning. His first motion picture, *The Jerk,* was a top-drawing movie in 1979. The film essentially offered the same absurdist Steve Martin humor as did his stand-up work. "*The Jerk* came at the crest of TV-induced Martin-mania," wrote Jack Barth in *Film Comment*. "It was the first chance to hear the Wild and Crazy Guy swear, and the first chance to pay to see him up close, since his concert venues by that time were too large for his own good. The film was stuffed with sight gags; a car towing a church or driving with no tires, Martin 'wearing' two dogs or dancing like Jerry Lewis in *The Nutty Professor*. The sheer density of the humor combined with the truth-in-advertising title put this one over the top."

Martin with Daryl Hannah in a scene from *Roxanne*, 1986.

Encouraged by the success of that film, Martin proceeded to make four others that simply died at the box office. He starred in a musical, *Pennies from Heaven*, and then turned out *Dead Men Don't Wear Plaid*, *The Man with Two Brains*, and *The Lonely Guy*. Although Barth noted that all of these movies "have had moments of mirth worth the price of admission," Martin tends to view them now as his apprenticeship in the motion picture business. "I see that whole stretch of time now as learning how to make movies," he told *Gentlemen's Quarterly*. "That was actually my transition period. By *All of Me*, I started to get a footing. I was insecure about doing *All of Me*, but only because I was insecure about my movie career. I thought the script was funny, but I really didn't know what to do. But I got on a plane, reread this script and said, This is funny. This is what I want to do. It was the beginning of the second phase."

That "second phase" has assured Martin's film stardom and brought him a substantial amount of respect as a screenwriter. In *All of Me*,

Instead of signing autographs when approached by his fans, Martin hands out autographed cards certifying "that you have had a personal encounter with me, and that you found me warm, polite, intelligent and funny."

released in 1984, Martin portrays a lawyer whose body becomes partially inhabited by the spirit of one of his female clients. Martin was coauthor of the script, with Rob Reiner. In 1986 Martin earned good notices for his cameo as a sadistic dentist in *Little Shop of Horrors.* The best was yet to come, however.

Roxanne, Martin's 1987 comedy, is based on the classic story of Cyrano de Bergerac, a love-smitten soldier with an oversized nose. In the movie, Martin appears as a fire chief—with a banana-sized nose—who helps a handsome coworker woo a beautiful young woman. "The script challenges its star to be at once noble and fatuous, strong and swooning, utterly in control, and desperately in love—all of which Martin handles as gracefully as if he'd written it himself (which he did)," remarked *Time* correspondent Richard Corliss.

Martin's surge at the box office continued with hits such as *Planes, Trains, and Automobiles* (1987), *Dirty Rotten Scoundrels* (1989), *Parenthood* (1989), and *Father of the Bride* (1991). Ironically, the last two vehicles found Martin playing parts far removed from his life. He is childless, but in *Parenthood* he convincingly portrays an anxious father of younger children, and in *Father of the Bride* he appears as the beleaguered dad in the midst of massive wedding preparations. Martin told the *Chicago Tribune* that he chose the two family-oriented roles because "they were warm and funny and touching." He added: "The emotions involved in rearing children or feeling about children, you don't have to have the experience to have them. It's just the emotions of life. It's like missing someone or caring for someone. It's not impossible to get to."

The Steve Martin of the 1990s promises to be as ambitious and unpredictable as the Steve Martin of earlier decades. In 1993's *Leap of Faith,* Martin let loose with an over-the-top portrayal of a semi-sincere preacher who cons his flock. He continues to write screenplays—1991's *L.A. Story,* in which he also starred, being one more recent example—and he is considering starring roles in several more comedies. Another challenge awaits him in serious drama. He played a cameo role in the Lawrence Kasdan film *Grand Canyon* in 1992, and he has told reporters that he will not rule out other non-comic roles.

Most recently Martin has talked about entering the third phase of his life, where he wants to do something more creative than acting. He has written a play, *Picasso at the Lapin Agile,* which concerns the early-twentieth-century artist Pablo Picasso and the famous scientist Albert Einstein.

The play premiered in Chicago in November 1993 and received excellent reviews. In an interview with the *New Yorker* Martin reflected on the previous night's performance: "I've been in show business long enough to know that these things are never perfect. And this was. I thought that the emotional parts worked and the funny parts worked. The whole cast came together. I couldn't be happier.... I really see this now as my future. I'll write plays and appear in films."

Martin and his wife, actress Victoria Tennant, live in Los Angeles. The comedian guards his privacy, saying little about his marriage or about his fine collection of modern American art. "People always expect me to, you know, do something funny when they see me," he told the *Miami Herald*. "They think I'm funny or outrageous all the time. But I can't show off, it's not bred in me.... It's embarrassing! But I just cannot be on." Except, of course, when the cameras are rolling. Then Steve Martin is ready to shine.

Sources

Chicago Tribune, January 2, 1992.

Film Comment, September 1984.

Gentlemen's Quarterly, July 1990.

Los Angeles Times, February 3, 1991; February 10, 1991.

Miami Herald, February 10, 1991.

Newsweek, April 3, 1978; January 11, 1994; June 22, 1987.

New Yorker, November 29, 1993.

People, May 1, 1978; May 23, 1994.

Rolling Stone, December 1, 1977; November 8, 1984; January 21, 1993.

Saturday Evening Post, November/December 1989.

Time, August 24, 1987.

Bobby McFerrin

Born March 11, 1950
New York, New York

"I consider myself a healer, using music as a potent force to bring people joy."

SINGER, SONGWRITER, MUSICIAN

In Germany they call him *Stimmwunder* (wonder voice), in America Bobby McFerrin is considered the most innovative jazz vocalist to emerge in 20 years. Singing solo and a cappella, he uses his four-octave voice to "play" a variety of instruments—such as the guitar, the trumpet, and the drums. "I like to think of my voice as being my body," he told Michael Bourne in *Down Beat*. "That's my equipment."

Discovered by Bill Cosby

The son of opera singers (his father was the first black man to perform regularly with the Metropolitan Opera), McFerrin was born in New York City. In 1958 his family moved to Los Angeles. McFerrin attended Sacramento State University and Cerritos College but dropped out to play piano for the Ice Follies. Over the next few years, he played keyboards with lounge acts and for dance troupes. In 1977 McFerrin decided, suddenly, to become a singer. "I was in a quiet moment when a simple thought just came into my head: 'Why don't you sing?' It was as simple as that, but it must have had some force behind it because I acted on it immediately," he explained to Bourne. He sang with various bands and was eventually discovered by singer Jon Hendricks. While on tour with Hendricks, McFerrin was again discovered— this time by comedian Bill Cosby.

On December 31, 1990, McFerrin organized "Singing For Your Life." This 24-hour singing and meditation event sought to promote world peace, understanding, and the uplifting of the human condition.

Through Cosby, McFerrin was booked in Las Vegas and at the Playboy Jazz Festival in Los Angeles. He later performed at New York's Kool Jazz Festival and began touring or recording with such jazz greats as George Benson and Herbie Hancock. In 1982 he released his first album, *Bobby McFerrin*. His fans were disappointed. "He sang with some of his vocal pyrotechnics fully alight," *Horizon*'s Leslie Gourse wrote, "but he had loud electronic instrumental accompaniment that essentially was pop." McFerrin learned from his mistake, and his next effort, *The Voice*, was widely praised. Recorded live during a solo concert tour of Germany, the album is all a cappella and displays the singer's virtuosity. "McFerrin coaxes up a daffy assortment of vocal effects and characterizations on *The Voice*," Francis Davis noted in *Rolling Stone*. "His circular breathing technique enables him to sing while inhaling and exhaling, thus allowing him to be his own background choir on 'Blackbird' and 'T. J.' He slaps himself into a percussive frenzy on 'I Feel Good' and creates the sound of static between frequencies on 'I'm My Own Walkman.'"

McFerrin's later works have also been well received. Of *Spontaneous Inventions* Susan Katz of *Newsweek* wrote: "[It] shows off his ability to Ping-Pong between sweet falsetto melody and what sounds like a walking-bass accompaniment ... McFerrin delivers a cappella improvisations on everything from Bach to 'The Beverly Hillbillies' theme song." Similarly, his more recent album, *Simple Pleasures,* contains versions of old pop and rock tunes, such as "Good Lovin'," "Suzie Q," and "Sunshine of Your Love." *Interview*'s Glenn O'Brien found that "the way he does these near chestnuts makes them new and restores the power that made them parts of your memory banks in the first place." The album sold over one million copies; one of its tracks, "Don't Worry, Be Happy," become a hit single.

Has won seven Grammy awards

McFerrin has received seven Grammy awards, two for his work on *Another Night in Tunisia,* recorded by Manhattan Transfer. His third, as best male jazz vocalist, was for "Round Midnight," the title song of the 1986 movie.

At the 1989 Grammy Awards, McFerrin won the remaining four. He took honors for best male pop vocalist, best song, and record of the year. He received the fourth Grammy for best male jazz vocalist, for the track "Brothers" on the album *Duet*. McFerrin has also recorded the theme for *The Cosby Show* and the soundtrack for "Just So," an animated series of specials that aired on cable television. He has appeared on *The Tonight Show* and *Sesame Street*, and he provides the vocals for Levi's commercials and appears in commercials for Ocean Spray fruit juices.

McFerrin tours extensively as well. During his concerts, he often improvises his material. Spontaneity is an important part of McFerrin's music. "I like being an improviser, expecting the unexpected," he told Bourne. "Even when something is rehearsed, I want it to be spontaneous."

Sources

Christian Science Monitor, April 17, 1987.

Down Beat, May 1985.

Horizon, July/August 1987.

Interview, August 1988.

Newsweek, October 6, 1986.

New York Times, November 20, 1987.

People, September 21, 1987.

Rolling Stone, March 28, 1985.

Time, October 17, 1988.

Utne Reader, December 31, 1990.

Bette Midler

Born December 1, 1945
Honolulu, Hawaii

ACTRESS AND SINGER

Bette Midler's show business career has been one of remarkable variety. Although she became famous in the early 1970s as "The Divine Miss M.," a powerful singer with a raunchy sense of humor, she has most recently made a name as an actress and one of the saviors of the ailing Walt Disney Studios, for whom she made a series of hugely successful family comedies. Between those two extremes, Midler endured a period of personal and professional difficulties that left her virtually unemployed. Considering her career as a whole, *Time*'s Richard Corliss asserted that Midler is "the most dynamic and poignant singer-actress of her time."

"Because the Improv was a comedy club, you had to be a little bit funny, so I added chatter between songs. There I was, singing my ballads and crying the mascara off my eyes, and in the next breath I'd be telling whatever lame joke I'd just heard."

Midler was born in Honolulu, Hawaii, where her father painted houses for the U.S. Navy. Ruth Midler named her daughter after her favorite actress, Bette Davis, whose name she mistakenly believed was pronounced "bet." Bette and her three siblings grew up in rural Aiea, living in subsidized housing in the middle of sugarcane fields and feeling out of place as the only Jews in a community of Chinese, Japanese, Samoans, and Hawaiians. At an early age, Bette's alienation and loneliness translated itself into a powerful desire to perform. In the first grade, she won an award for her rendition of "Silent Night." "After that you couldn't stop me from singing," she recalled in *Time*. "I'd sing 'Lullaby of Broadway' at the top of my lungs in the tin shower—it had really good reverb. People used to gather outside to call up requests or yell that I was lousy." Midler's father, a strict man who flushed the girls' makeup down the toilet and locked his eldest daughter out of the house if she missed her curfew, disapproved of Bette's ambitions, but his wife was encouraging. She sent her daughters to hula lessons and shared with them her great love of musicals.

Midler attended a stage show, *Carousel*, for the first time when she was 12 years old. "I couldn't get over how beautiful it was," she remembered in *Time*. "I fell so in love with it. Everything else in my life receded once I discovered theatre, and my mother was all for my starting on this journey and going full-speed ahead." Her father remained skeptical even after his daughter became world-famous, however: "He never chose to see me perform— except on Johnny Carson," Midler admitted. "He said I looked like a loose woman."

Begins professional career

After a year at the University of Hawaii, Midler quit school to dedicate herself to drama. Her first professional job came in 1965, when she played the bit part of a missionary's seasick wife in the film adaptation of James Michener's novel *Hawaii*. When the production company returned to Hollywood to complete the movie, Midler went with them. She hoarded her weekly salary until shooting was complete, then headed for New York City. There, she worked variously as a hat-check girl, typist, go-go girl, and sales clerk while expanding her theatrical range with work in children's theater, revues in the Catskills, and experimental plays. In 1966 she landed a part in the chorus of *Fiddler on the Roof*. Shortly thereafter she graduated to the part of Tzeitel, Tevye's eldest daughter, which she played for the next three years.

During her stint with *Fiddler*, Midler met two men who profoundly influenced her career. One was Ben Gillespie, a fellow cast member, who introduced her to soul and R&B music. Midler referred to him as her "mentor" in a *Rolling Stone* interview with Nancy Collins, explaining: "He opened up the world for me.... He taught me about music and dance and drama and poetry and light and color and sound and movement.... I never lost the lessons he taught me." The other influential man in her life at this time was Tom Eyen, author of offbeat plays such as *Sarah B. Divine!* and *Who Killed My Bald Sister Sophie?* He began casting Midler in the dizzy bimbo leads of his productions and gave her a sense of camp. She cultivated a retro-chic look created from thrift-shop clothes from the 1930s and worked up a repertoire of songs from the past, which she performed at any club that would have her. The best known was the Improvisation, where aspiring stars often went to be discovered. Here Midler's unique blend of humor and song began to gel. She reminisced in *Time:* "In my velvet dress with my hair pulled back and my eyelashes waxed, I was convinced I was a torch singer. Because the Improv was a comedy club, you had to be a little bit funny, so I added chatter between songs. There I was, singing my ballads and crying the mascara off my eyes, and in the next breath I'd be telling whatever lame joke I'd just heard."

In 1969 Midler left *Fiddler on the Roof,* only to find she was unable to get another Broadway job. For about a year, she devoted herself to psychoanalysis sessions, singing lessons, and acting lessons at the Berghof Studio. Her acting coach told her that the Continental Baths, a public bathhouse catering to gay men, was looking for weekend entertainment. Midler landed the $50-a-night job and began rehearsing with her pianist and arranger, Barry Manilow. Performing at the Baths forced her to expand her material and set her more firmly on the road to comedy, she stated in *Time:* "By the time I got to the Baths, I had 20 minutes of material but needed 50. So I had to wing it. The Baths was gay, gay, gay in a heartfelt way. The guys would check their clothes, get towels, and sit on the floor. They thought my show was fabulous. So eventually the big brassy broad beat the crap out of the little torch singer and took over." Her attention-getting outfits ranged from a simple ensemble of wedgies, a bath towel, and a flower for her hair to rhinestone girdles, glittery strapless tops, and sequinned gowns. Her repertoire came to include bawdy jokes, novelty songs, blues, and rock. "I was able to take chances on that stage that I could never have taken anywhere else," she wrote in her book *A View from a Broad.* "The more outrageous I was, the more they liked it. It loosened me up."

Finds success at the Baths

"The Divine Miss M.," as Midler now billed herself, was emerging as "one of the first—and few—distinctive personalities of the Seventies," according to *Rolling Stone* contributor Nancy Collins. Word quickly spread about this exciting new performer, and soon the Baths were flooded with people from all walks of life wanting to see the woman whose motto was "Flash with class and sleaze with ease." Offers came pouring in from big nightclubs, television, and record companies. Midler's career was given an additional boost from the shrewd business sense of Aaron Russo, who became her manager in 1971. Their eight-year alliance, which was both personal and professional, was stormy but productive. "Aaron began booking me in theatres," Midler noted in *Time*, "and lo and behold, I was a big success." Her material had to be toned down for mainstream audiences but retained its bite, and the first album sold over 100,000 copies in the month after its release. She showed her usual irreverence during her 1972 New Year's Eve performance at Lincoln Center, where she rose from the stage clad only in a diaper and a vinyl sash marked "1973."

Exhausted by the hectic pace of her initial success, Midler stopped working for several months, then came back strong with a record-breaking Broadway show, *Clams on the Half Shell Revue*. Richard Corliss commented on the physicality of her style, which was evident in this show: As singer or comedian, "Midler has put her body to non-stop work. Harnessing the energy of some Rube Goldberg perpetual-motion machine, prancing on those fine filly legs like the winner of the strumpet's marathon, Bette uses her body as an inexhaustible source of sight gags." Of her singing, he stated, "Her phrasings were as witty as Streisand's, her dredgings of a tormented soul as profound as Aretha's, her range wider than all comers.'" Midler's next challenge was a major film role. She and Russo selected *The Rose*, a serious script about a self-destructive rock star modeled on Janis Joplin. "The picture did good business, I got fabulous reviews, I was nominated for an Oscar," Midler told Cathleen McGuigan in *Newsweek*. "But the fact is that I never got another offer. I died. I was devastated. I really felt I had been shut out." Marjorie Rosen speculated in *Ms.* that perhaps "no one could separate the real Bette from her boozy screen heroine, so convincing was her performance."

Other failures followed: *Divine Madness*, a concert film that was panned by both critics and audiences, and *Jinxed*, a black comedy notable mainly for the vicious power struggle that took place between Midler, her costar Ken Wahl, and director Don Siegel. "*Jinxed* was the worst working experience of my life," Midler told Collins. "I wanted to make the best movie I could, but not everyone felt that way. And they resented me because I did." Siegel and Wahl put out the word that Midler was impossible to work with, and she entered a prolonged depression, turning to psychotherapy to restore her shattered self-confidence. She continued to make recordings and to do concert tours, but her career seemed hopelessly stalled.

Overcomes depression

"I couldn't face the world," Midler told *Time*. "I slept all day and cried all night. I was drinking to excess—I was miserable." Just as she reached her lowest ebb, however, Midler got a phone call from Martin Von Haselberg, a commodities trader who occasionally went onstage as Harry Kipper, one half of a bizarre performance-art duo known as the Kipper Kids. He and Midler had met briefly some time earlier, but in October 1984 they began an intense relationship that culminated two months later in an impromptu Las Vegas wedding ceremony, conducted by an Elvis impersonator. Von Haselberg helped Midler to revitalize her personal and professional lives. "He asked what I really wanted to do," she told *Time*. "Singing? Comedy? I realized I didn't care that much about singing anymore. Nobody else seemed to like it either. But I knew they liked it when I was funny."

It was about this time that Midler signed a contract with Touchstone Films, a new division of Walt Disney Studios. Disney hoped to find its way out of serious financial trouble by releasing films through Touchstone that were more sophisticated and adult-oriented than the studio's traditional fare. The decision to hire Midler was made in part because her career problems meant she could be hired relatively cheaply. She turned out four comedies in quick succession: *Down and Out in Beverly Hills*, a comedy about the newly rich; *Ruthless People*, in which she played a wealthy kidnap victim whose husband refuses to pay her ransom; *Outrageous Fortune*, which teamed her shrill, vulgar character with a prim Shelley Long; and *Big Business*, in which she and Lily Tomlin portrayed sets of identical twins separated at birth. The films proved very popular, all grossing over $60 million, and were largely responsible for Touchstone's becoming the most powerful studio in Hollywood. A reviewer noted that these roles "do not stretch Bette; they shrink her to farce-sized roles." Midler joked about the formulaic quality of the Touchstone comedies—"Was it Outrageous Ruthless People in Beverly Hills?"—but voiced no real complaints in *Time*, explaining: "I'm too happy that anybody noticed I had any talent at all." She concluded: "The whole package is a surprise: to be a box-office success hand in hand with Disney.... I mean, Walt Disney never would have hired me." The star's fifth film for Touchstone and one which she coproduced, *Beaches* was a more serious look at two women from radically different backgrounds and their evolving friendship. Rosen reported in *Ms.* that "critics have panned *Beaches* for its

Among Midler's honors are the After Dark Ruby Award in 1973; an Antoinette Perry "Tony" Award in 1973; a Grammy Award for best new artist in 1973; an Emmy Award for outstanding special for *Bette Midler: Old Red Hair Is Back* in 1978; an Academy Award nomination for best actress for *The Rose* in 1979 and for *For the Boys* in 1992; and a Grammy Award for best pop vocal performance by a female in 1980. She also won Grammys for the singles "Wind Beneath My Wings" and "From a Distance."

unabashed sentimentality, [but] the picture—very much in the fashion of *Love Story* and *The Way We Were,* other soap operas about doomed love, transcends critical objections quite simply because of Bette. For the first time on-screen we're treated to the full force of her personality—the comedienne, [the singer], the romantic leading lady."

Following *Beaches* Midler had a string of films that met with only moderate box-office success. In 1991 Midler produced and starred in *For the Boys,* a film that focused on a USO performer's experiences entertaining the troops during a number of wars. Despite favorable reviews and a strong soundtrack, the film was a disappointment. This same year she also appeared with Woody Allen in *Scenes from a Mall,* which was both a critical and commercial failure. The 1993 *Hocus Pocus* was only moderately successful. In it Midler plays a witch put to death in 1693 Salem only to return on Halloween night 1993 intent on regaining her own youth by sucking the breath out of the town's children. Leah Rozen of *People* called it "[a] cluttered muddle of a movie. Hocus can't make up its mind whether it's a campy vehicle for Midler and her witchy siblings ... or a thriller aimed at kids, about how three plucky children foil this evil sister act."

After these three less-than-successful films Midler decided to return to the concert stage. Her first tour in ten years, "Experience the Divine" broke box-office records wherever it played. In a review of her Radio City Music Hall performance Richard Corliss of *Time* stated: "After 25 years as a singer, comedian, actress and a heavenly blend of all three, the lady has earned her halo. It may be mild hyperbole to call Midler the greatest entertainer in the universe—there are, after all, other galaxies yet to be explored—but who can doubt she's the hardest working woman in show business?" She has also conquered the small screen with a television production of the musical *Gypsy,* which aired in December 1993. David Hildebrand praised her performance in *People:* "Midler combines the brassy flamboyance of Ethel Merman, who played Rose in the original Broadway production, with the broader emotional range of Rosalind Russell, who starred in the 1962 film version. For three hours, Midler is a dizzy delusional dynamo, utterly dominating the rest of the cast."

Sources

After Dark, May 1971.

Detroit News, January 31, 1986.

Midler, Bette, *The Saga of Baby Divine,* Crown, 1983.

Midler, Bette, *A View from a Broad,* Simon & Schuster, 1980.

Ms., March 1989.

National Observer, March 2, 1973.

New Republic, August 2, 1975.

Newsday, July 9, 1970; August 6, 1972.

Newsweek, May 22, 1972; June 30, 1986; January 26, 1987.

New Yorker, June 27, 1988.

New York Sunday News, February 20, 1972.

New York Times, December 3, 1972; December 29, 1972; January 14, 1973.

People, November 14, 1983; February 3, 1986; July 26, 1993; December 13, 1993; March 7, 1994.

Rolling Stone, December 9, 1982.

Savvy, July 1988.

Time, March 2, 1987; October 4, 1993.

Midori

Born October 25, 1971
Osaka, Japan

"When I am on stage, those are some of the happiest times of my life."

VIOLINIST

At age 23 Japanese violinist Midori Goto, who performs under the name Midori, is no longer considered a mere child prodigy. With her virtuoso technique, pure tone, and artistic interpretations, she is quickly dispelling doubts about her future as a violinist. Midori has appeared with many of the world's best orchestras, including those in Berlin, Chicago, Cleveland, Philadelphia, Boston, Montreal, and London, performing some of the most technically difficult works in the solo violin repertoire.

Born in Osaka, Japan, on October 25, 1971, Midori demonstrated her musical ability at an early age. Her mother, a violinist, regularly took young Midori with her to orchestra rehearsals, and one day she noticed that the toddler was humming a piece that the orchestra had been practicing several days earlier. Midori, fascinated by her mother's violin, often tried to touch the instrument, so on her third birthday, her mother gave her a 1/16th-size violin and began to teach her to play it. Later Midori maintained that learning to play the violin was as natural as learning to talk.

Talent discovered

At age six, Midori gave her first public recital with a performance of a free-form instrumental piece by Niccolo Paganini. She progressed rapidly during the next few years, practicing diligently, and she often went with her mother to the auditorium where orchestra rehearsals were conducted, practicing in one of the hall's empty rooms. An American colleague of Midori's mother chanced to hear the young girl play and, astonished by her technique, took a recording to renowned violin instructor Dorothy Delay at New York City's Juilliard School of Music.

Delay, who taught at the music festival in Aspen, Colorado, during the summer of 1981, invited Midori to participate and arranged for a scholarship. Midori's performances that summer confirmed Delay's estimation of her talent, and a year later Midori and her mother moved to New York City so that Midori could enroll on a full scholarship at Juilliard in the precollege division.

After enduring years of an unhappy, arranged marriage, Midori's parents divorced. Midori and her mother began a new life in the United States. Remembering those early years in New York, Midori told *Los Angeles Times* contributor Donna Perlmutter, "When she decided to bring me here—for the study opportunities, for a school like Juilliard—we had no money and could not even speak English.... It took amazing conviction to come alone to a foreign country with a little kid, and to go against the family wishes. I like to think I have some of that strong-mindedness." Midori's mother obtained a position at the Hebrew Arts School in Manhattan, teaching violin to support the family. While studying at Juilliard, Midori attended the nearby Professional Children's School for academic subjects. She also began performing with the New York Philharmonic Orchestra for young people's concerts and galas, but her agent strictly limited her schedule.

In the summer of 1986, 14-year-old Midori took the stage with the Boston Symphony at Tanglewood, in the Berkshire Mountains of Massachusetts. She performed Leonard Bernstein's *Serenade* until a string on her violin broke. As is the custom, Midori calmly approached the concertmaster and borrowed his violin, a much larger one than her own. A short while later a string on this instrument broke. After Midori borrowed the associate concertmaster's violin and finished the performance, the audience, orchestra members, and Bernstein, who was conducting that night,

Midori was named Best Artist of the Year by the Japanese government in 1988; won the Dorothy B. Chandler Performing Arts Award from the Los Angeles Music Center in 1989; and was presented the Crystal Award from *Ashani shimbun* newspaper for her contribution to the arts.

burst into hearty applause. The next day Midori's photograph appeared on the front page of the *New York Times*.

Leap to fame

Despite the sudden fame, the number of Midori's annual performances was increased gradually. By 1990 she was appearing in a total of 90 concerts or recitals per year. Midori claims she does not suffer from stage fright. "I never get nervous or anything," she told Michael Fleming of the *St. Paul Pioneer Press-Dispatch*. "For me it is such fun and so comfortable to play the violin." Surprisingly, however, Midori maintains that she is always a bit disappointed with her performances, insisting that she will do better the next time. "I'm always fighting to be better, to improve, to express new ideas with my violin," she explained to *Denver Post* writer Marian Christy. "After a concert I rate my performance: What was good? What was not so good? Then I tell myself that I'm not a robot." While traveling, Midori practices several hours each day, and until she graduated from the Professional Children's School in June 1990, she also did several hours of homework daily.

Earlier—in 1987—Midori left Juilliard because of personal differences with Delay, which she declines to discuss. "Between school homework, rehearsals and practice there was no time for anything else," Midori explained to Perlmutter. "Since dropping out of Juilliard the world has opened. I go to concerts and movies and have a special curiosity to hear how this one plays and that one plays. I love it." Midori enjoys reading, writing short stories, studying karate, and attending concerts. In addition, she regularly contributes a column on life in the United States to a Japanese teen magazine.

Budding recording career

Midori has successfully ventured into the recording industry as well, releasing double concertos of Johann Sebastian Bach and Antonio Vivaldi with Pinchas Zuckerman, two violin concertos by Bela Bartok, the violin concerto of Antonin Dvorak, and caprices by Paganini. Under an exclusive contract with CBS Masterworks, Midori chooses her own repertory for recordings and also selects the conductor and orchestra, though some orchestras and conductors are unavailable because of contracts with other record companies. After listening to some of the records she made in the 1980s, Midori confessed to Fleming: "I sound like a little girl. But now ... I'm different; I'm sure I will sound different when I'm forty. That's the great advantage of playing from an early age, that you get to see yourself change."

Sources

Atlanta Journal, April 12, 1989.

Berkshire Eagle (Pittsfield, MA), August 26, 1988.

Boston Herald, July 22, 1988.

Buffalo News, March 26, 1989.

Denver Post, March 21, 1991.

Los Angeles Times, April 8, 1990.

New York, October 11, 1993.

New York Times, July 28, 1986.

Ovation, August 1987.

Reader's Digest, March 1987.

San Francisco Examiner, February 7, 1991.

St. Paul Pioneer Press-Dispatch, September 8, 1990.

Strad, May 1987.

Washington Post, January 24, 1988.

Arthur Mitchell

Born March 27, 1934
New York, New York

"The young people today, particularly minority and inner-city kids, they need some kind of motivation as well as compassion. We live in a very technological society. Very few people are spending time to develop the soul."

DANCER, CHOREOGRAPHER, DANCE COMPANY FOUNDER AND DIRECTOR

Members of the Dance Theater of Harlem call Arthur Mitchell the "Pied Piper of Dance." Mitchell, one of the first blacks to succeed in the field of classical ballet, founded the Dance Theater of Harlem in 1969 in an effort to provide minority students with a chance to learn and perform classical ballet. He has been leading the troupe ever since and has presided over an extensive ballet school, worldwide tours, and performances of both classical and modern dance. *Boston Globe* contributor Christine Temin called Mitchell "a preacher of sorts," an artist whose "gospel is one of discipline, hard work, education, goals set and then met. His own goal, of course, was to show that blacks could dance classical ballet. He realized that aim with his Dance Theater of Harlem, now famous for its energy, purity of style, dedicated dancers and diverse repertory." In 1993 Mitchell was awarded the National Medal of Arts, which is given for exceptional work and contribution to the performing arts.

Mitchell's Dance Theater of Harlem includes a school of some 500 would-be dancers, as well as a group of professionals—graduates of the school who perform. The school is located in Harlem and draws many of its pupils from that struggling neighborhood. Most are on scholarship, and all are encouraged to pursue a well-rounded education. Mitchell told the *Philadelphia Inquirer* that his goal is to use dance "to build better human beings."

Mitchell didn't want a publicity frenzy surrounding his becoming the first black NYCB Dancer. "I didn't want any Jackie Robinson stuff about breaking the color barrier. I wanted to be tested on the merits of my dancing. Balanchine ... felt the same way. Of course I knew I was the only black person there, but there was no issue about it. No problem. Balanchine cast me in ballets like he cast everyone else."

No one—least of all Arthur Mitchell—would have predicted that he would become a classical ballet star, an artist of the first rank in one of the nation's best companies. He was born and raised in Harlem, and his early interest in dancing and dramatics was encouraged by his school teachers. As a teenager he enrolled in New York's High School of the Performing Arts, a public institution made famous by the television show *Fame*. There he excelled in jazz and modern dance but was determined to try his luck with classical ballet.

He came to the demanding art form relatively late, and of course he was one of only a few black students in his classes. Instructors told him he had little chance of breaking into the all-white ranks of classical ballet, but he persisted. Mitchell told the *Philadelphia Inquirer* that he chose ballet because of "prejudice." He explained: "I wasn't getting work, and I thought I'd better get classical technique, because then I'd be so good I couldn't be turned down." He soon landed a scholarship with the School of American Ballet, where he became the student of renowned choreographer George Balanchine.

In 1955 Balanchine invited Mitchell to join the New York City Ballet. The imaginative Balanchine even created a duet called Agon specifically for Mitchell, a work *Philadelphia Inquirer* dance critic Nancy Goldner described as "Balanchine's profoundest exploration of partnering as both a physical exercise and a metaphor of the tensions in love relationships." As a principal dancer with the New York City Ballet Mitchell traveled all over the world giving performances. He was the first black man to perform classical ballet in the Soviet Union, where ballet is considered a pinnacle art form. The dancer told the *Washington Post* that the Soviet hosts "were mind boggled at the sight of a black man dancing classical ballet." In fact, Mitchell began to find such special notice annoying. He knew that other black dancers could perform ballet as well as he could, if they were allowed the same opportunities—especially dance scholarships—that helped launch his career.

Started his own school

Mitchell was in a taxicab on his way to the airport in 1968 when he heard over the radio that civil rights leader Martin Luther King, Jr., had been assassinated in Memphis. The news stunned Mitchell, and it proved a turning point in his career. He had planned to continue his work with the National Ballet Company of Brazil, which he had established two years earlier. Instead, he told the cab driver to turn around and head back into Harlem. Mitchell told the *San Jose Mercury News:* "After hearing of King's death, I came back to Harlem and set up a dance school in a garage. Nobody said I could do it. I started with 30 kids and two dancers, and inside of four months I had 400 kids."

Mitchell wanted to give black children another route out of the ghetto—one through the arts, especially dance. He also wanted to prove, once and for all, that classical ballet need not be the exclusive realm of whites. "What we started out to do, to prove, was that black children, given the same opportunity as white children, could be great dancers," he told the *Lexington Herald-Leader.* "We proved that in just a few years. Then we wanted to take that company of black dancers and showcase them in the city, the country, the world, to show people what black artists could do. We did that."

The energetic Mitchell had strong opinions about how he wanted his company to perform. He sought to preserve an American dance repertory, calling attention to the unique contributions this country has made to ballet. Over the years his repertory has included balletic versions of *A Streetcar Named Desire* and *John Henry,* the latter based on the American ballad pitting a man against a machine. He also drew widely on the works of Balanchine, his former mentor. Mitchell told the *Chicago Tribune:* "In the early days, I figured, 'What better way to grow but to dance Balanchine's repertoire?'... But it's the eclecticism of the American dancer that is his and her strong point—their versatility.... I was criticized as being too eclectic, not knowing what kind of company I wanted. We did jazz and classical, for instance." Mitchell defends his action by pointing out that his productions appeal to a broad base of people, rather than those who merely like classical ballet. "Notice we used the word dance and not ballet," he said in the *Philadelphia Inquirer.* "That other word tends to turn people off. Then, we chose theater, so audiences will know that we want to attract more than just the dance public. We're after the public."

Initial fears that the nation's dance enthusiasts would not support an all-black ballet troupe soon vanished, and Mitchell's Dance Theater of Harlem forged a reputation for both innovative modern works and imaginative staging of classics. "When the curtain goes up, the first thing the audience sees is that the dancers are black," he told the *Philadelphia Inquirer.* "If they don't see it, something is wrong. The real questions are, 'What are they doing? And, how well are they doing it?' Dance Theater of Harlem is a major ballet company." In the *Philadelphia Daily News,* Mitchell explained that his decision to cater to mass tastes is actually one of the company's strengths. "Dance Theater of Harlem is an example of American classicism," he said, "and by that I mean that we stress eclectics and strong dramatic elements. There's a difference between being classic and being classical. When you are classical, you are an imitation of an original. But if you're a classic, you are unique. This notion I got from Balanchine."

For 20 seasons the Dance Theater of Harlem has toured America and abroad. The company even mounted a full-length ballet for the Public Broadcasting System several years ago, an honor accorded only the finest of troupes. A high point came in 1987, when the group made a two-month visit to the Soviet Union for a series of performances. Not only was Mitchell invited to teach in Russia—the first American artist of any race to receive such a request—but his company met full houses and standing ovations everywhere it went. Mitchell told the *Chicago Tribune:* "In Leningrad, on the stage where the Kirov Ballet performs, they came onstage and gave us a champagne salute. It was like being a rock star. I think that brought the company as artists to another level, that feeling of acceptance by the best."

Company faced troubled times

Early in 1990 the Dance Theater of Harlem faced a major crisis. The cancellation of several performance dates and the withdrawal of some corporate sponsors led to a significant reduction in revenues. Mitchell was forced to lay off his dancers and most of his staff and cancel much of the 1990 season's roster. At the time Mitchell told the press that the move did not mean the end of the company; instead, it was a means to keep the operation from plunging into deep debt. Fortunately, new corporate sponsors appeared to help defray expenses, and the troupe was back in business by early 1991. Mitchell was far from relieved, however. "We have taken our first step back on land," he told the *Boston Globe.* "But if we take a wrong step, we'll be back in the sea."

The Dance Theater of Harlem's financial problems are not unique in an age when federal funding of the arts is dwindling and corporate sponsorship must be spread broadly across numerous charities and organizations. Mitchell has been able to sustain his dance company because of its fine reputation, his own personal charisma, and the laudable goals of the company and its satellite school. Mitchell offers art as a solution for the ills of the ghetto. "Put the arts first, give us the children first, and there won't be any AIDS or homelessness," he asserted in the *Boston Globe*. "The kids you see in the street get their hope from something chemical and it doesn't last. Our society doesn't have enough real hope. That's what the arts give you." Mitchell sees the dawn of the twenty-first century as a precarious time for art, and hence for the health of American youth. Voicing his concerns in the *Boston Globe*, he expressed a fear that someday, "people [will] wake up and realize there is no art in their lives. And then it will be too late."

Sources

Arizona Republic, November 23, 1987.

Boston Globe, November 11, 1990.

Chicago Tribune, May 7, 1989.

Dance, December 1993.

Jet, September 27, 1993.

Lexington Herald-Leader, June 25, 1989.

Orlando Sentinel, March 11, 1990.

Philadelphia Daily News, November 17, 1987.

Philadelphia Inquirer, November 15, 1987; February 13, 1991; June 14, 1991; July 24, 1991.

San Jose Mercury News, February 14, 1988.

Washington Post, March 14, 1989; March 13, 1990.

Rita Moreno

Born December 11, 1931
Humanacao, Puerto Rico

ACTRESS, SINGER, AND DANCER

A remarkably versatile performer, Rita Moreno has received all four of show business's top awards. For her acting in *West Side Story*, Moreno won an Oscar in 1962. A Grammy followed her vocal performance on the *Electric Company Album* for children in 1972. Her role as Googie Gomez in *The Ritz* (1975) on Broadway won her a Tony. And finally, Moreno has been awarded two Emmys: one for guest appearances on *The Muppet Show* in 1977, and another for an episode of *The Rockford Files* in 1978. Although impressive, this long list of prestigious awards merely suggests the variety of Moreno's excellent performances, and it cannot convey the determination with which she has worked to become a respected actress.

"I have had to learn to laugh at myself— otherwise there would be lines of sorrow from my forehead to my toes."

Moreno—her given name is Rosa Dolores Alverio—was born to Paco Alverio and Rosa Maria Marcano Alverio in the small town of Humanacao, Puerto Rico, on December 11, 1931. Moreno's parents divorced soon after her birth, and her mother left her with relatives while she went to New York to work as a seamstress. When Moreno was five years old, her mother returned for her and, along with other members of the family, they found a home in a Manhattan tenement. It was at this point in Moreno's life that she began to take dancing lessons. Paco Cansino, an uncle of the legendary actress and dancer Rita Hayworth, was a very effective dance teacher: the young Moreno soon began to dance professionally.

Moreno, who attended New York Public School 132, soon found herself performing in the children's theater at Macy's Department Store and entertaining at weddings and bar mitzvahs. By the time she was 13, Moreno had exchanged the life of a schoolgirl for that of an actress.

Under the name Rita Cosio, she had her first role on Broadway as Angelina in Harry Kleiner's *Sky Drift*. Later, she performed in nightclubs in Boston, Las Vegas, and New York, and dubbed the Spanish for actress Elizabeth Taylor, Margaret O'Brien, and Peggy Ann Garner in foreign releases of their movies. Moreno's first film, *So Young, So Bad,* led to a meeting with Louis B. Mayer, who contracted her with Metro-Goldwyn-Mayer (MGM).

Gains recognition with stereotypical roles

Under the name Rosita Moreno (her stepfather's surname) and, later, Rita Moreno, the actress garnered minor roles in some 25 movies. The most notable of these included *The Toast of New Orleans* and *Pagan Love Song,* with Esther Williams. Free-lancing after she lost her contract with MGM, Moreno found only stereotypical, ethnic roles. With the exception of her part as Zelda Zanders in *Singin' in the Rain,* Moreno portrayed Latin vamps in *The Fabulous Senorita, The Ring, Cattle Town, Latin Lovers,* and *Jivaro.* She was hired to play an Arab in *El Alamein,* and an American Indian in both *Fort Vengeance* and *The Yellow Tomahawk.*

Although Moreno became a recognizable actress after these movies, the "Latin Spitfire" roles created a troublesome and unfair image for her. She became known as "Rita the Cheetah"; her highly publicized relationships with legendary actor Marlon Brando and Geordie Hormel of the Hormel meat family only made this image worse. Disheartened by these roles which, she later told a *New York Times* contributor, she "played ... the same way, barefoot, with my nostrils flaring," the petite actress attempted to return to the stage. She lost a part in *Camino Real* because the playwright, the renowned Tennessee Williams, did not think her voice was suitable.

It seemed as if Moreno's career had taken a turn for the better when she was featured on the cover of *Life* magazine. She immediately signed a contract with Twentieth Century Fox, singing in *Garden of Evil*, and doing a Marilyn Monroe takeoff in *The Lieutenant Wore Skirts*. Once again, however, she was given stereotypical roles which failed to challenge the serious actress. The casting was difficult for Moreno emotionally as well as professionally. As she recalled in the *New York Times*, she spent six and a half years in therapy "trying to get my ethnic problems untangled." Moreno did not find a truly satisfying role until she was given a part as a Burmese slave girl in the hit musical *The King and I* in 1956.

Wins Academy Award for West Side Story

Despite these professional successes, Moreno found the latter half of the 1950s to be less rewarding; she made few movies from 1956 to 1960. In 1960 Moreno returned to the stage in Arthur Miller's *A View from the Bridge* in theaters in Seattle, Washington, and La Jolla, California. Although she was well received during this summer theater tour, Moreno could no longer cope with the frustration she had been experiencing—she attempted suicide with sleeping pills. When she woke in the hospital, however, she realized that she wanted to live. She recovered beautifully, and went on to star in the movie for which she is most famous, *West Side Story*.

Moreno had been asked by Jerome Robbins a year after her performance in *The King and I* to try out for the role of Maria in the original theater production of *West Side Story*, but Moreno, busy as well as intimidated, did not. By the time the movie version of the play was being made, Moreno's face had matured, and she was better suited to the character of Anita, the more experienced friend of Maria, who was ultimately portrayed by Natalie Wood. As Anita, Moreno illuminated the screen with her singing and dancing. *West Side Story* was an instant success. It won ten Academy awards, one of which was Moreno's Oscar for best supporting actress.

During the ten years from 1961 to 1971, Moreno found that she could not rest on her laurels. While she played Rosa Zacharias in Tennessee Williams's *Summer and Smoke*, and a camp follower in *Cry of Battle*, she did not find these parts entirely rewarding; seeking better roles, she left Hollywood for London. There, in 1964, she portrayed Ilona Ritter in Hal Prince's *She Loves Me*. Forced to return to the United States because of British performance laws, Moreno made her way to Broadway once again. This time she won the role of Iris Parodus Brustein in Lorraine Hansberry's *The Sign in Sidney Brustein's Window*, a play which ran for 101 performances. Marlon Brando, the man whom Moreno had dated on and off for eight years, assisted Moreno as she renewed her movie career with her portrayal of a drug addict in *The Night of the Following Day.* This led to appearances in various movies; she found roles in *Marlowe, Pop!,* a comedy focused on East Harlem, and *Carnal Knowledge,* in which she played a prostitute visited by Jack Nicholson.

Marries and launches television career

It was during these ten years that Moreno met and married Dr. Leonard Gordon, a cardiologist and internist at Mount Sinai Hospital in New York. When they were introduced near the end of 1964, Gordon asked Moreno to attend a New Year's party with him. When she accepted, Moreno instructed Gordon to pick her up at the Henry Miller Theater, but as Gordon later told a *Hispanic* contributor, he "couldn't figure out the sense of it." "Why would this attractive young lady be going to the theater on New Year's Eve? Was she going on a date with some other guy and then planning to dump him and go out with me?" Gordon, still perplexed, waited and waited for Moreno to leave the theater long after the audience had exited, while an angry Moreno waited inside her dressing room, thinking she had been stood up. It was not until Gordon checked the marquee to see if he was at the right theater and saw Moreno's name in lights that he realized his date was *the* Rita Moreno. Moreno and Gordon finally went on their date, and they were eventually married in June 1965.

Moreno took a break from both theater and film to perform for television in 1971. When the Children's Television Workshop, which produces the popular preschool series *Sesame Street,* asked Moreno to star in *The Electric Company,* a television series for older children, she was enthusiastic. Moreno's performance was delightful, and in 1972 her participation, with Bill Cosby and others, in the soundtrack recording of *The Electric Company* won her a Grammy Award for the best recording for children.

Laughs at stereotypes in **The Ritz**

This success did not develop into any other television ventures, though. Moreno's next role was that of the shoplifter in the play *Detective Story,* which ran in Philadelphia in 1973. She then portrayed staff nurse Norton in *The National Health,* first in New Haven, Connecticut, from 1973 to 1974, and then in the Circle in the Square, in New York City, in 1974. It was around this time that Moreno displayed the character that would eventually win her the Tony Award. While at a party she began singing "Everything's Coming up Roses" to playwright Terrence McNally. With her mother's Spanish accent and the mannerisms she had developed during the filming of *West Side Story,* she was hilarious. McNally later invited Moreno to attend his new play, *The Tubs,* at the Yale Repertory Theater, and she was shocked to see the character she had created singing onstage. McNally asked her to portray this character, which he named Googie Gomez, when the play, renamed *The Ritz,* came to Broadway in 1975, and she accepted.

Moreno was a hit. While the *New York Times* noted that her performance as the Puerto Rican singer was "variously hailed as 'pure beauty,' 'wonderfully atrocious' and 'a comic earthquake,'" a writer for the *White Plains Reporter Dispatch,* quoted in *Current Biography Yearbook,* said it best: "In fractured English, she [Moreno] creates a portrait of tattered glory.... Hot, cold, tempestuous, wiggling, seething, cursing, ... so that she tears the house down every time she opens her mouth or does a bump and grind, she is showing a new generation of theatergoers what stars are all about." *The Ritz* ran for 400 performances, and it was no surprise when Moreno received the Tony Award for best supporting actress.

Moreno's next appearance was in the motion picture version of *The Ritz.* While this performance was not as appreciated as the one on Broadway, many believed this was the fault of the director, Richard Lester. Later, however, guest appearances on *The Muppet Show* in 1977 won her an Emmy for outstanding continuing or single performance by a supporting actress in variety or music. She won another Emmy for outstanding lead actress for a single appearance in a drama or comedy series in 1978 for her appearance in "The Paper Palace" episode of the series *The Rockford Files.* Moreno went on to portray a Jewish mother in *The Boss's Son,* and to develop a nightclub act which she has since performed in Chicago, New York City, Lake Tahoe, Toronto, Atlantic City, and on various cruise ships. Her next motion picture role did not come until 1980, when she played an Italian American mistress in *Happy Birthday, Gemini.* And in 1981, Moreno was given the opportunity to star with Alan Alda and Carol Burnett in the motion picture comedy *The Four Seasons.*

In 1982 Moreno found herself on television once again. She appeared as a secretary named Violet Newstead in ABC's *Nine to Five.* This situation comedy, based on the Jane Fonda/Dolly Parton/Lily Tomlin movie of the same name, promoted the rights of working women. While it did relatively well from 1982 to 1983, its ratings fell after a time-slot change, and it was taken off the air. Despite the failure of the series, Moreno was nominated for an Emmy. Moreno's next career move was to return to the stage. With James Coco and Sally Struthers, she appeared in *Wally's Cafe* on Broadway for 12 performances in June 1981. In 1985 she was again starring with Struthers, this time as the slobby Olive Madison in a revision of Neil Simon's comedy *The Odd Couple* on Broadway. The play, which was originally written for two male principals, was not well received despite its talented cast.

Since then, Moreno has been involved in a variety of activities. In early 1994 Moreno began doing the voice of Carmen in the cartoon version of the popular computer game and quiz show *Where in the World Is Carmen Santiago?* Although she loves to spend time with her family in their homes in Pacific Palisades, California, and Manhattan, Moreno also finds ways to spend time with Leonard Gordon and Fernanda Luisa professionally. She has appeared several times with her daughter, Fernanda, in theaters around the nation in *Steel Magnolias* and *The Taming of the Shrew.* With her husband, Gordon, as her manager and partner, she is committed to the Hispanic community. She remarked in *Hispanic:* "Lenny and I are very involved in trying to make the Hispanic community understand that education is everything." She was also a member of the board of directors of Third World Cinema and the Alvin Ailey Dance Company, and she was included on the theater panel of the National Foundation of the Arts.

While Moreno is aware of the responsibility she has as a Hispanic role model, she is, as she explained in *Hispanic,* an actress with career aspirations. It is to Moreno's credit that she attempts to combine her love of acting with her desire to assist the Hispanic community. In 1989 she worked on two movies which would provide inspiration to Hispanics. It was her aspiration to play the part of a Hispanic woman who created an organization to fight gang warfare. Before she won one of *Hispanic*'s ten 1989 women of the year awards, Moreno spoke of this character: "She's the kind of Hispanic woman I want desperately to portray on television, and that is a woman of some sophistication, who speaks English very well, who is quite political. She is the emerging Hispanic woman, the one that nobody has gotten to see yet on television." Whether she portrays them in television movies or provides an example with her own career and personal life, Moreno is a leader of these emerging Hispanic women. She told another *Hispanic* interviewer, "When I was a young starlet, I wanted to be an all-American girl.... But when I grew up and developed a sense of self-esteem as a Hispanic, I learned how essential it was to cling to one's own heritage, for only in that way can we truly understand our ancestors, our culture, and ultimately understand ourselves."

Sources

Boston Globe, September 5, 1986; September 8, 1986.

Chicago Tribune, May 3, 1988; November 15, 1988.

Cosmopolitan, August 1981.

Current Biography Yearbook, H. W. Wilson, 1985.

Harper's Bazaar, May 1981; September 1981.

Hispanic, October 1989; December 1989; September 1990.

Los Angeles Times, November 17, 1988.

Ms., January-February 1991.

Newsweek, May 25, 1981.

New Yorker, June 22, 1981; June 24, 1985.

New York Post, March 13, 1955.

New York Times, March 1975.

Nuestro, October 1981; March 1986.

People, May 3, 1982.

TV Guide, January 15, 1983.

Variety, February 26, 1986.

Washington Post, March 19, 1990.

Noriyuki "Pat" Morita

Born in 1932
Isleton, California

"[The] only thing I wanted to do for 10, 12 years out of my life, was just to be a good journeyman stand-up comic."

ACTOR AND COMEDIAN

Noriyuki "Pat" Morita is best known today for his big-screen portrayal of a legendary character, the karate sensei or teacher. By the mid-1980s, most of the country's youth knew him as the thoughtful, usually nonviolent sage in *The Karate Kid*, parts I and II. Interestingly, there were several major ironies regarding his success in these films. First, Morita gained fame playing a traditional Japanese, even though his knowledge of Japanese culture was limited. Second, he portrayed a karate expert, even though his karate moves were ungainly and his appearance anything but athletic. And third, and perhaps most ironic of all, was the fact that Morita seemed to achieve his success in a single role in a blockbuster movie—after laboring in numerous roles and as a nightclub comic for more than two decades. In fact, Morita's career has displayed great resourcefulness and adaptability, and his success has come with hard work and persistence.

That persistence began early. His childhood was not easy. His parents were migrant fruit pickers, and, as a child, he spent nine years in a sanitarium recovering from spina tuberculosis. When he was about 11, he and his family were interned—like most Japanese Americans on the West Coast during World War II—in a detention camp. The Moritas spent the war years in the Manzanar camp near the Arizona border. "I feel great sorrow and have many deep, emotional scars from what happened," he told Diane Haithman of the *Detroit Free Press*, "but the key is the 'ed' of the word happened. It's in my past. I am not trying to belittle it in terms of scope, how it affected my life, but because of that incarceration, I think, therefore, I am always connected to black people, and barrios and ghettos and substandard ways of having to live in this, the land of riches.... I don't like to talk about it too much.... I'm fortunate that through the Great Spirit I was able to survive it, and go beyond it, longer than the memory."

After the war, as a young adult, Morita worked in his family's Chinese restaurant in Sacramento. ("You get the picture?" he asked a *Los Angeles Times* interviewer, "a Japanese family running a Chinese restaurant in a black neighborhood with a clientele of blacks, Filipinos and everybody else who didn't fit in any of the other neighborhoods.") Then came a variety of computer jobs, including one as a supervisor at an Aerojet-General facility. Around 1960, he made the decision to become a stand-up comic—a move his family did not appreciate. It ultimately destroyed his first marriage. "It was absolutely nutty, against the grain of the family, every wrong you could have picked," he told the *Detroit Free Press*.

Begins career as comedian

Morita eventually would have a successful career, but before it was over, it would run from high to low. He is said to have played everything from the Hollywood Palace to third-rate clubs in the Catskills and the "Chop Suey" circuit of Chinatown. He often opened for headliner acts in Las Vegas. Morita thrived on thoughtful, gentle, fresh humor. "His is one of the quiet acts, more of a conversation with the audience, than anything else," said a *Detroit Free Press* critic who saw Morita in 1968.

On one memorable occasion in the mid-1960s, Morita had been booked as a replacement for singer Don Ho at a club in Hawaii. As he was waiting in the wings before the show, he told the *Los Angeles Times*, "a waitress walks by me and almost drops her tray. 'You're the act?' she says. 'Aren't you terrified?' 'Why should I be terrified?' I ask, all confidence. 'Don't you know who has the club tonight?' 'No,' I say, still confident. 'It's the 25th anniversary reunion of the Survivors of Pearl Harbor.' O... K... Well, I tell myself I've got the heart of a comic and I'm going to stay. I turned on all the angelic, cherubic charm I could find and I went out and I said, 'Before I begin, I just want to say I'm sorry about messing up your harbor.' There was a second of silence, and then a big wave of laughter started at the back and rolled forward. That was all it took. I did all the regular material—'I'm really Italian but I had an eye job'—and then I even turned it around and started kidding them about using any excuse to go out and get loaded."

In one part of his routine during the late sixties, Morita described his first trip to the Orient. It showed just how American he was. "It was weird. All those people who look like me and I couldn't understand any of them." He also told his audiences that he drank Cutty Saki and Jap Daniels, a play on the whiskeys Cutty Sark and Jack Daniels. A put-on dialect was also part of his routine. "Though he speaks English as if born to it, which he was, he has great fun mixing his R's and L's, as his audience expects," the *Free Press* critic wrote.

For all the Japanese jokes, Morita's humor has always been typically American. In fact, he knows little about true Japanese humor. Until some acting roles came along in the mid-1970s, he could not do an accurate Japanese accent—although he could understand some Japanese from contacts with his older relatives. For one role, he developed an accent with the aid of comedian and voice actor Mel Blanc. At times, Morita even waxes comical about his shortcomings as an ethnic Japanese. "About four years ago I was playing the Copa in New York and tried an old-country accent," he said to the *Detroit Free Press*. "On opening night, Bill Dana told me that I had the worst [Japanese] accent he ever heard. And what does Dana know. He's Hungarian. My brother can read and write Japanese and speak the language too. I can understand it pretty well, but I can barely make myself understood in Japanese. I guess I'm the yellow sheep of the family."

Begins work as actor

Morita's career as a comic rolled ahead for about a decade. Then the entire nightclub entertainment industry hit a slump during the early seventies, and the bottom fell out of Morita's own career. "There wasn't any work—even the headliners weren't getting any work—even the Ella [Fitzgerald]s and the Vic Damones," he said. "So I became an actor. Sure, I couldn't do Shakespeare, but I could quote him funny."

A number of roles have made Morita a familiar sight to American television audiences. The first ones were a far cry from his role as the adroit karate master in *The Karate Kid*. He played the excitable Arnold on *Happy*

Days and then starred in *Mr. T. and Tina.* As Mr. T., Morita played an immigrant widower, with a couple of young daughters, who couldn't quite fit into the American culture. "He's taken a Berlitz course in English and is willing to jump into the mainstream of American life. But he messes up," Morita explained in an interview with *United Press International.*

Morita spent much of the late seventies and early eighties outside the limelight. But he briefly surfaced in the Los Angeles press when a mudslide struck his home in fashionable Tarzana, California. A series of storms caused the slide, which left a small mountain of mud on the street in front of the Morita house. According to press accounts, the mud severely damaged the $300,000 home and destroyed the Moritas' household goods. Yuki Morita told the *Los Angeles Times* that she and daughters Aly and Tia escaped with nothing in the way of personal possessions, "except with the clothes we were wearing." To make matters worse, the mudslide briefly caused a row between the Moritas and the Tarzana city government—which wanted the Moritas to clean up the huge pile of mud.

Finds success and recognition for Karate Kid *series*

For a time, that was the most publicity Morita would receive, until his role in *The Karate Kid* gave him new box-office appeal. Many critics described it as basically a teenage version of the original *Rocky* (both featured the same director). In the movie, Morita used his given first name, Noriyuki, to give his role greater authenticity—something the producers and director were after. In fact, they originally wanted a Japanese, not a Japanese American actor, to play the part of Miyagi, the sensei. But Morita won them over with an impressive audition—and especially the skill he displayed in working with sidekick Ralph Macchio. Before shooting could begin, though, Morita—who had no previous martial-arts experience—had to complete six weeks of intensive karate training. "Ralph and I had to go through all sorts of preparation: body exercises, agility, flex and a lot of basic karate moves," he told the *Detroit Free Press.*

The film became a tremendous success and was recognized as the "sleeper" of the year. Critics who expected just another teenage trash film praised *The Karate Kid* for its unusual sensitivity. Stated a *Sports Illustrated* writer: "I know this will tax your imagination, but try to envision one summer movie that doesn't feature ghosts, gremlins, space-ships, snakes, special effects, or cardboard cutout characters, and that actually deals with people. Believe it or not, such a movie really and truly exists." A *Peo-*

ple critic pointed out that "the wonderful parts of this film are those involving the kid and the old guy; there is something magical about the old man's balanced, compassionate view of life. Morita also proves that economy is effective when it comes to acting." Agreed the *Sports Illustrated* reviewer, "With a lesser actor, Mr. Miyagi could have come off as no more than the stock Hollywood Oriental, but Morita has invested him with both humor and humanity." For his performance, Morita received an Academy Award nomination.

Although sequels are often not very well received by reviewers, *The Karate Kid, Part II* drew considerable praise, again due mainly to the performances of Morita and Macchio and the interaction between their characters. *Detroit Free Press* critic Catharine Rambeau stated that "the picture was a natural choice for a sequel: It had characters with whom diverse audiences could identify; it had heroes, and it appealed to teenagers." Concluded Rambeau, "It's a little more self-conscious, a good deal slicker and more Americanized than the original, but *The Karate Kid, Part II* is entertaining enough." A *Maclean's* reviewer found the film to be "every bit as effective as the original due to the special relationship between teacher and student." And Tom Matthews, writing in *Boxoffice*, stated: "It is surprising ... to find that *The Karate Kid II* is not only a fine piece of filmmaking, but that it far surpasses the original in style and genuine emotion.... The photography of the new film is finely textured, the spirit of the story is befitting of Miyagi's peaceful and reverent interpretation of the martial arts, and the relationship between the two leads is both humorous and warm." In 1989 *The Karate Kid III* was released to somewhat less enthusiastic reviews, but still drew an audience.

Morita has reacted humbly to the acclaim. "This is a marvel to me," he told the *Detroit Free Press*. "It's a phenomenon. I am enjoying it." But he is also interested in the future. He has co-written and is starring in a film entitled *Fate of a Hunter*, currently in production for MGM. It is a drama about two American airmen who were shot down over a small Japanese village during World War II. "I'd like to play a variety of characters. I'd like to play a politician sometime, and a greasy, slimy villain type maybe somewhere down the line. But I don't think it's my time to do that right now.... I want to stay the huggable, warm, compassionate ... kind of guy. I get a kick out of people's reaction to me."

Sources

Boxoffice, August 1986; March 1987.

Detroit Free Press, September 5, 1968; June 20, 1986; March 25, 1987.

Detroit News, June 23, 1986.

Jet, July 21, 1986.

Los Angeles Times, March 3, 1980; June 22, 1986.

Maclean's, July 7, 1986.

New York Times, March 9, 1985.

People, July 9, 1984; June 30, 1986; July 7, 1986; March 9, 1987.

Sports Illustrated, July 9, 1984.

Time, July 2, 1984.

United Press International, June 26, 1976.

Variety, August 20, 1986; March 7, 1990.

Mike Myers

Born in 1964
Scarborough, Ontario, Canada

"Wayne's sort of like everybody I grew up with in Scarborough. It's just the suburban, adolescent, North American, heavy-metal experience, as I knew it."

COMEDIAN AND ACTOR

For a generation who grew up in paneled basements listening to heavy metal music, Mike Myers is nothing less than a genius. Myers has drawn upon his own years in suburbia to create the character Wayne Campbell, a metal freak with a colorful vocabulary and a dogged dedication to having fun. Wayne and his nerdy sidekick, Garth, have appeared in skits on *Saturday Night Live* and in the 1992 sleeper hit *Wayne's World*. No one was prepared for the film's phenomenal success—it eventually earned more than $170 million worldwide and spawned a sequel, *Wayne's World 2*, which was released in 1993.

Perhaps one of the strongest indicators of the *Wayne's World* success is the way in which the movie's vocabulary, or "Waynespeak," has invaded American culture. "Babes, parties, brew and tunes: the four pillars of Wayne's excellent world," wrote Laura Blumenfeld in the *Washington Post*, describing the credo of Wayne and Garth. "Hanging out is what you do, 'Party time!' is what you say, and when you spot a major babe you go

'Schwing!!' Wayne Campbell is a long-haired, baseball-capped, guitar-jamming dudester.... If he ran this land, the Constitution would outlaw wedgies. The national anthem would be 'Stairway to Heaven'; the national bird would be the chick." Myers, who is still amazed by the success of *Wayne's World,* told the *Washington Post* that his alter ego offers no message beyond the fact that "adulthood isn't all that interesting."

Myers has said that he always thought his *Wayne's World* characters would make a good movie, but he was still unprepared for the phenomenal success of his debut film. "It's very strange, you see," he was quoted as saying in the *Miami Herald,* "because Wayne is me. I am Wayne. Who knew it would come to this?" Myers admitted that Wayne is based on himself and his friends who grew up in the predominantly white suburb of Scarborough, outside Toronto, Ontario. "I had a great childhood. A great childhood," he said. "And now, I hate adulthood. I really do. I like adulthood to the extent that I'm more free to be a child, because I'm the master of my own destiny." That destiny includes the very stuff of Wayne's most excellent adolescent fantasies: kisses from pop icon Madonna, one-on-one hockey with Wayne Gretzky, and the respect of rock and roll legends like Alice Cooper and Aerosmith. Myers acknowledged to a *Miami Herald* correspondent, "I only realized that the character had become this, like, big thing when Aerosmith came on [*Saturday Night Live*] as musical guests and requested to be on 'Wayne's World.' That blew the top of my head right off. I could not believe it.... And then Madonna called, and she wanted to be on with Wayne! So then I knew.... I knew Wayne had become a true legend in his own time."

In *Entertainment Weekly,* Myers called himself "a feral child raised by television." He described his native Scarborough as "a very suburby suburb of Toronto, very flat—there are a lot of doughnut stores and factory carpet outlets." The trappings may have been conventional, but Myers's parents were delightfully eccentric. His mother was a retired actress who steered Myers into commercials at the age of eight. Myers's father sold encyclopedias for a living but was fascinated by comedy and pop music. Myers recalled in the *Los Angeles Times* that his father would "sing 'Psycho Killer' by the Talking Heads while cooking breakfast. He'd wake us up to watch *The Goon Show* and *Monty Python* on television." Myers and his father were also great fans of two comedy programs, *Saturday Night Live* (SNL) and *Second City T.V.*

Grew up a lot like Wayne

Mike Myers actually did grow up hanging out in a paneled basement with his friends, watching television and listening to rock music. "We used to have a lot of teachers' strikes in Canada, and my best friend and I would hang out and watch episodes of *I Dream of Jeannie, Happy Days, That Girl,* and *The Dick Van Dyke Show,* which I adored," he remembered in the *Miami Herald.* "It's because of Dick's show that I probably became a comedy writer." After becoming disillusioned with straight acting as a youngster, Myers found inspiration watching *Saturday Night Live,* which debuted in 1975.

"I've wanted to be on *SNL* since I was eleven," Myers declared in *Rolling Stone.* He idolized the original *SNL* cast members, including Dan Aykroyd and the late John Belushi. More importantly, though, he began to look around at his own environment with an eye toward exploiting it for comedy. "I knew this guy who was an artist who came to Toronto from Stuttgart [Germany]," Myers recollected. "He was working as a waiter. One day I went in the restaurant and ordered a hot dog. He said, 'Your order has become tiresome.' Then a song came on the loudspeaker, and he said, 'That is my favorite song,' and began dancing. He would say things like [*F-Troop* star] 'Larry Storch is a much-maligned genius.'" Myers quickly made friends with the would-be artist from Germany, who provided inspiration for Myers's future *Saturday Night Live* skits "Sprockets," an artsy talk show hosted by the turtleneck-wearing Dieter. Meeting the man, Myers assessed, "was like hitting a streak of ore."

Another streak of ore was found closer to home, among Myers's 30 or so metal-freak pals. "There were twelve Waynes in my class," Myers related in *Rolling Stone.* "Wayne is everybody—including myself—who I used to hang out with. I was always a student who liked to hang out with guys who partied—and get my homework done. People just thought I was an idiot who liked to party. People always underestimate Wayne's intellect." While Myers will lovingly describe a permanent vomit stain on the old car he and his friends drove around, he admits that he never shed his wholesome values completely. "I hung out with those guys, but I was always the guy who would say, 'Hey, we shouldn't break windows. They just paid for that window and I think it's not a good idea,'" he recounted in the *Washington Post.* "I couldn't really be mean. It was exciting hanging around these guys because they were interesting, but I could never, like, really be mean."

Begins work on the "Wayne" character

By the time he was an older teen, Myers had discovered punk music. The character of Wayne developed when Myers began to make fun of his suburban metal-loving friends. As early as 1981 Myers went on the air in the guise of a Wayne prototype, performing on an all-night talk show produced in Toronto. As Bill Flanagan put it in *Rolling Stone,* "Wayne has followed Myers to the big time like an idiot twin."

Most comics struggle for years before earning enough to pay the rent. Myers is the exception to that rule. The same day that he graduated from high school, he auditioned for the prestigious Second City comedy troupe and immediately landed a job. He began doing routines in Toronto and then joined the Chicago troupe in the mid-1980s. After developing several characters, including Dieter, Middle-Aged Man, and Wayne while in Toronto and Chicago, Myers flew to New York City in 1989 to interview for a job on *Saturday Night Live.*

Joins Saturday Night Live

Fellow Canadian Lorne Michaels, the producer of *Saturday Night Live,* hired Myers after their first meeting. In the *Washington Post,* Myers described his first moments in Michaels's office: "I was blown away, are you kidding? I stayed in New York City, where I'd only been once before and only drove through it. I went into that famous Lorne Michaels office and behind his head was [a view of] the Empire State Building. I'd only seen it in movies and stuff. And I turned to him and said, 'Is that the Empire State Building?' ... In mid-interview! I couldn't believe it. And then he said, 'Would you like a job?' And I was like, 'Of course I'd like a job.' I started the show January 21st [1989]." Myers was 25 years old, the youngest member of the ensemble at that time.

Myers's natural humility and solid work ethic endeared him to the other *Saturday Night Live* cast members, who had been working together for three years. Within six months Myers was promoted from featured performer to full cast member, and his sketches about Wayne, Dieter, and Lothar of the Hill People earned increasingly more air time. *Washington Post* correspondent Todd Allan Yasui noted that Myers is "a standout in an ensemble, no doubt due to his ability to create vastly different personas with a rubbery face, manic gestures, and dialects. Unlike other *SNL* members who are basically one-dimensional in characterization ... Myers is a Chaplin kind-of-guy, a physical comic actor. He's a skeletal mishmash of body language—a jangly gawky teenager for Wayne and a measured, robotic Teuton for the hyper-pretentious Dieter, host of the German culture show 'Sprockets.'" Yasui continued, "But all the attention and star treatment one gets from being the newest and funniest cast member on a beloved nationally televised show apparently hasn't changed Myers much. It's that neat/nice guy thing again."

Myers's "Wayne's World" sketches did not appear frequently on *Saturday Night Live*, but they nevertheless drew a following. An early fan was *SNL* cast member Dana Carvey, who agreed to take the supporting role of Garth. While the full extent of the Wayne phenomenon began to hit Myers when *Saturday Night Live* guest stars would request a "Wayne's World" segment, the impact was most fully felt in the domain of hip language, where such Wayne-isms as "hurl," "schwing," and "No way! Way!" have entered the cultural code. *Esquire* correspondent Alex Gross wrote, "A parody of the ubiquitous talk show format, 'Wayne's World' is also about a world in which our last common experience is the joy of watching and deconstructing bad TV. Wayne's trademark exclamation—'Not!'—is the kind of all-obliterating riposte that TV in the cable era demands. No more and certainly no less."

Makes transition to the movie screen

It remained to be seen whether "Wayne's World" could be translated from a five-minute sketch into a full-length feature film. Not since Belushi and Aykroyd had taken their Blues Brothers skit onto the large screen had any *Saturday Night Live* sketch parlayed its way into moviedom. Myers was confident, though, that the idea would work. "I'd always envisioned 'Wayne's World' a movie," he disclosed in the *Los Angeles Times*. "Its heart is a movie. It's a sketch, more than others on the show, that does get out of the basement."

In the movie *Wayne's World*, Wayne and Garth trade their freewheeling public-access cable show in Aurora, Illinois, for a chance at the big time on a local Chicago station. They quickly discover that making it big means having to do on-air interviews with their profit-hungry sponsor broadcast from a high-tech studio built to look like Wayne's basement. Wayne also suffers when the show's producer tries to steal Wayne's new girlfriend. The duo escape and return to the real basement, where cable is king. They even get their babes in the end.

Wayne's World was filmed in 12 weeks on a shoestring budget of $13 million. In the first two months after its release in 1992, it earned more than $40 million and made stars of Myers and Carvey. Since they were both still regular cast members of *Saturday Night Live*, they were required to shoot the movie on a tight schedule so they could be back in time for the season opener in September 1991. The film eventually earned $170 million worldwide.

Makes sequel

Wayne's World 2 was released in late 1993. In this film, Wayne and Garth have moved out of the basement and now share an apartment they call their "babe lair." After being visited by the ghost of Jim Morrison (the lead singer of the 1960s legendary rock group, The Doors), Wayne tries to stage a rock concert. "It's the further adventures of two guys who want to have fun," Myers told *Maclean's*. "It's about faith and spirituality. It's also about the threshold of adulthood." The sequel enjoyed only moderate success, something of a disappointment after the tremendous impact of the first *Wayne's World*.

The film *So I Married an Axe Murderer*, which starred Myers, was also released in 1993. The movie concerns the marriage-as-death theme. Myers plays a character who is afraid of the finality of marriage—viewing it as a kind of death. In the film he meets a woman he is willing to marry, and it turns out that she might literally kill him. The film did not perform well at the box office.

The film's philosophy is one that Myers shares. "Getting married has a lot in common with dying," Myers told *Cosmopolitan*. "Think about it: 'We two are now one.' Mathematically, something's got to go." He managed to overcome his fear, however, marrying his live-in companion of five years, Robin Ruzan. The couple met in Chicago in a bar across the street from the Second City Theater, where Myers was working. All kidding aside, Myers seems to appreciate marriage. He told *Cosmopolitan*, "Being able to say 'This is my wife, this is my husband' has real clarity, as opposed to 'This is my l-l-lover,' a creepy term with a fifteen-minute aftertaste."

Sources

Cosmopolitan, May 1993.

Entertainment Weekly, May 17, 1991.

Esquire, March 1992.

Los Angeles Times, November 3, 1991.

Maclean's, July 26, 1993.

Miami Herald, February 12, 1992.

Rolling Stone, November 16, 1989; March 17, 1992.

Washington Post, April 22, 1990; February 16, 1992.

Photo Credits

The photographs appearing in *Performing Artists: From Alvin Ailey to Julia Roberts* were received from the following sources:

AP/Wide World Photos: cover photographs (Robert Townsend, Julia Roberts, Andy García), pages 1, 4, 10, 15, 24, 30, 49, 67, 71, 77, 93, 106, 113, 120, 126, 138, 152, 157, 159, 166, 175, 178, 190, 208, 212, 220, 226, 249, 258, 264, 271, 275, 284, 289, 295, 299, 302, 306, 309, 314, 319, 323, 347, 350, 355, 357, 363, 371, 374, 380, 384, 400, 404, 407, 417, 425, 432, 435, 446, 458, 464, 492, 502, 512, 516, 519, 523, 533, 537, 547, 552, 556, 567, 571, 575, 585, 593, 599, 606, 610, 620, 623, 628, 656, 662, 666, 668, 675, 681, 693; UPI/Bettmann: pages 22, 53, 185, 255, 544, 596, 635, 650; The Bettmann Archive: pages 35, 38; UPI/Bettmann Newsphotos: pages 40, 55; Reuters/Bettmann: pages 61, 101, 104, 131, 182, 280, 393; Archive Photos/Fotos International: pages 81, 168, 172, 335, 641; Patrick Harbron/Sygma: page 87; Archive Photos/Saga: page 97; Courtesy of A&M Records: page 146; Archive Photos/Popperfoto: page 162; Copyright © 1985 Columbia Pictures Industries, Inc.: page 195; Archive Photos/Saga/P. Iovino: page 201; Archive Photos: pages 252, 282; Courtesy of Arista: page 330; Photograph by Harrison Funk, © 1991 Sire Records Company: page 341; Archive Photos/American Stock: page 369; Archive Photos/Express News: page 413; Courtesy of ICM Artists, Ltd.: page 442; Photograph by Chris Cuffaro, © 1991 The David Geffen Company: page 487; Courtesy of Priority Records: page 498; Photograph by Lance Mercer, © 1993, Sony Music, courtesy of Epic Records: page 527; Photograph by Ernie Panicioli, © 1991 Sony Music: page 561; Photograph by Chris Cuffaro/Visages, © 1991 Warner Bros. Records: page 580; Archive Photos/Darlene Hammond: pages 615, 624; Springer/Bettmann Film Archive: page 638.

Index

Bold denotes profiles and volume numbers.

C

G

R

Rabbit Test **1:** 148
A Rage in Harlem **2:** 317
Ragtime **1:** 13
Rain Man **1:** 143, **2:** 319, 322
Raising Arizona **1:** 83
A Raisin in the Sun **3:** 545, 547
Rambo **3:** 639
Rambo: First Blood, Part II **3:** 639
Rambo III **3:** 639
Rapid Fire **2:** 382
Rashad, Phylicia **1:** 10, 129
Rastaman Vibration **2:** 419
Raw **3:** 660
Raw Deal **3:** 612
Rawhide **1:** 184-185
Rebecca **3:** 509
Redford, Robert **3:** 571-579
The Red Hot Chili Peppers **3:** 527, 530, **580-584**
The Red Hot Chili Peppers **3:** 581
Red Rock West **1:** 85
The Remains of the Day **2:** 327
Renacer **1:** 191
Repo Man **1:** 195-197
Resource Center for Nonviolence **1:** 43
Revelations **1:** 5, 8, 10
Revolver **1:** 56
Rhinestone **3:** 521, 639
Rhyme Pays **2:** 342
Rhythm Nation 1814 **2:** 347, 349
Rich and Famous **1:** 65
Richardson, Patricia **1:** 19
Richard III **3:** 510
Ricochet **2:** 344
The Right Stuff **3:** 685
Ringo **1:** 59
Rising Sun **1:** 125, **3:** 633
Risky Business **1:** 141-142
The Ritz **2:** 451, 455

A River Runs Through It **3:** 571, 577-578
The Road to Wellville **1:** 105, **2:** 328
Roberts, Julia **3:** 585-591, 667
Robin Hood: Prince of Thieves **1:** 136, 230
The Rockford Files **2:** 451, 455
Rock the House **3:** 625
Rocky **3:** 637, 639
Rocky II **3:** 637
Rocky III **3:** 637
Rocky IV **3:** 637
Rocky V **3:** 637
Roddenberry, Gene **3:** 643
Rogers, Ginger **1:** 37
Rogers, Mimi **1:** 143
The Rolling Stones **3:** 592-598
Romero **2:** 362
A Room With a View **1:** 168-169
Ropin' the Wind **1:** 71, 74
The Rose **2:** 438
Roseanne **3:** 606-609
Roseanne **1:** 18, **3:** 606-607
Roseanne: My Life as a Woman **3:** 609
Rose, Axl **3:** 599-605
Rose, Leonard **2:** 405
"Round Midnight" **2:** 433
Roxanne **2:** 425-426, 430
Royal Wedding **1:** 38
Rubber Soul **1:** 56
Running Man **1:** 31
Running Scared **1:** 150, **2:** 317
Russia House **3:** 542
Ruthless People **2:** 439

S

Sarafina: The Movie **2:** 269
Saturday Night Live **1:** 89-90, 101-102, 104-105, 146, 149-150, **2:** 428, 464, 466468, **3:** 504-505, 677
Scandal **1:** 208-209